Adventure in the Classroom

Using Adventure to Strengthen Learning and Build a Community of Life-Long Learners

by Mary Henton

KENDALL/HUNT PUBLISHING COMPANY
4050 Westmark Drive   Dubuque, Iowa 52002

To my parents,
Keith and Janet Henton

Contents

Foreword

Education is at a critical crossroads. Traditional methods—a teacher lecturing to students sitting in ordered rows of desks with textbooks open, assigning follow-up homework—remains the norm for learning around the world. Yet adult workers in the present information economy increasingly learn within a realm of teams, experiential and self-directed processes, creative project-based R&D and a technology driven curricula.

Past experience tells us that eventually the world of our educational institutions will follow the world of our economic needs. This happened with the change from an agrarian to the industrial economy, as the factory model of instruction became the norm in the twentieth century. There is a growing segment of the education community dedicated to finding ways to reform education to meet the current and future needs of the information age.

The central idea behind *Adventure in the Classroom* is that using adventure techniques can help create a stronger community of learners and result in greater, deeper learning for individuals. And this learning encompasses all academic curricula; math, science, reading and writing, etc. This idea of using adventure as a *hook* for learning is increasingly accepted by leading edge theory and practice. But the strategies and methods of how to integrate this approach in a classroom setting have not been widely shared.

Our hope is that the teachers, principals, curriculum developers and parent groups involved in the educational change process will find this book a useful tool to help them in their efforts. *Adventure in the Classroom* is a model that presents a unique and exciting approach to learning and teaching; a model that we encourage you to use and adapt to your specific needs. Our experience has been that the AITC model can be useful to many different teachers and schools, across geography, discipline, age, population and cultures.

Mary Henton and I started working together as teachers at Manchester High School, in Massachusetts, in the 70's. As colleagues at PA, we have worked on the development of Project Adventure's academic approach for over a decade. It is with pride and anticipation that we offer you the work of PA in this area, so well crafted and interpreted by Mary, in the knowledge that many students at all levels will benefit.

I look forward to communicating and collaborating with many of you to help us shape the future of education. Learning together how to make the inevitable happen will be an adventure! I look forward to sharing that adventure with all of you.

— Dick Prouty
Executive Director
Project Adventure, Inc.

Acknowledgments

Many people have been involved in the journey this book has taken. My thanks and appreciation go to them all.

To begin with, I thank my parents, Keith and Janet Henton. Teachers to others, they have been my teachers by word and example. Their unwavering commitment and support, along with substantial aid in maintaining household and family through this project, are beyond measure.

My husband, Gary Nussbaum, also deserves my deepest gratitude and thanks. Gary has been a wellspring of encouragement, advice, good humor and counsel. He has contributed important perspectives from his work in the fields of recreation, leisure and experiential education. In addition, he has provided professional and personal support in countless ways.

My children, Ann, Molly and Carl Quinion, have grown up with this book. They have endured my cycles of joy, enthusiasm, worry, frustration and panic. They have learned to work and play around my needs for uninterrupted quiet time to think and write. Most importantly, their intellectual and social growth has inspired me numerous times as real examples of what learning is about.

Tom Zierk, Project Adventure's Director of Publications, has been my coach throughout. His clear focus, unwavering and practical support, honest feedback, sense of humor, broad shoulders and open ears have guided me through a process that, before this book, had been a mystery to me. His advice to "Just write it down, then work it later," helped me break through writing blocks and step into action when my divergent thinking stymied me.

I offer sincere thanks to Dick Prouty, Executive Director of PA, who was instrumental in getting this book going. The concept for the book was his. He had an active hand in the early stages of the writing and offered helpful feedback during the outlining and formulating stages. I thank him heartily for the opportunity to push myself and learn through this process.

As my immediate supervisor through much of the project, Nancy Terry protected my time from other company needs so that I could remain focused and on task. In addition, she contributed substantially to the theoretical base of the model. In particular, she introduced me to organizational development and change theory and its application to schools.

Lisa Furlong has been influential in this effort. On many occasions she helped me grasp the unformed ideas, organize and reorganize, write and rewrite. When I was consumed in the abstract, she found the concrete. She gave me words when I had only concepts and examples when I had blank pages.

Jim Schoel has been a guide in helping me balance my personal and professional responsibilities. His reminders of the importance of this project encouraged me and highlighted the reasons for carrying out the effort—to give voice to the teachers who are doing this good work and through that, to help students grow into the people they were created to be.

My good friends and colleagues T. C. Motzkus and Laurie Frank offered significant insight regarding curriculum integration, processing, the use of adventure activities and the role of the teacher in the AITC model. They brought practical experience as well as theoretical understanding to the model. Excellent teachers and gifted facilitators, they have taught me much.

Beth Acinapura, Susan Fossmeyer, Mark Glasbrenner, Rick Osterhaus, Linda Click, Pat Price, Susan Pine, Mary Rykowski, Jan Gruber, Cathy Moore, Shirley Nyhan, Suzanne van Schaik, Linda Innis, Sheri Gittins, Melissa Weber, Susan LaBonte, Pat Petersen, Michele Harkins, Denise Blank, Jill Reinhart, Karen Loehr, Jill Smith, Kathy Ligocki, Pam Miller and David Joseph are the teachers and principals who have graciously accepted me into their schools, allowed me numerous visits to their classrooms and answered my many questions. They have molded the concepts, raised the questions, developed the strategies and refined the model. Along with their students, these teachers and principals have not only defined, but have also lived *Adventure in the Classroom*.

Hector Lopez, Tracey Dickson, Terri Corlett and Joy Casteel contributed timely and pertinent information. The particular expertise which each offered as teacher, facilitator, counselor, curriculum developer and/or student opened my eyes to important perspectives and enriched my understanding of the model's concepts.

Richard Segien entered this project at the point of laying out the book and creating graphics to illustrate concepts for which I had only words. He has transformed pages of text into a readable format and enlivened words with images.

For the contributions to this project that these people have made, I am deeply grateful. This book, I hope, is a worthy reflection of their efforts and dedication.

How Does This Book Work?

Although I have not checked the research, I am certain that just as there are different learning styles preferences, there are different reading styles preferences. Some folks begin a book at page one and follow the numbers to the end, regardless of how pleasurable the experience. Other readers hunt and peck, scanning a page here, jumping on to another topic there. There are readers who maintain libraries of reference books which they investigate as specific needs arise, and others who collect texts that they study thoroughly. It is my hope that the structure of this book satisfies your reading preferences, as I have tried to present material sequentially and build upon the various facets of the model cumulatively.

To begin with, this book is written for teachers, curriculum developers, administrators and teachers of teachers. I have written with the general assumption that the reader is unfamiliar with the language and practices of experiential and adventure education. At the same time I have focused the discussion so that readers experienced with these two educational approaches might see them in a new light. I expect that some readers will be new to discussion about educational practice and pedagogy, and others will have far more experience than I do. But then, my hope is that I convey here the attitude with which I enter into a workshop—that we are all learners and teachers together. Each of us brings knowledge and experience, gifts we share as we learn from each other.

For some of you, as well as for me, understanding both the historical and contextual background of a model is necessary to understanding the larger set of concepts. Those questions of, "Where did this come from?" "What is the big picture?" and "What is this all about?" demand early answers for many folks. Section One attempts to lay the background for the model. This includes discussion about the core of the model, about its very name, *Adventure in the Classroom*, Project Adventure's history with education and the contextual background of the model, the *community of adventure learners*.

Another section of the book needs to focus on the operating principles of the model. The Experiential Learning Cycle, Challenge by Choice and the Full Value Contract support virtually all of Project Adventure's work. These operating norms ground each of PA's instructional models and all of its curriculum. While the basic concepts of each principle remain constant throughout all of PA's work, there are nuances that each model either brings to those norms, or which the operating principles tease out of the model. Section Two attempts to describe not only the basics of the Experiential Learning Cycle, Challenge by Choice and Full Value Contract; but also to describe the unique role that each plays in the AITC model.

Section Three presents the four primary teaching strategies of the Adventure in the Classroom model. The order of presentation is not a hierarchy of elements but simply a way to isolate each aspect of the model. While two strategies (team teaching and learning and integrated curriculum) are rooted in other areas of educational research and practice, two grow directly from PA's own work (adventure activities and processing).

Appendix II offers descriptions of curricula that practitioners have developed and used with their students. Throughout the book the elements of the model are examined separately, as if with a magnifying lens. The sample curriculum are offered as another lens to view the AITC model. The curriculum section is more like a periscope that surfaces to scan the scene above, taking in the horizon as well as the near view.

Finally, I would like to make a few comments about two other aspects of the book: the theoretical framework supporting the model and the vignettes opening each chapter. Regarding theoretical support for the AITC model, it is accurate to say that I anticipated and even tried several approaches to its presentation. My logical, sequential preferences suggested that I devote a chapter in Section One to summarize the theory. After all, theory is part of the background. Through the process of writing, however, I eventually decided to also integrate theory directly into the discussion of the various aspects of the model. Several researchers and writers offer theories supporting particular aspects of the AITC model. An integrated approach to theoretical discussion seemed to lend itself to the processes of sifting out those points and illustrating their influence on the model. In addition, integrating theoretical background throughout the book meant that readers, regardless of their approach to the book, would have that information readily available.

The classroom vignettes at the beginning of each chapter are distilled from the experiences of teachers whom I have had the privilege of knowing. While examples from numerous sources inform each chapter, these opening scenes, I hope, offer the reader a snapshot to introduce the particular background element, operating norm or teaching strategy of that chapter.

Whether you follow the dots or hunt and peck your way through, it is my sincere desire that this book assist you in your challenges as an educator, and support you and your community of learners as you pursue the *adventure* of learning.

Note to the Reader

Several years ago circumstances and colleagues presented me with the opportunity to put into words an approach to teaching that Project Adventure had begun to shape sixteen years earlier. Project Adventure staff, trainers and classroom teachers had been doing Adventure in the Classroom; but the model was a work in progress. There were sketches and scenes, characters and snatches of dialogue, but the play had yet to be written.

Very soon into the process of writing this book, I discovered the challenges of identifying and analyzing existing pieces, conceptualizing the whole model and then finding words to express it all. New puzzle pieces spilled onto the table at every turn. For example, at one point I described the model as a spiral, where the five teaching strategies identified at that time (cooperative learning, adventure activities, processing, integrated curriculum and thematic instruction) were drawn in to support the model. In time the limitations of this concept and the inability of this model to demonstrate the significance of the Full Value Contract, Challenge by Choice and the Experiential Learning Cycle became clear. I also began to see that the AITC model advocated an adaptation of cooperative learning—team learning and teaching, where students and teachers share the roles of learners and teachers together. At another point I chose to eliminate thematic instruction as a strategy, emphasizing, instead, a broader definition of integrated curriculum than existing literature suggested. Eventually, the pieces fell into place, and the current model, with its focus on learning in the context of the adventure community, emerged.

While this project has taken more time than any of us had planned or even desired, I am convinced that the AITC model as presented here is closer to the truth of the model than an earlier birth would have offered. And just as the children in your life and mine have years of change ahead of them, the AITC model will continue to grow and mature with each child and each teacher that lives it.

Background to the Adventure in the Classroom Model

The goal of Section One is to paint the background for the Adventure in the Classroom model. This background includes a definition of *adventure,* a review of Project Adventure's history and a description of the context within which the AITC model operates.

A discussion of the nature of adventure is an important first step in describing the AITC model. While traditional notions of adventure indicate something of its nature, a broader view indicates that *adventure* is a set of qualities more than a set of activities. The qualities of *significance, support, stimulation* and *satisfaction* are characteristics not only of adventure in the outdoors, but of Adventure in the Classroom

A review of Project Adventure's history reveals the organization's long-standing and active commitment to education. This review also sketches significant changes in the AITC model. Among these changes have been the adoption of its name and the conceptualization of the model that places learning at the center, supported by three operating principles and four instructional strategies. PA's model

for teaching and learning in the academic classroom was built upon the very foundations of all of Project Adventure's work—commitment to experiential learning and to adventure as a vehicle for personal and professional growth. Putting adventure out front demonstrates this commitment as well as PA's confidence in the roles that experiential learning and adventure learning play in academic classrooms.

The third important aspect of the background of the AITC model is the context within which the model operates—the community of adventure learners. As teachers, we cannot neglect the fact that learning takes place in context, not the least of which is the context of personal relationships within the classroom and within the school. More importantly, that set of relationships forms a community that supports learners in their educational endeavors. That the learning community in the AITC model is an *adventure* learning community highlights the significance, stimulation, support and satisfaction that accompany learning and teaching in this model.

Qualities of Adventure

Here is Adventure in the Classroom.
Here is a community of adventure learners
that teaches, challenges, trusts and
supports each other.

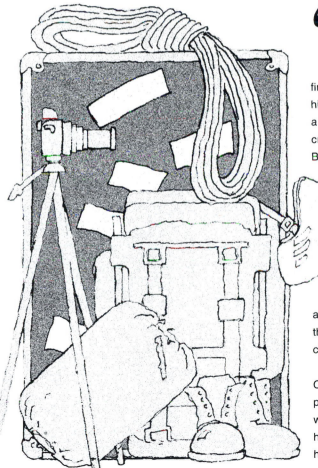

"**W**hat are the things you can do about finishing your homework?" asks second grader Seth, his dark eyes intent while he chews his lower lip. Tom, a fifth grader from the classroom next door, sits cross-legged in a corner of the second-grade room. Blond bangs drape his forehead as he bends over the "Problem-Solving Worksheet" in his lap. He has been reviewing the five steps listed on the sheet and thoughtfully writing answers.

Tom reads from his worksheet. "Come right into class in the morning and finish work. Have Alisha call me at night to check. Have Mom check my work at night. Take half of recess and do homework." Seth listens attentively to Tom, then asks the next question. "What is the best idea?" "Well, I think I'll do two things. Have Alisha call me at night to check, and spend half of recess on homework."

Like every other student at the Devonshire and Cedarwood elementary schools, Seth is familiar with this procedure for problem solving. He has learned to use it when he is confused by a book report assignment, when he gets into a fight with a classmate, or when he forgets his lunch money. Tom knows the steps, too. The two

Name Brian   ✓ Ashley

① Do you have a problem? yes no

② What is the problem? I took somebodys chair

③ What can you do?
Say sorry
Give it Back
Give my chair

④ Best idea Say Sorry

⑤ TRY!
Goal: not do it again

⑥ Do you have a problem? yes no

boys share a language and a strategy for dealing with the challenges of school.

Tom has chosen to "cool off" in the second-grade room and talk with someone else after an argument in his own classroom. His team members had been angry that he had neglected his homework for the fourth day in a row. Tom's incomplete homework meant the group's project on marshlands was also unfinished. Tom's family was preparing for a move, and the household was

disrupted. Tom's learning group had been patient. They had offered assistance and encouragement. But Tom hadn't taken any steps to follow through on his work.

Around Tom and Seth the other students work with large sheets of newsprint in cooperative learning groups of four or five. The class, with teacher guidance, has generated a list of topics that everyone needs to complete during these last six weeks of the school year. Each student lists on the group's sheet tasks to be accomplished. At one table, soft-spoken Micah writes, "Finish three more *Arthur* books. Pass addition and subtraction timed tests. Do *Charlie and the Chocolate Factory* project." Rasheeda itemizes, "Making change. Write letter to pen pal. Pass the timed subtraction test. Three more spelling sheets."

The signed goal sheets will be posted in the room. As the children complete their tasks, they will check off the items. Although the children will stay in their learning teams for the last six weeks, they will join with other children on the assignments they have yet to finish. Rasheeda and Micah will practice subtraction problems with three other students who have to pass the timed test. Tina will work with the four children who have spelling units. They will check each other for understanding.

Here is Adventure in the Classroom. Here is a community of adventure learners that teaches, challenges, trusts and supports each other.

For some people the word *adventure* conjures up images of National Geographic explorations into Tibet or rafting on the Colorado River. Other people list backpacking in the White Mountains, canoeing

Children beginning school expect this new adventure to be big and important. Witness their excitement about getting a lunch box or finding out which bus to ride. Note their anxiety about "going to school" reflected in disruptive behavior, sleeplessness, excessive energy. One six-year-old, after two days of first grade, complained that she didn't have any homework. "It's not first grade if there isn't homework," she lamented. In her mind, homework was a significant part of school. Homework was important. It was "doing school" at home. It was testing out new skills and showing off new knowledge.

a local river or exploring the depths of a limestone cave as adventure. While these various adventures represent a range of activities, the observer's response to such intriguing challenges is either, "I'd love to do that," or "I can't imagine!" Whether the adventure occurs in an exotic location or in one's back yard, it is the setting of physical challenge in an outdoor environment that characterizes the popular understanding of adventure.

While there is nothing inherently wrong with this view of adventure, it limits our ability to harness the power of adventure to other settings. After all, adventure is more than equipment, more than physical risk taking, more than remote vistas or the outdoors. Adventure is a matter of *significance, support, stimulation* and *satisfaction.* —characteristics of quality education.

Significance

Individuals embark on an adventure conscious that something about it is important. The adventure may have scientific importance, cultural significance or personal meaning. An adventure demands effort and commitment beyond the routine. It requires some amount of planning and preparation. In some cases it may stress financial resources. It requires some form of physical exertion. The adventure may demand personal sacrifice or even cause emotional strain. Adventures require some amount of risk taking.

A trek into Tibet requires considerable planning and effort. Significant personnel and financial resources are required to fund an expedition, support the logistics and negotiate the various bureaucratic requirements. Regardless of the goal—researching metabolic changes at high altitudes or the religious practices of Tibetan monks—the adventure is important, it has significance to the adventurer.

A science student experiments with basic principles of chemical reactions, ignoring the bell that signals the end of class. She comes in early and stays after school to complete her investigations. A pianist practices and studies a musical phrase in order to best express the composer's intent. He disciplines himself to practice for hours at a time. A beginning reader proudly sounds out words and eagerly demonstrates her developing skill. She ekes out precious minutes at bedtime and at breakfast to plunge into the exciting world of books. Such focus fuels new insights and understandings, forging intellectual growth.

Our challenge as teachers is to sustain this excitement by teaching to high expectations, exploring the profound questions and assisting our students in their intellectual growth. Our challenge is to make school, to make learning, significant to our students.

Support

Some level of support is necessary for the risk taking of adventure. The expedition to Tibet requires financial, medical, diplomatic and logistical support. The backpacker needs reliable equipment. The adventurer relies on some sort of emotional or spiritual support—confidence in one's skill and knowledge, religious faith, the encouragement of family and friends.

A journey into the intellectual unknown also requires support to encourage the healthy intellectual and social risk taking that characterize adventure learning. Children and teachers in adventure classrooms support each other. Students read their compositions to each other for feedback. They explain new and unfamiliar math concepts to each other. They give thank-yous and put-ups to acknowledge each other's contributions. Teachers admit when they don't have the answers and ask for help from their students.

The *adventure* in Project Adventure nourishes itself in emotional and physical support and safety. A supportive environment gives permission to "go for it," to put out all effort, to defy pre-conceived notions of success and failure, even to be silly. Affiliation and social support enable the student to stretch herself intellectually, as social support promotes achievement, successful problem solving and persistence on challenging tasks (Johnson and Johnson, 1991). Students are more willing to take academic risks, offer ideas, read from their own writing or propose an experiment if they know that they will be rewarded for the risk taking and encouraged in the effort, even if the result is less than perfect.

Because support and safety are its cornerstones, a community of adventure learners cultivates high expectations for its members, prompting individuals to stretch themselves intellectually and socially. Students assume new and greater responsibilities. They do not accept mediocre work from themselves or each other. They take ownership of the goals they set and hold each other accountable for individual achievement.

Stimulation

In many cases if a child does something other than what you expected, it's not "No;" it is another "Yes," The more different yeses we have in a classroom, the more everybody learns.

— *Eleanor Duckworth*

Adventures are intellectually, psychologically, emotionally and physically stimulating. While an adventure is well planned, it nevertheless retains that adrenaline-pumping feeling of "What will we see? How will it go? Can I really do it?" There is an element of surprise and anticipation.

The processes of discovery, personal meaning making and construction of knowledge that accompany stimulating intellectual pursuit transform experience into the certainty of knowledge. The intellectual challenges of the adventure classroom breed a healthy excitement and stimulation of thought that set the stage for the "Aha's!" (Duckworth, 1987) of learning. There is, then, an element of the unknown. Just how will the experiment turn out? Will this essay be good enough to send to the literary journal?

The teacher provides resources, and along with the students, establishes guiding questions for the topic of study. The teacher instructs in the necessary skills to embark on the study and sets parameters and requirements to be met. Rather than detailing the precise steps to carry out the inquiry, the teacher poses questions and provides opportunities for the students to grapple with the material. Surprises often occur in the processes students follow, the strategies they develop, the way they teach each other, the questions they raise. But developing skills, understanding concepts and learning the processes of complex problem solving are as much a part of the lesson as getting the right answer.

Adventure lies at the intersection of emotional involvement and unexpected outcomes, where adventure is more than the sum of its parts, more than fun, more than high expectations, more than support. This is the turning point, the point of transfer.

Satisfaction

A sense of satisfaction in meeting the challenges of an adventure encourages the adventurer to continue in that activity and even pursue new challenges. The hiker returns to a favorite trail. The rock climber tries new routes. The adventurer enjoys the adventure. She takes pleasure in the activity and pride in her accomplishments. In a similar way the satisfaction that comes from meeting academic challenges encourages further intellectual pursuit.

Individuals of all ages learn better and retain more when they are immersed in the process, when they feel the excitement, when they enjoy the learning. People learn, retain what they learn, and use what they learn when they have fun with what they learn (Caine and Caine, 1991). When students experience personal satisfaction with the material, they engage more deeply and learn more effectively. An adventure classroom is a fun place to be. It demonstrates and celebrates the learning processes. It encourages the natural joy of mastering new skills and embracing new concepts that characterize early childhood.

In addition, the adventure classroom opens many doors to the material through the orchestration of various modes of perceiving and processing information. Paper-mâché models of the planets hang from the ceiling, and a robot made from recyclables guards the doorway of a second-grade class studying space exploration. Living plants and menageries of reptiles, mammals and amphibians reside in high school science rooms where students take responsibility for tending to the animals' needs. During a unit on *Charlotte's Web*, the doorway into a first-grade classroom is decorated like a barn door, complete with hay and a spider's web. Students pick through a miniature feed bin to locate creative writing challenges and language arts activities. Students chatter about next week's visit to a local ropes course and plan math and writing challenges that incorporate their outdoor experience. These classrooms are satisfying places to be, both because of the atmosphere and the various avenues by which the students meet the material. Satisfaction in the classroom derives, among other things, from the opportunities to use the various strengths or intelligences of human learning (Gardner, 1990).

Adventure in this Classroom?

The Adventure in the Classroom model challenges teachers to view adventure through a new filter, a broader more inclusive lens. The AITC model asks teachers to examine the *qualities* of adventure rather than get caught up in the *appearance* of adventure. The psychological, physical and intellectual needs challenged through outdoor adventures are the same

needs that occur in our daily lives and that must be addressed in our educational endeavors: Significance, Support, Stimulation, Satisfaction.

Inattention to these needs leads to mediocre curriculum, inept pedagogy, apathetic students and frustrated teachers. Deliberate attention leads to student engagement, commitment to learning, professional development and strong, healthy schools.

Seth and Tom are actively engaged in their discussions and problem solving, just as the other students around the room are engrossed in their planning. Teacher and students contribute to a positive, nurturing atmosphere as they ask questions, give feedback and encourage each other. Group and individual planning do not have predictable outcomes, and students are not certain about what partners they will have during their last weeks of study. Tom must return to his own classroom where he will work out his difficulties with his peers and try a new strategy to complete his homework. The children are immersed in their work, sharing ideas and information, smiling, learning new skills. They are enjoying their time in class. This is a community of adventure learners.

History and Background

Essential to the original Project Adventure curriculum, the AITC model has a rich history.

HOW CAN the school become a true learning community where teachers, counselors and students support each other in a cooperative setting that is challenging and educationally sound?

HOW CAN students help solve problems in their communities, serve real needs and learn valuable curricular and social lessons in the process?

HOW CAN the school truly operate in partnership with the larger community and collaborate with parents, business leaders and social service agencies to provide quality education for its youth?

Educators twenty years ago posed the same questions often asked today. In 1970 the search for answers to these concerns prompted Jerry Pieh, principal of Hamilton-Wenham Junior/Senior High School in Hamilton, Massachusetts, and his colleague, Gary Baker, to write a three-year development proposal to the federal Office of Education. Their desire was to distill the essential characteristics from the experiential/adventure process of Outward

Bound programming and apply them to the secondary public school setting. Their intent was to imbed this new program in the structure of the public school. They called the new program Project Adventure.

Pieh and his partners wanted more than an outing club format or a specialized curriculum isolated from the mainstream schedule and goals of the school. They envisioned something bigger than expeditions, rock climbing and ropes courses. Their goal was to see Project Adventure and the processes of experiential and adventure education embraced as standard curriculum.

Project Adventure was funded in 1971, and the first PA staff began to work with several classroom teachers at the Hamilton-Wenham High School to write and experiment with curriculum. Bob Lentz, the Project's first director, himself a former teacher and principal, found in the Project Adventure curriculum a way to help students become more engaged in learning and more responsible to their schools and communities. In addition, he was committed to institutionalizing the process. He recognized the need for faculty and staff to accept and validate the program as part of the general curriculum and to be given authority and resources to make curricular changes as they saw appropriate.

Original Curriculum

Two basic goals drove the sophomore interdisciplinary curriculum that formed the original Hamilton-Wenham model: that the students would 1) learn to solve problems more creatively and efficiently, and 2) learn to overcome preconceived barriers to

their agreed upon objectives. Every sophomore participated in a year-long Project Adventure physical education class of sequenced, innovative warm-ups, trust-building exercises, initiative problems and low and high ropes course elements. Concurrently, the sophomore English, social studies and biology curricula reinforced the same goals in pursuit of traditional academic course objectives. Educational goals and curriculum were interdependent and interdisciplinary.

In physical education class students learned how to plan and allocate group resources in order to complete initiative problems. In biology class students implemented those same skills as they devised procedures to investigate a freshwater swamp and collect data. The four-period Action Seminar curriculum was an interdisciplinary class combining adventure activities and service learning. Among the community service projects the students implemented were a tutoring program at local elementary schools and a community-wide recycling program.

The experiential units of this class were largely cooperative. They culminated in peak experiences of two- and three-day camping trips that used the environment of the campsite to introduce additional material. Peak experiences were also opportunities for final practice, implementation and evaluation of academic skills, content learning and group process. During the annual trip to Maine's Acadia National Park, for example, students gathered and classified specimens for a saltwater tide pool unit. They managed the many jobs necessary for a successful camping experience, and they chronicled their experiences.

Evaluation and National Demonstration Award

The 1974 evaluation of the first two years of the program utilized six instruments. Strong positive results with statistically significant changes on two of the instruments, the Tennessee Self-Concept Scale and the Rotter Scale of Internal vs. External Control, led to the 1974 awarding of National Demonstration School Status by the federal Office of Education. Funding from the National Diffusion Network, along with the awarding of Model Program status, put Project Adventure on the map by subsidizing the adoption of Project Adventure programming at other school sites. By 1980 more than 400 schools across the country had adopted at least one component of the original PA program.

Adventure Based Counseling

While the academic and physical education curricula were the cornerstones of Project Adventure in the Hamilton-Wenham High School, a third model, which became known as Adventure Based Counseling, had begun to take shape in 1974. The new school curriculum, along with outpatient counseling practice

at the Addison Gilbert Hospital in Gloucester, Massachusetts, helped to mold this emerging model. From its inception, the Adventure Based Counseling model combined intake strategies, consultation and adventure activities to facilitate behavior change.

Between 1980 and 1983, funding from a Massachusetts State Department of Education grant supported the development of a counseling curriculum. PA staff worked with personnel from three Massachusetts school systems to refine the processes of intake, grouping, staffing, activities selection and staff training. Extensive evaluation of this program showed significant statistical results, and the Massachusetts State Department of Education awarded the program validation as a State Model Program (Schoel, Prouty, Radcliffe, 1988).

Project Adventure and "Back-to-Basics"

In 1982 Project Adventure incorporated as a non-profit entity. The mission of the newly-organized Project was to help others design and implement model PA programs. Simply stated, the goal was to "help bring the adventure home." Although home for clients included businesses, corporate training centers, hospitals, drug treatment facilities, camps, family and youth service agencies, schools were PA's own "home base."

Schools faced tough times during the early 1980's. Federal funding of public education

decreased. A back-to-basics movement and a climate intent on the reclamation of behaviors and values of the pre-Vietnam era exerted pressures on American schools. Public schools experienced decreased enrollment with changing demographics. Adding to this dilemma was an increase in the number of students choosing to attend private schools. Student acquisition of basic skills became the goal of education; and the public, along with many in education, seemed to frown upon any instructional methods that appeared to contain an element of fun. Fun, it seems, was considered subversive to serious education.

Concurrently, the expediency of delivering curriculum was considered more important than the depth of student understanding. Schools relied heavily on textbooks and curriculum workbooks. Teachers designed and mimeographed individual instructional packets aimed at keeping kids busy at their desks with paper, pencil and carefully chosen resource materials. Workbooks and paperbacks appeared as line items on school budgets under the heading *Consumables*, evidence of the attitude that children simply needed to ingest curriculum materials, like vitamin C, in the daily recommended dose.

In spite of the public's demand for more traditional methods of education and its skepticism of alternative approaches, the flow of people to PA training workshops and subsequent adoptions continued. Although most school adoptions were physical education and counseling curriculum, the

academic model managed to survive the powerful currents of "basic education" for several reasons.

First, there was a commitment to the philosophy of the model—that people learn best when they are engaged in the learning process, work cooperatively and take ownership of their learning. Second, key individuals within Project Adventure remained committed to the concept of the academic model. They were convinced of its viability in the mainstream of educational practice. The Project continued to offer one or two workshops in the model each year as evidence of its commitment. These provided opportunity for the model to continue its evolution. Finally, students and teachers scattered throughout the national PA network learned and grew in adventure classrooms, testimony to the model's effectiveness, viability and impact. These classrooms were the action labs that further developed and refined the model.

Classroom Model Comes of Age

By the mid-1980s the academic model embraced the name "Adventure in the Classroom." David Joseph, a teacher in Essex, Massachusetts, who

The model was Adventure in the *Classroom,*
not in the gym or on the playing field
or in the group therapy session.

suggested it, pointed out that Project Adventure's interdisciplinary model encompassed more than academic material. It included adventure. In fact, *adventure* was the catalyst for learning. The model was Adventure in the *Classroom,* not in the gym or on the playing field or in the group therapy session. In classrooms such as David's there was significance, support, stimulation and satisfaction. The adventure was built through team learning and teaching, integrated curriculum, processing and adventure activities—elements consistent with the academic model from its inception.

The roles and expectations of schools had come under new scrutiny. The American public, along with government and business leaders, were identifying goals for education that included skills to process information, make decisions, work collaboratively, solve complex problems and provide leadership. The 1982 Carnegie report, *A Nation at Risk,* heralded the need for individual excellence, "performing on the boundary of individual ability in ways that test and push back personal limits, in school and in the workplace." It also challenged the school to be a place of excellence that "sets high expectations and goals for all learners, then tries in every way possible to help students reach them."

New expectations regarding the need for students to apply knowledge to a wide range of complex problems were being espoused. Basic skills acquisition had been a short-sighted objective. Educators were now being challenged to look at not only *what* they taught, but *how* they taught.

A Call for Cooperation

American service and manufacturing industries, recognizing the importance of teamwork for their own survival in an increasingly competitive global market, also challenged schools to reconsider the competitive and individualistic goal structures prevalent in the classroom. Cooperation in the boardroom, on the production floor and in the research lab leads to more creative approaches, better products, effective strategies and a stronger bottom line. Self-managed teams, quality circles and more flexible approaches to management demand different skills than does the traditional production line. As supervisors and on-line workers gain increased satisfaction about their jobs, they demonstrate higher productivity.

The early 1980's was also a time when educators and researchers at the university level were designing and carrying out experiments, field tests and studies on the effects of cooperation in the learning environment. The research documented the positive effects of cooperative learning in the classroom. The identification of components necessary for effective implementation—positive interdependence, individual accountability, face-to-face interaction, group skills and processing (Johnson and Johnson, 1988)—focused curriculum development efforts. With the call from future employers and the validation from their own arena of expertise, local school administrators and classroom teachers began to acknowledge and integrate cooperative learning strategies in their classrooms.

Cooperative strategies had been a hallmark of Project Adventure from the start. The first curriculum at Hamilton-Wenham Regional High School had relied heavily upon a team approach to learning and teaching. Classroom lessons were structured for student collaboration. Students had worked in project groups outside the classroom to gather information about water quality in the community and made recommendations to the town planning board. By the late 1980's, the Adventure in the Classroom model began to benefit from more concrete guidelines to assure effective instruction along with a growing body of research to support what its practitioners had known intuitively.

Processing, Problem Solving and Critical Thinking

Despite the earlier basics movement in education, classroom teachers in the late eighties recognized the need to teach problem solving, processing and critical-thinking skills. By the end of the decade, increasingly complex curriculum goals and rapidly changing content in the established disciplines challenged existing curriculum. New courses in environmental science, drug and alcohol awareness, global politics, computer technology and literature of developing nations demanded school time alongside the standard curriculum of English, biology, algebra and American history. It became clear that as information continued to expand exponentially, the skills young people needed to develop were the skills of inquiry, research, assimilation, analysis, synthesis, prediction and transfer.

The Four Pointer

One of the original problem-solving initiatives developed by PA is *The Four Pointer.*

Object:

To attempt to get a group of seven students across a thirty-foot area, using only four points of simultaneous contact with the ground (for example, foot, hand, knee, etc.).

Rules:

1. All seven students must start at the marked starting line and end at the finish line.
2. No props (logs, wagons) may be used.
3. All seven students must be in contact with each other as they progress across the ground.

Note:

A large group can be divided into many groups of seven. The groups make the attempt simultaneously so they will discover solutions independently. This problem can also be done with five people on three points.

Business leaders and education futurists remind us even now that citizens of the twenty-first century will not need to know information as much as they will need to know how to find, process and use information. Technology continues to outpace the human ability to master an ever-expanding knowledge base. The information explosion demands that our students develop skills to identify, explore and solve complex problems. Students need to be able to gather, analyze and synthesize information and then apply new knowledge. They must be able to critique opinions and arguments, prioritize, infer meaning, deduce facts, make decisions. Knowledge bases will continue to grow at startling rates. Today's

The goals of public education as we moved into
the last quarter of the twentieth century were remnants
of the goals of public education a century earlier.

discovery may well be tomorrow's outdated information. To be positive, contributing members of the larger community, citizens of all ages need to learn a complex array of skills to meet these challenges.

This is what the AITC model has been about from the beginning. The problem-solving initiatives of the early activity base were designed to push individuals to look for new answers, apply existing knowledge, develop new applications. Initiatives were geared for creative problem solving. Attention to processing the activity meant that students were learning metacognitive skills. What the public dialogue around life-long learning goals did for the AITC model was to challenge Project Adventure to be more articulate and transparent about the ways the model met these goals.

The Whole Student

The back-to-basics movement had stressed acquisition of information and development of literacy and computation skills. Departments of education and school boards wanted hard evidence that students could read, write and compute. Yet, in spite of the move to competency testing, the students who were in school during this period of education reform did not demonstrate significant performance gains over their counterparts a decade earlier. The students of this era also lacked the ability to use higher order thinking skills and maneuver the more complex environments of self-managed work teams and multidimensional managerial tasks in the work world. The back-to-basics movement had been woefully inadequate to meet the complex needs of American students in the latter part of the twentieth century. It addressed only one facet of learning—the mechanics. In their attempt to isolate skills, educators drained skills of contextual meaning. Curriculum barren of anything connected to students' daily lives further alienated them from the classroom and contributed to flagging interest in the work of the school.

The insidious alienation of content from meaningfulness to students managed to illuminate another significant issue in education. The goals of public education as we moved into the last quarter of the twentieth century were remnants of the goals of public education a century earlier: to train a labor force disciplined to operate within the authoritarian hierarchies of a growing manufacturing industry and to mold an immigrant population into a homogenous American citizenry with shared common values (Tyack, 1974). Operating within the framework of these goals meant a commitment to systems rather than students, and a conviction that learning is as much a matter of will as of intellect. The debilitating effect of this attitude was, and is, a blindness to the needs of the whole student.

Changing economics, family patterns, concepts of diversity and increasing pressures on citizens in the twentieth century demand that education concern itself with the child as a whole person, not just an entity reduced to intellect and will. Children are a complexity of needs. We are daily reminded of the effects of the accumulation of unmet needs on individuals, families and entire communities. Fluctuating home environments, economic deprivation, drug and alcohol use and ineffective social institutions mean that our children come to school with bags full of unmet needs that demand satisfaction before children are able to grasp any segment of state mandated academic curriculum.

The AITC Model Today

Education today must concern itself as much with collaboration as it does content, process with problem solving, human needs as much as human intellect. The demand for an inclusive, multi-layered approach to improving academic achievement grows almost daily. The challenge today for the AITC model is to strengthen its stride and continue in the directions already set.

Refinement of the Model

The ardent efforts to refine the model have resulted in a clearer articulation of a conceptual model consisting of four main components: (see Fig. 2.1)

Goal — Learning is the goal at the center of the model. The learning may be in a subject area, such as reading, calculus or global politics. The learning may be of a particular skill, such as estimation, computation, short story analysis or scientific methods of investigation. The learning may be about a theme or an interpersonal skill. In all cases, the focus of the model is learning—the construction of knowledge.

Context —The context for the learning is the community of adventure learners (see Chapter Three). The learning community is both setting and participant. The adventure learning community as a whole, as well as individuals in that community, challenge, support, teach and hold the members to standards of excellence. The healthy functioning of that group, then, is as important as the healthy functioning of a family is to its various members.

Operating principles — The operating principles of the Experiential Learning Cycle, the Full Value Contract and Challenge by Choice (see Section Two) support the goal by providing ways for students to develop the skills necessary to becoming quality, positive members of the adventure learning community.

Strategies for teaching and learning — Finally, teaching and learning strategies of Adventure Activities, Processing, Team Learning and Teaching and Integrated Curriculum (see Section Three) are the vehicles of instruction. Project Adventure's legacy is rich in adventure activities and processing. One of the organization's strengths is research and development in these two areas. Educational research and practices around cooperative learning and curriculum integration from other sources have significantly benefited effective implementation of Team Teaching and Learning and Integrated Curriculum in the AITC model.

Alignment with Current Practice and Research in Education

The AITC model is mutually supportive of many of the positive directions in education today. The growing body of work in metacognition, applica-

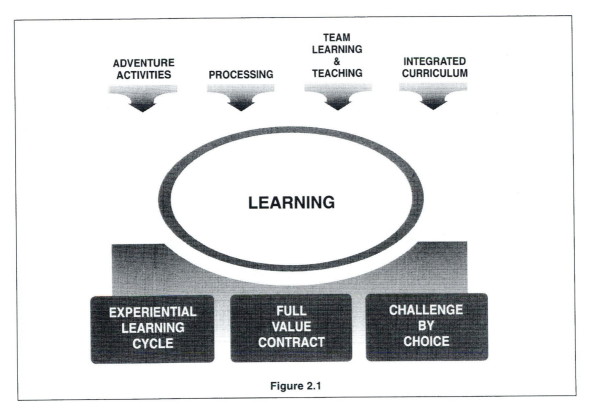

Figure 2.1

tion of multiple intelligence theory, development of service learning curriculum, and authentic assessment supports and is supported by the AITC model.

Project Adventure has incorporated ideas from compatible programs and has created new directions within the context of the original philosophy. The model continues to benefit from collaboration with practitioners across the country. These teachers and administrators bring practical experience as well as expertise within their particular areas of professional development.

The context, operating principles and strategies of the AITC model have been validated in the workplace and the classroom. The benefits of divergent thinking, of working in teams and of open dialogue are no longer relegated to the fringes of educational practice from a decade or more ago. The AITC model has come of age.

Broader Definitions of Activity and Adventure

The definition of activity inherent in the AITC model invites a variety of teaching methods to contribute to this approach to teaching and learning. Challenge ropes course elements, cooperative games and problem-solving initiatives are still cornerstones of the activity base. But by expanding the definition of adventure in terms of *significance*, *support*, *stimulation* and *satisfaction*, a wider range of activities is available to the AITC teacher. The adventure activities, after all, have their significance within the entire context of the model.

The work of one team of teachers who developed an AIDS curriculum illustrates the broader definition of *adventure*. The teachers developed a research unit which included various activities designed to teach factual information about AIDS.

The teachers also created a problem-solving initiative which required students to apply information about HIV and AIDS. These students spent their time in either the classroom or library for the duration of this curriculum. They did not go out on a challenge ropes course. However, the curriculum and its activities required students to study and learn content, to support each other in the very same ways had they embarked on a more physical adventure. They worked together, maintained a safe environment in which to learn, involved themselves in significant and meaningful work, and participated in stimulating intellectual pursuits throughout the process.

School Climate and Structure

The effects of school structure and climate have enormous impact on the classroom and the quality of education. The restructuring dialogue of the last decade has pressed everyone in education to more consciously address issues of structure and climate. Collaborative visioning, individual and group goal setting, norm articulation, feedback and process skills are among the skills necessary to support the culture change which accompanies effective school restructuring. Project Adventure's attention to the entire learning community and a long history in team building have served us well in working with administrators, faculty and staff involved in the school change process. PA's experiential and adventure approaches effectively introduce and nurture profound changes in organizational behaviors throughout the school.

Strength in Flexibility

The strength of the AITC model is its flexibility to meet a wide range of content and a variety of needs and abilities. Teachers who have developed their craft over years in the classroom can incorporate the AITC model as easily as apprentice teachers. An instructor can integrate the operating principles on an incremental basis or comprehensively. The AITC model is as effective for the first-grade classroom as it is for sixth-grade health and college physics. It is a comprehensive approach built upon a commitment to the adventure learning community, a system of operating principles and methodologies that actively involves the student and responds to her cognitive, affective and behavioral development.

Summary

Essential to the original Project Adventure curriculum, the AITC model has a rich history. Grounded in the philosophy that people learn best when they are engaged in the learning process, work cooperatively and take ownership for their learning, the AITC model has survived various winds of educational reform. In addition, the collective efforts of practitioners have contributed to the model's growth and development. Increasing demands for team models and collaborative skills for the workplace, highly developed problem-solving abilities and attention to a wholistic view of learning have highlighted the strengths of the AITC model.

Through the years of development, the model has become shaped according to its four components:

1. **Goal** — Learning

2. **Context** — Community of Adventure Learners

3. **Operating principles** —
   - Experiential Learning Cycle
   - Full Value Contract
   - Challenge by Choice

4. **Strategies for teaching and learning** —
   - Adventure Activities
   - Processing
   - Team Learning and Teaching
   - Integrated Curriculum

At the same time that the AITC model maintains strong roots, it continues to break new ground. The model's strength continues to grow from its firm foundation and flexibility.

CHAPTER THREE

The Community of Adventure Learners

*There can be no peace —
and ultimately no life — without community*

— M. Scott Peck

For the first few months of school, Toni, an easy-going fifth grader, wouldn't do her homework. This hampered her ability to participate in class, and before too long she was falling behind. No amount of cajoling, discussion or consequence had any impact on her. Parents and teacher were at wit's end. "The turning point came when I finally decided to turn it over to the class," explains Toni's teacher, Ms. Acinapura. "After all, that's what it's about—trusting the process and building on the community." She continues her story:

"We began with a half-hour feedback session with Toni. The kids asked her about her afternoon schedule; what did she do when she got home, what jobs she had at home. Toni said that she had to take care of her younger brother until their parents got home. Other children told about how they had to do the same thing.

"Next the kids wanted to know the layout of the house. Was there a place where Toni could do homework and be undisturbed by her brother's play, yet still keep an eye on him? They made suggestions about things the brother could do that would be safe, so she didn't have to be right with him. Then they made suggestions about how Toni could manage her time and complete her homework.

"But it wasn't over with the advice. After about twenty minutes of this, the students gave Toni 'put-ups.' One child said, 'You've done great sitting here and listening all this time. I couldn't have done it.' Charley, another classmate, told Toni that he was proud that Toni could sit through it all without crying—quite a compliment from Charley.

"At the end of the day, I asked one of the children to review the homework assignments with Toni. She had already done that!

"This was a turning point for Toni. For the first few weeks she consistently completed and returned homework on time. She was more active in class, invested in the work. She really contributed to class.

"Then there were a few missed assignments. The three students who sat with her checked it out with Toni. They held a small feedback session, like the entire class had done earlier. There were more periodic check-ins, and eventually Toni became more consistent with her work and her grades improved. Keeping up with her homework meant she was spending more time with the material, studying, fulfilling her potential. She seemed to feel better about being in class, too. She participated more actively and really became a member of the team."

Toni's classmates valued each other enough to take the necessary risks to first confront then commit themselves to helping Toni. While the problem at hand involved time management at home, the decision to attend to Toni's problem in the classroom meant the difference between succeeding and failing in school.

Community

The root of *community* is the word *common*. Among other things, a community shares a common government (as does a city), a common set of values (as a professional group), a common locale (as in the case of a neighborhood) or a common purpose (as a school). Even though schools sometimes neglect to articulate their goals for education, the institution of school serves the purpose of learning. In other words, schools are a place of learning. But learning is such an intricate web of subject matter, cognitive skills, attitudes, habits of mind and social interaction that the community needs skills to negotiate those intricacies. The web either snags or supports the school community members. Issues ranging from block scheduling to inclusion to discipline codes hang themselves up on the snares of personalities, history and territory. The healthy functioning of the community depends upon the integrity of its relationships. For a community to promote a common goal, it must consciously nurture the relationships in a healthy manner.

The members of Ms. Acinapura's classroom share the common goals of adventure learning. Their academic work matters. School is *significant*. These students care enough about each other to *support* each other. They are committed to *safety* even in confrontation. They are *stimulated* to take interpersonal and academic risks.

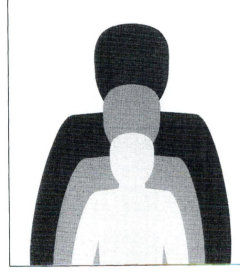

Community

- Meeting needs of safety and belonging as a prerequisite for growth
- Learning occurs in context and relationship

Adventure

- Cognitive growth a product of intellectual risk taking

Learner

- Individual benefits from collective endeavors of the group

Theoretical Framework

The notion of a *community of adventure learners* emerges out of the interplay between several theoretical perspectives, each of which recognizes the relationship between the learner and the learning community:

- Learning occurs in context and relationship.
- Meeting basic human needs for safety and belonging is a prerequisite for cognitive growth.
- Cognitive growth is a product of intellectual risk taking.
- The individual benefits from the collective endeavors of the entire group.

Learning Occurs in Context and Relationship

Humans, as social beings, mature intellectually in reciprocal relationships with other people.

— *Art Costa*

Brain research (Caine and Caine, 1991), learning as social interaction theory (Vygotsky, 1978) and challenges to hierarchical paradigms of education (Noddings, 1992) confirm the role of relationships in cognitive development.

Research reveals that the brain actively searches for and creates patterns of information in order to construct meaning (Caine and Caine, 1991).

The higher functions of the brain search for ways to connect the past and present experiences of the learner in order to deepen understanding. Information in isolation is soon lost to long-term memory and future accessibility. Similarly, the brain is a socially-oriented organ whose efficacy improves or weakens in direct response to the individual's sense of belonging. Safety and support enhance learning, while threat and intimidation inhibit learning.

Toni and her classmates dealt with the problem of completing homework and juggling school work because the two issues were interrelated. Inability to concentrate at home meant incomplete homework and lack of understanding of material.

Consideration of the social nature of learning (Vygotsky, 1978) is another angle from which to understand the theory that learning occurs in context and relationship. The premise is that cognitive development is the internalization of social speech, and interaction between peers is necessary for cognitive growth. The dialogue that characterizes this interaction is a necessary step for internalization of the material to be learned. The "more able peer" pushes the "less able peer" into the "zone of proximal development," where optimal learning occurs. Simultaneously, as the more able peer verbalizes, rehearses, explains the material to the less able peer, she internalizes that material and develops the cognitive structures necessary for in-depth learning. Learning is a social activity characterized by verbal interaction. Learning unleashes the many internal developmental processes that operate only when the child interacts with others and cooperates with peers.

The discussion of caring as it relates to education, both in terms of human/human relations and human/non-human relations (relations between people and ideas, between people and the human-made world, or between people and the world of other living organisms) pushes the issue of relationship and context even further. Relationships between people within the classroom invite new learning. "Relation, except in very rare cases, precedes any engagement with subject matter. Caring relations can prepare children for an initial receptivity to all sorts of experiences and subject matters" (Noddings, 1992). The reverse, unfortunately, also holds true, as "merely contractual relations can keep students busy for a long time at work for which they have no real talent or interest." For many children, "human relations are simply irrelevant to the knowledge we profess to value. There is no connection at all" (Noddings, 1992). In other words, as learners, we embrace new experiences in the classroom as we feel a positive connection to those experiences and to the people around us.

Relationships are what learning is about. People truly learn as they care about what they are learning. It is the kind of relationship we see when someone is engrossed in a book, intent in working on a piece of sculpture or bending over a new computer program.

Meeting Basic Needs for Belonging and Safety — Prerequisite for Cognitive Growth

The basic needs for safety and affiliation are undeniable. The infant cries to be held. The third grader looks anxiously down the bus aisle to find a friend with whom she can sit. Adolescents consume themselves with friendships, anxious to belong to a group. Human development, brain research, organizational development, public health and policy verify the human need for affiliation. Unless an individual feels safe and experiences positive affiliation, she is unable to engage in the kind of cognitive activity that supports in-depth learning.

Maslow's hierarchy of needs (1962) identifies safety as a primary need that must be met before other needs can be successfully satisfied. Lacking the confidence of safe affiliation, the student remains shackled to very limited patterns of behaving. This deficiency thwarts attempts at behavior change or intellectual challenges. On the other hand, the feelings of validation that emerge from mastering needs encourage the individual to reach further both academically and behaviorally.

The benefit of a state of "relaxed alertness" that a student experiences in a safe environment is the release of adrenaline and noradrenaline during eustress (or good stress), stimulating the individual to handle challenges. Conversely, cortisol, released during periods of distress, inhibits the brain's capacity to recognize and create patterns, to tap short- term memory and to form new permanent memories. Brain research challenges teachers to "take students beyond their comfort zone without undue threat" and "establish an environment that allows for safe risk taking" (Caine and Caine, 1991).

In order to meet this challenge, the personal relationships within the community of adventure learners cannot be left to chance. Relationships must be developed so as to create a learning environment that supports the safe risk taking of intellectual challenges. This is the kind of safety and belonging that both challenged and supported Toni in her efforts to meet her academic responsibilities.

Cognitive Growth — A Product of Intellectual Risk Taking

The aspect of *adventure* in the community of adventure learners is a reminder that cognitive growth is a product of intellectual risk taking. Healthy risk taking is an adventure. It requires an atmosphere of safety and support. Healthy risk taking involves significant, meaningful endeavor and elicits that optimal arousal that stimulates the individual to develop new levels of competence (Ewert, 1989). Appropriate levels of challenge or adventure produce a dynamic that leads to intellectual growth. Whether we use the language of zone of proximal development, the place where the student has emerging abilities which need to be exercised and challenged in order to develop (Vygotsky, 1989); disequilibrium, and the theory that the mind develops via appropriate interactions which introduce disequilibrium (Piaget, 1968); or active uncertainty, where learning is a matter of reorganizing, rearranging or enlarging the self (Pribram, 1987), it is clear that the process of learning involves periods of uncertainty or ambiguity followed by moments of "felt meaning" (Caine and Caine, 1991) or the "Aha!" (Duckworth, 1987). In each case, there is a place of pushing into unknown territory. There is risk taking, or uncertainty about the outcome.

Toni, her classmates and their teacher faced a challenge whose outcome was uncertain. The teacher had hopes, even expectations based on the values, skills and knowledge possessed by the students. Toni certainly was entering the zone of proximal development, or disequilibrium. There was a problem that needed resolution. For growth or positive change to occur, the challenge needed to be appropriate—confrontational yet realistic challenges to behavior change. The interaction needed to be at that zone of proximal development where Toni had some emerging skills or knowledge but needed the challenge to test and to develop those skills.

Individual Learner Benefits from the Collective Endeavors of Entire Community

There is developing support for the notion of a collective intelligence—one that is greater than the sum of its parts. Literature from the fields of organizational development and management (Senge, 1990; Wheatley, 1992) enrich our understanding that humans learn collectively as well as individually. In addition, this collective intelligence reveals truth and understanding otherwise lost to the individual. This notion is not only applicable to the creative factor in the learning process, but to collective understanding of known concepts. During dialogue people question positions, challenge answers and develop new ideas. A new intelligence emerges during the interaction within a community of learners.

In turn, individuals benefit from this new intelligence. Scientific research teams, for example, are effective models for investigation because the output of the group is greater than the collection of individual efforts. Each member of the team becomes the beneficiary of whatever knowledge the team produces, just as Toni learned from the collective efforts of her classmates.

The School as Community

The classroom as a community of adventure learners is, of course, a microcosm of the larger learning community—the school. Current discussion concerning the structures of the learning organization emphasize the shared vision and language of the organization members (Barth 1991; Senge 1990). Members of the learning organization engage in continuous dialogue to support active participation of each and every participant. In this large community students, faculty, administrators and staff share the roles of teacher and learner. The Carnegie Council's challenge to schools to become "a community of adults and young people embedded in networks of support and responsibility that enhance the commitment of students to learning" (1989) echoes Project Adventure's vision of the larger community of adventure learners.

Members of a community of adventure learners control their learning goals. Teachers participate in administrative decisions and create curricular units that support appropriate student decision making, promote healthy life-styles, make connections between current knowledge and new concepts, and teach students the skills to be responsible for their own learning. Parents share in the decision making process and participate in curriculum development.

The traditional isolation of students and teachers stifles the sharing and continuous dialogue necessary for the development of real community. For a whole school to become a community of adventure learners, then, there must be a deep and abiding change from the traditional models of school structure (Fullan, 1982). As they develop new norms, adventure learners need to look within their community to where the greatest resources exist to address its problems. The community then mobilizes these resources to expand its members' views about learning and schools. The community must identify its goals, clarify its common values and construct a common vocabulary to initiate such changes.

Stated Goals of the Community and Individual Members

Goals direct the efforts of an individual and a community. It is against the stated goals that we make choices about activities, policy, instructional strategy and behavior norms. Articulating individual and group goals allows community members to choose their role in supporting those goals.

Common Values

Similarly, the values that a learning community lives color its complexion. A learning community that recognizes competition and rewards winners nurtures very different behaviors than the school that emphasizes cooperation. In the latter case, students are rewarded for their contributions to others and their ability to listen and incorporate divergent ideas. In the competitive classroom, individualistic behaviors and performance gain stature. The competitive student, driven by personal desire to demonstrate success by quantitative measures, flourishes. The student who thrives on personal relationships falls short against these competitive standards.

Vocabulary

Embedded in an organization's communications are expressions of what it prizes. Scan any newspaper and you will find a reflection of a society's values in its major sections: sports, business and finance, and entertainment.

— Art Costa

What we say, what we talk about reflect our values. A community speaks a common vocabulary. You can not mistake the slang of truck drivers with that of computer programmers. The vocabulary of the adventure learning community illustrates commitments to challenge, risk taking and collaboration. The hallway banners that proclaim *Trust, Risk* and *Challenge* at Cedarwood Elementary School, and the corridors painted *Cooperation Climb* and *Problem-Solving Path* at Devonshire Elementary School proclaim the values in action throughout the schools.

To call school work and home work "challenges" (see Chapter Five) reminds students and teachers of the high degree of interest and support in the classroom. When students speak of "put-ups" and consistently thank each other for them, the students internalize this value as they effortlessly use this vocabulary. When students in an eighth-grade class ask, "Will you be 'on belay' for me?" or offer, "I'm 'on belay' for you," they remind each other of their commitment to mutual support.

Membership and Roles in the Community

Membership in a community changes as our lives change. For instance, a parent who volunteers in his younger daughter's school may not have been able to volunteer regularly when his older child was in elementary school. As the individual's participation changes, so do relationships surrounding those roles. In the community of adventure learners, the teacher is a co-learner with his students as well as his peers. Sometimes that teacher takes an administrative role, making policy decisions and refining the budget. The administrator is a leader and vision builder but also a coach, a member of a curriculum team, a facilitator and a co-learner. A student assumes the roles of mentor, learner or peer coach. In each case, there is fluidity in the roles and a responsibility of the community to support the various strengths that each member brings to that community to the best advantage of both the individual and the group.

Fluidity

The woodwind section has a decidedly different place in Vivaldi's *Four Seasons* than it has in a Grieg piano concerto. The solo instrument of one movement may be *sotto voce* in another. Similarly, roles and membership in a community are dynamic and fluid. The adventure community calls upon the various strengths of members so that the variety of existing knowledge, skills, leadership abilities and group skills can be tapped.

In the early phases of a classroom coming together, for example, the teacher more actively manages the roles and responsibilities of the class members. As the students learn self-management skills and begin to take more responsibility for their own learning, the teacher moves into a facilitative mode. If, at the end of the semester or the year, the relationships among students and between students and teachers look the same as they did at the beginning, there has been no growth. Students may have learned material, but that they have developed greater reasoning, thinking and creative powers is highly suspect.

Teacher as Conductor, Co-learner and Coach

After many years of teaching, I must admit that mine is not the primary voice in the classroom. Only rarely, for example, do my words find their way into the children's stories. I may draw attention to the storyteller's ideas, but I remain the commentator and not the inventor.

— *Vivian Gussein Paley*

The teacher in the AITC classroom assumes several roles. As a conductor, she is an artist with an ear for excellence. She demands the best from each member of the orchestra. The orchestra, this community of adventure learners, develops skills as individuals, as sections and finally as the entire orchestra. Like the conductor who knows the history of the piece, the influences on the composer, the delicious intricacy of sounds, the teacher draws from the richness of the community of learners and helps the students to create a sound that is truly their own.

As a co-learner the teacher models learning in her own efforts to grow. She is not afraid to say, "I don't know," or, "I'd like to try this and see what happens." As a co-learner in the larger school community, the teacher actively engages in professional development and collaborates with colleagues in the change process. The willingness to admit weaknesses or lack of knowledge in the classroom is the same willingness to admit vulnerabilities and lack of knowledge with colleagues. Members of the school community support each other in their professional risk taking just as they support the students in their endeavors.

Finally, as a coach, the teacher is actively involved with the material and the students. The teacher may not be an expert player, but she is a good player who knows good technique. Like the coach, the teacher has an eye for form. She also understands her players' strengths and helps the players make best use of their abilities. The teacher knows how to tap into the leadership strengths of one student, the logical thinking abilities of another, and the inquisitiveness of still another student. Nurturing these strengths benefits those individuals as well as the entire team.

Administrator as Conductor, Co-learner and Coach

The administrator of the community of adventure learners is also conductor, co-learner and coach. The administrator shares her experience and ability with the team, but also challenges the orchestra members to play to the best of their own abilities. She draws from a spectrum of knowledge and resource to help this orchestra create a sound that is truly its own. She provides the context in which to build the vision of the school and helps create the values that echo in school halls and classrooms. She creates opportunities for dialogue among students and staff which define the community and keeps a constant ear for the tone of the whole building so that it vibrates with the joy of growth.

As co-learner, the administrator acknowledges vulnerabilities and remains open to new learning. If she wants to be heard, she needs to listen and participate openly and honestly in the dialogue around approaches to student learning, classroom management and curriculum development.

Finally, the administrator carries a vision for her team, knows the individual and collective abilities of the members, and coaches them to excellence. She assesses the strengths of each team member and nurtures an atmosphere in which they can flourish. She asks for practice and demands excellence, and at the same time, provides a safe place for experimentation and growth.

Students as Resources Responsible for Learning

Students in this community of adventure learners carry the responsibility for their own learning. Like musicians, they practice in order to develop their talent and the music they bring to the group. Students are responsible for assisting each other. They are accountable for meeting their own goals. Unfortunately, not all classrooms expect students to be responsible partners in the learning process.

Teachers often view students as "objects" of the educational process. The attitude can be expressed by, "We know what's best for these students. We know how to prepare them for their future." Students have no input regarding curriculum or pedagogy. Student choice is limited to the selection of courses within a specified framework. Teaching as though students are objects means that there is little room for a consideration of what young people think about the design of the opportunity. It is the responsibility of the young person to take advantage of the opportunity designed by adults (Lofquist, 1989).

A slightly different approach to student roles in the classroom treats students as "recipients." Students have some choices, but primarily for the reason that making choices is a valuable experience. Wider latitude in course selection, choosing books for free reading or selecting a science fair project help prepare young people for the *future* by providing them with present opportunities to develop responsible decision-making skills.

A third way to view students fits more completely with the Adventure in the Classroom model. This orientation sees students as "resources" in the learning process. With this perspective, teachers involve students in the decision making and design of curriculum; not because those experiences will be good for them, but because students have valuable knowledge, experience and perspective to bring to bear on their education. Students do not just choose whether to write a play or produce a video, but they help to design the curriculum, choose resources and write the guiding questions. Students, teachers, administrators and parents become partners in the process.

Summary

Learning does not occur in isolation. It is embedded in relationships, events, histories and perspectives. This rich milieu is too important to be left to chance. The AITC model acknowledges the role of the community in an individual's learning experience and attends to that community as the context within which the learning occurs. Safety and belonging, so essential for cognitive growth, must be nurtured within the adventure community. Only then can the individual undertake the kind of intellectual risks that foster cognitive growth. The learner also benefits from the collective strength and intelligence of that community.

The fluidity of roles reflects the growth of the community of adventure learners. That community, in turn, responds to the particular needs of its members, shifting to better support individual learners while maintaining the integrity of the whole. This means that the teacher must employ the skills of the conductor and coach, while at the same time be a co-learner with the students, who are resources in their common educational endeavor.

SECTION TWO

Operating Norms

The foundation of the Adventure in the Classroom model is a set of three operating norms. The Experiential Learning Cycle, Challenge by Choice and the Full Value Contract are basic to all of Project Adventure's work, and guide the adventure learning community and its individual members as they work and learn together.

Project Adventure's own foundation is in the Experiential Learning Cycle—a notion that has a rich history of literature and practice. For the AITC model, the Experiential Learning Cycle provides a pattern or standard for developing and facilitating educational experiences that emphasizes reflection, generalizing and abstracting, and transfer of the learning from the educational or instructional experience. For Project Adventure, and for the AITC model, experiential education is much more than "hands-on learning" or "experience." Experiential learning intentionally integrates the cognitive and metacognitive activities of processing the experience in order to draw out, construct and apply the learning.

Challenge by Choice and the *Full Value Contract* are Project Adventure's own contributions to the fields of experiential and adventure education. As it applies to the AITC model, Challenge by Choice is the notion that in-depth learning occurs when individuals choose and commit to academic and personal goals that are challenging and

meaningful. Risk taking, within the supportive atmosphere of the adventure learning community, is essential for cognitive, metacognitive, interpersonal and personal growth. Consequently, the AITC classroom facilitates individual and group goal setting to harness the power of Challenge by Choice.

The Full Value Contract is the norm within which the adventure learning community respects the integrity, diversity and strengths of individuals at the same time that the individuals respect and support the group as a whole. The Full Value Contract calls for each group member to value self, others, the group and the learning. To do this, the group must establish basic guidelines of emotional and physical safety. This safety supports the educational processes of individuals and the entire adventure learning community. The Full Value Contract also provides a context within which students set and work to attain their goals.

It is the intentional and consistent integration of the Experiential Learning Cycle, Challenge by Choice and the Full Value Contract that makes the AITC model unique among other models for education. While other pedagogical designs incorporate various of the instructional strategies employed by the AITC model, this potent combination of operating norms transforms effective education in the classroom into Adventure in the Classroom.

Experiential Learning Cycle

*Experience is the child of Thought, and
Thought is the child of Action. We cannot learn
men from books.*

— *Benjamin Disraeli*

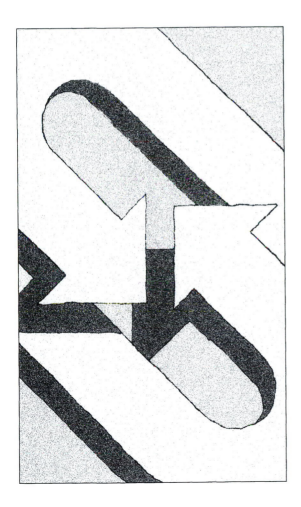

An urban classroom of thirty-two high school students, ages fourteen to seventeen, swarms with activity. Students cluster in groups of five or six around a half-dozen worktables. At two tables, they line up dominoes on end, carefully adjusting the space between them with a meter stick. The students then topple the line of dominoes and record their observations. They try different spacing, topple and record observations again.

At a couple of other tables students drop meter sticks and catch them as they fall. They record observations and document procedures for measuring reaction time. Lively discussion punctuates the room as students argue and defend their techniques. They ask questions and challenge each other's ideas. "Do we need to do it again? How accurate does the measurement have to be?"

Their teacher, Hector Lopez, moves from table to table, observing and asking questions. "Why do you question the accuracy of your measurements? What do you think is happening?"

Akim asks, "Do you think there is any difference between boys and girls?"

"What do you mean?" asks Hector.

"Do you think boys are faster than girls?"

"What about girls faster than boys!" challenges Rita, a student new to the school.

Soon Rita, Akim and their other teammates are working out a method to test out their theory about gender differences and reaction time.

At another table students compare sets of averages from a previous experiment and discuss sources of statistical error they have encountered. Chandra proposes some research using a computer program she has been learning. Another student joins her in drawing up a plan that will combine the dominoes activity, reaction time and two other activities to evaluate the testing, measurement and assessment techniques used by their classmates.

The students of this interdisciplinary Motion class study averages, predictions, margins of error, statistical analysis, square roots, decimal conversion and experimental design. At the same time they develop problem-solving, thinking, analytical and collaboration skills. Students have their hands on measuring instruments. They design experiments and generate data. They write quality reports. They take time to process their work and their working together to better understand concepts and develop skills. When they talk about averages, margin of error and velocity, their direct experience brings life to abstract concepts.

Experiential learning supports the classroom where high expectations and academic standards of excellence are the norm. Although students can learn facts by listening to a well-delivered lecture and taking notes, there is no replacing the depth, breadth, and permanence of learning that is the outcome of high quality, experiential lessons.

Overview

Experiential learning is central to all Project Adventure models. Often captured by the proverb, "What I hear I forget; what I see I remember; what I do I understand," quality experiential learning is much more than simply *doing*. Quality experiential learning attends very carefully to the entire cycle of learning—Activity, Reflection, Generalizing and Analyzing, and Transfer.

The following topics shed some light as to how experiential learning both grounds and directs the AITC model:

- Current research and theory that informs experiential learning theory
- The Experiential Learning Cycle
- Metacognition and the Experiential Learning Cycle
- Learning styles preferences and experiential learning
- The teacher's role in experiential learning

Current Research and Theory

Literature regarding the necessity of full experience in learning (Dewey, 1938) and the conceptualization and articulation of the four phase Experiential

Learning Cycle (Kolb, 1985) shape much of current experiential practice. Three positions current in educational research today offer additional information that complements this theory base:

- Discovery is essential to learning and the construction of knowledge.
- There are many avenues of learning and various "ways of knowing."
- Learning is an act of caring and reciprocity.

Discovery

The virtues involved in not knowing are the ones that really count in the long run. What you do about what you don't know is, in the final analysis, what determines what you will ultimately know.

— *Eleanor Duckworth*

Experiential Learning is discovery. Dr. Jane Goodall's story of learning how chickens lay eggs paints a picture of discovery learning. A radio interviewer asked the renowned scientist about her childhood curiosity. Dr. Goodall explained that during a visit to a family who owned chickens, she had the task of retrieving eggs from the hen house. A curious four-year-old, Jane was puzzled by how so large an object emerged from the hen, especially since Jane's careful inspection of the hen revealed no opening to match the size of an egg. To satiate her curiosity, the young scientist hid under the straw in the hen house for four hours, waiting for a chicken to lay an egg. Jane waited patiently until one of the hens settled herself and laid an egg right before the astonished child. "I can still vividly see the entire process," she commented in the interview. Teased by her own question, the child discovered the answer. Driven by innate curiosity, she created the opportunity and persevered.

What is exciting about the discovery process is that what we discover becomes our own. We possess the new knowledge much as we possess treasures we unearth. The child who finds an arrowhead while he digs in the yard insists, "It's mine!" No appeal can wrest the found object from the young owner's grip. In the same way, knowledge of our own discovery and making is something we hold onto with assurance and tenacity.

In much the same way, children in the Adventure classroom probe questions by handling the material, thinking about it and pouring their whole being into it. The discovery process is theirs because the experience is theirs.

Avenues of Learning and "Ways of Knowing"

The stages of the Experiential Learning Cycle build upon the various learning styles preferences that individuals bring to new situations. The activity stage of the cycle engages the learner who needs to get right into a problem, play with the computer, plunge into the story. The *reflective* stage meets the student who prefers to get all the facts down first, take notes or read through the entire lab project before beginning to assemble the equipment. The *generalizing* and *analyzing* stage prompts the student who processes new information by direct experience and thoughtful analysis and synthesis—who wants to identify the key variables in the experiment or comb the poem for mythological allusions. Finally, the student for whom concepts make sense through practical application thrives at that place in the cycle where *transfer* and *application* occur.

Experiential learning opens the door to the range of abilities that students bring to the classroom. In virtually all experiential lessons, students must utilize a variety of intelligences (Gardner, 1990). Adventure activities in the Motion class require mathematical/logical skills as students measure, predict and plan. The activities demand interpersonal skills, since the students must work together. This interaction calls upon verbal strengths. Many activities are physical in nature so that students also become engaged at a kinesthetic level.

The Experiential Learning Cycle also supports the theory that there are different "ways of knowing" (Belenky, et al., 1986). This literature, drawing as it does from studies regarding the ways that women construct knowledge, sheds light on the processes of learning. The epistemology outlines how one initially relies on authority as the source of knowl-

> "Few students learn to care for ideas in school. Perhaps even fewer learn to care for objects. I am not talking about mere acquisitiveness; this seems to be learned all too well. I am talking about what Harry Broudy (1972) called 'enlightened cherishing' and what the novelist and essayist John Galsworthy (1948) called 'quality.' This kind of caring produces fine objects and takes care of them. In a society apparently devoted to planned obsolescence, our children have few opportunities to care lovingly for old furniture, dishes, carpets, or even new bicycles, radios, cassette players, and the like. ...one wonders how long a throwaway society can live harmoniously with the natural environment and also how closely this form of carelessness is related to the gross desire for more and more acquisitions. Is there a role for schools to play in teaching care of buildings, books, computers, furniture, and laboratory equipment?"
>
> — *Nel Noddings*

edge, then learns to listen to the inner voice and the voice of one's own experience to construct new knowledge. The ability to apply one's own reasoning powers and the growing confidence in one's ability to develop ideas and reshape experience into an integrated whole parallel the cyclic model of experiential learning.

Reciprocity and Caring

The activities of toppling dominoes, taking measurements, handling equipment, testing theories, collaborating and strategizing require reciprocity (Noddings, 1992). The physical activity, intellectual involvement and interpersonal dynamics

require a give and take between learner and material and between learner and learner. It is easy to see this reciprocity between members of the adventure learning community in the dialogue, sharing of ideas and the building of the collective intelligence (Senge, 1991). But reciprocity also happens in the relationship between the learner and ideas, the learner and the non-human living world, and the learner and the human-made world.

Experiential learning nurtures a caring attitude in the learning process. The learner is directly involved physically, intellectually and emotionally. This strengthens the attentiveness and responsiveness the student experiences in regards to the material. An attitude of caring elicits a deep sense of connection between the individual and others, between the individual and non-human life (plants, animals, the earth), and between the individual and the "human-made world" of objects and ideas. "Robert Frost insisted that 'a poem finds its own way.' And we know that well-tended engines purr, polished instruments gleam and fine glassware glistens. The care we exert induces something like a

response from fields of ideas and from inanimate objects" (Noddings, 1992). Experiential learning nurtures an attitude of caring that elicits responsiveness from material, from the ideas, from animate and inanimate participants in the learning process. This reciprocal relationship, in turn, supports the individual's cognitive, metacognitive, interpersonal and personal growth.

The Experiential Learning Cycle

*Experience is not what happens to you;
it is what you do with what happens to you.*

— *Aldous Huxley*

A misunderstanding about experiential learning that often persists among educators is that experiential learning is simply children being physically active with the material. In fact, activity comprises only one phase of the four-stage cycle. Activity offers first-hand experience with the material and a place to become engaged with the topic. From there learners must process the experience in order to find the meaning of it, construct knowledge from it and then put this new learning into action.

The Experiential Learning Cycle begins with activity, moves through reflection, then to generalizing and abstracting and finally to transfer. This cyclical process repeats itself, as learning identified in the transfer phase applies itself to the next activity. (see Fig. 4.1)

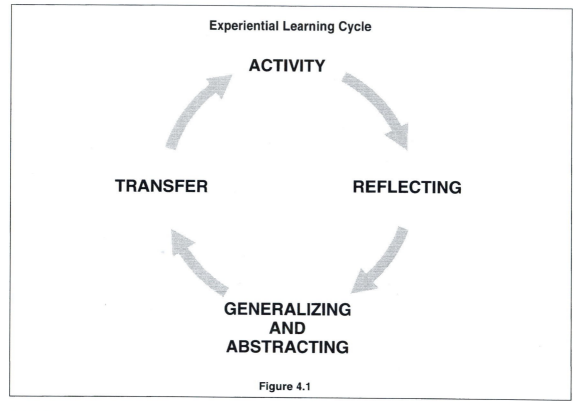

Experiential Learning Cycle

ACTIVITY

TRANSFER

REFLECTING

GENERALIZING
AND
ABSTRACTING

Figure 4.1

Activity

The activity that prompts the process may be any one of a number of activities implemented for a variety of instructional goals. The activity may be an adventure game that introduces a topic. For example, the adventure activity *Predator and Prey* (see Appendix I for descriptions of adventure activities) works well as an introduction to a study of the food chain. Activities can demonstrate a concept or raise questions. *Quail Shooters* initiates discussion about statistics and probability. The activity can be an exploratory science and math activity, where students use magnifying glasses and measuring instruments to isolate and identify plant specimens in a square meter of the school yard. Students in the physics and math Motion class measure the speed at which dominoes collapse and the reaction time of classmates. The activity can be a combina-

tion of collaborative writing and visual arts. Regardless of the specifics, the primary goal of the activity is to initiate as many connections with the material as possible. What affects measurement? How does one measure reaction time? What affects reaction time? The attention is on doing and experiencing.

The activity may take fifteen minutes or fifty. An entire class period or only a portion may be devoted to it. It is not mandatory that this phase be completed in one time block. In fact, with many middle school and high school schedules, it is not unusual for experiential lessons to carry over a couple of class periods.

Doors open to the student's many intelligences at this phase of the cycle: logical/mathematical, visual/spatial, kinesthetic, interpersonal, intrapersonal, verbal/linguistic and musical. The activity phase of the Experiential Learning Cycle allows students to engage with the material according to their individual strengths. Students who value accuracy and detail think in logical/mathematical terms, focus on methodology and precise measurement. The physical action captures concepts for the kinesthetic learner who volunteers to demonstrate. Verbal students explain the experience in an essay. The young scientist with highly developed interpersonal skills assumes a facilitative role. Instead of just one entrance, many doors open onto the subject at hand. Students can enter a front, side or even back door into the subject. Having stepped into the lesson, they are poised to learn.

Reflection

"So, what just happened? What did we do?" The second phase of the cycle, reflection, is a time of questions. During this part of a lesson, students review what they have done. The focus is on facts:

- How did the group solve the problem?

- How did we measure off the square meter of soil?

- Who did which jobs?

- What was our definition of *specimen*? What is the scientific definition of *specimen*?

- How many specimens were identified?

- How are time and distance related to speed?

- How is the equation derived?

- What were the rules of the game?

Reflection is important for at least two reasons. From the perspective of content, this is the time to clarify facts. Straightening out rules about the game and describing the experimental method occur here. This is a check-in time for the teacher and students to see what the students' level of factual understanding is with regard to the activity. This place in the cycle is comfortable for those teachers and students who want to know the facts— what actually happened, how things were "supposed to go," what the experts say. However, the reason for clarifying facts is not to substitute facts for learning, but to pave the road to in-depth learning with accurate information and the beginnings of a metacognitive framework.

Reflection on the *what* of an activity is like reviewing post-game videotapes, where the players see their actions from different angles. Students compare what they saw during the experiment and check to see if their individual perception fits with what others saw. With the information gleaned from reviewing, students move ahead to assess, evaluate, compare and contrast, and later apply or test out new knowledge. The examination of different answers that occurs here is an early step in developing skills for critical thinking.

Asking "What?" also provokes examination of learning patterns. In reflecting on the classroom activity, students find out how other students approached the activity, strategized, organized information, designed their experiments. As students look how they learn, their analytical skills and metacognitive processes improve. Their intellectual development increases.

During an analysis of a poem in an urban high school class, one team concentrated hard on the overall impact and statement that the poet was making. They discussed the time and context in which the poem was written. Another team examined references to various Greek myths and discussed the role of these allusions in the poem. Both teams came to similar interpretations. Both had valid approaches. Through reflection each team articulated its method of literary analysis. In turn, each team learned a new method from the other.

Reflection is also important for interpersonal and intrapersonal growth. In acknowledging *what* happened during an event, teachers and students validate individual experiences. Learning is often thwarted because teachers and students do not confirm each other's experiences, positive or negative. A student who feels embarrassed, frustrated or isolated downshifts to more primitive behaviors and thought processes (Caine and Caine, 1991). Cornered, he is unable to stretch intellectually or creatively. The student who opts out of the lesson withdraws in silence or disrupts other classmates. He no longer cares what the teacher or other students have to say about species classification or quadratic equations or the use of simile and metaphor. The sad outcome is another child isolated and harmed by the classroom experience.

A scene I witnessed in a fourth-grade class at Cedarwood Elementary School (Columbus, OH)

demonstrates the crucial nature of reflection in the learning experience. During a cooperative lesson on prediction and graphing, Billy, a member of one of the five-person learning teams, repeatedly blurted out numerous suggestions to his group while they worked on a logic and spatial problem. As his teammates consistently ignored Billy's ideas, some of which would have expedited their work, he withdrew. Pulling his chair against the wall, Billy propped back on two chair legs and folded his arms protectively across his chest.

After twenty minutes of the activity, the teacher, Mary Rykowski, facilitated a reflection time during which the children reviewed their steps. Billy's group explained that they had divided a circle to make a pie chart, made calculations and estimations, then became stumped, unable to proceed. Billy seized the opportunity to make one of his suggestions again, and complained, "If you had listened to me before, we might have finished this." The door was open.

Billy's team members defended themselves by explaining that they had been put off by what they felt was Billy's rude way of making suggestions. Billy told them he felt "dissed" and put down. Group members aired their feelings, and all five students identified what they could have done differently to manage their group's problem-solving process. Within fifteen minutes, the students were able to return to the logic problem, listen to Billy's ideas, implement his suggestions and complete their task.

Had it not been for this reflection time, a standard part of this teacher's lesson design, Billy would have been lost to the class, and his teammates would have missed some important points about graphing. Instead, everybody learned something new about ratios, pie charts and collaboration. These were lessons necessary to improve math and computation skills as well as collaborative problem solving.

Generalizing and Abstracting

The third phase of experiential learning is a time for examining abstract concepts and making connections between ideas and experience. Students connect previous experiences with present ones. They look at commonalities and differences in order to discern principles that can be applied broadly. Learners ask "How?" "What if?" and "So what?"

- How is this solution to the problem like the solution to the activity last week? How is it different?

- Does the process here apply to other problems?

- How can we be certain that our data collection is accurate?

- What would affect accuracy?

- How does this archetype fit with the others we have studied?

- Are we sharing responsibilities?

- Are some people doing most of the talking or most of the writing?

- What contributes to shared responsibility?

This type of questioning plays to the thinking and analyzing strengths of students. Teachers and students look at the larger context and find the relationships between the material under study and other information. This is the time to extrapolate, infer, deduce, analyze and evaluate. While analyzing and generalizing, students look at what has been learned and hypothesize about where to go next.

Various teaching strategies work in this part of the cycle: reading, small group discussion, teacher or student lecture, research that requires the new skills and information. The focus is on sifting out concepts that have a larger application in order to test them out, practice the new skills, master the content and raise new questions. In this phase students look at information they have gleaned from an activity and make decisions about other places to apply it.

Creative writing projects, conducting interviews, making a video or writing a stage script are other methods that can help students generalize and abstract. Studying the character development in a play they are producing and the techniques that the author used, both in the spoken word and actions, enables students to apply similar techniques to their own work. Can those techniques be generalized only to plays, or do they also work in videos? What are the similarities and differences? Might some of those techniques also work in short stories but not in novels?

Transfer

A return to action characterizes the fourth phase of the Experiential Learning Cycle. By this time students have identified causes of error in their experimental method. They have analyzed the playwright's characterization techniques and assessed the consistency of the characters' motivations and actions. They have identified the roles and responsibilities of the team members and established guidelines for feedback. The guiding questions of the transfer stage are "If…?" and "So What?"

- If we present our recommendations to the planning board, will they implement curbside recycling?

- If you increase the sample population to one hundred, how will the validity of the experiment be affected?

- Now that we know that we need to listen to each other more carefully, so what? What are we going to do about it?

- What are we going to do about the fact that we have set unrealistic goals and repeatedly frustrate ourselves?

The previous step of the cycle, generalizing and abstracting, teases out transfer possibilities for the learning that is emerging. In this fourth step, the transfer, students test those hypotheses. For example, if certain steps worked in the calculation of mean response time, and the test to see if the differences between boys and girls can be assumed to be more than simply individual differences among the students in the class, then what other kinds of differences can be examined? Can the same kinds of calculations be made in these other instances? Can the same design be used to see if age makes a difference in response time?

As students attempt to transfer what they have learned from one situation to another, they learn more about the practical limits to their newly acquired knowledge as well as broader applications. Their questions become more sophisticated and their understanding deeper. The characterization techniques the playwright uses have some application to videos. But what about to short story development and the novel? Statistical tests require that certain conditions be met. When they are not, we need to alter units of comparison and search other methods to examine differences. Only certain elements of that very successful presentation to the school administrators will be appropriate in the new presentation to the Planning Board.

Just as the cellist needs to play the concerto with the orchestra, students studying literature, scientific inquiry and calculations need to put their new learning into action.

The Cycle Continues

Evaluation and assessment are embedded in the experiential learning process. Students consistently ask themselves, What worked? What didn't? What do I need to do differently to improve? Because goal setting informs the process of experiential learning in the AITC model, expectations for student work are clear from the start. Students constantly evaluate their progress. Subsequent goals reflect evaluation of earlier goals. To the degree that assessment is a thoughtful process, students set additional goals, as well as more realistic and measurable goals, in the future.

The Experiential Learning Cycle is a fluid cycle. The results of the last phase lead into the next cycle. The questions raised and the answers not yet clear fuel further action, reflection, generalizing and abstracting, and transfer. The new set of lessons might begin with a play by a different playwright. Students might write their own play. There might be a new experiment involving the next level of mathematical inquiry and skills.

The transfer step often leads immediately into the activity phase, so that after the students put their new learning into practice, they move into a reflective phase again.

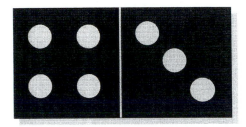

Students in the Motion class have finished their project with dominoes. They have drawn conclusions about accuracy of spacing, whether there are differences between straight- and curved-line placement. What does this all mean? Where can these principles be applied?

There is further application in physics but it would be interesting to look to other disciplines. Is there a domino effect in economics? What happens when there is a sell-off in the stock market? Timing of each factor would seem to be important. If negative news, such as higher interest rates, increased unemployment or fewer housing starts is spaced regularly, then stock prices will begin to tumble. The sell-off fuels further sell-offs. There are limits to the parallel, however. The domino effect assumes a one-on-one effect, while more variables influence the stock market. What can we do to show and explore this difference?

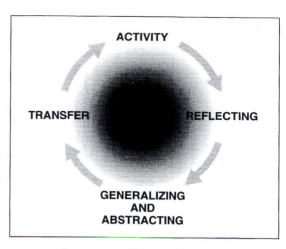

Metacognition and the Experiential Learning Cycle

The Experiential Learning Cycle reminds us of the importance of metacognitive activity to cognitive development. At least half of the cycle prompts metacognition, or thinking about thinking. Once students move past reflecting on the activity, they draw generalizations and abstractions then work to extend and apply. The work of this phase of the cycle is to step back from the activity and look at it from new perspectives and with the goal of learning from it. As students seek to integrate the learnings from a variety of previous activities and process their learning before, during and after the actual activity (see Chapter Eight), they learn about learning.

For some students, active metacognitive activity occurs early in the cycle and/or early in the students' participation in experiential learning. These students step outside of the experience easily and analyze not only the activity but also their processes in the experience. For other students, the ability to think metacognitively develops slowly and with considerably more direction and facilitation.

In the early stages of experiential learning, metacognitive learning is likely to be narrow in scope, and limited in depth. The goal, however, is to develop more sophisticated thinking skills about the processes of learning. The conscious attention to processing learning develops in an upward or outwardly expanding spiral, so that with each new experience, the student not only develops greater ability to generalize, abstract and transfer learning, but also recognizes how each level is linked and interconnected to the other.

Other Theories of Learning

Of the other theories of learning that currently influence instructional practice, the four-stage learning preferences models and the theory of multiple intelligences dovetail with the Experiential Learning Cycle and enhance the AITC model.

Learning Style Inventory, True Colors and 4MAT®

The Kolb Learning Style Inventory (1985), Bernice McCarthy's 4MAT (1981, 87, 96), and True Colors (1989) enrich the AITC model and offer additional tools to meet the needs of students. These models remind us that each of us has a preference or strength, a favorite place in the cycle. These models help us to understand that there are several ways. The issue is not how many preferences can be identified, but how best to meet students' different strengths. Each inventory provides vocabulary along with strategies to encourage the learner to stretch into other, perhaps unfamiliar stages of the cycle.

True Colors® Learning/Teaching Styles

Orange

Core need is for action, excitement, freedom and spontaneity.

Characteristics
- Charismatic and fun-loving
- Competitive and adventurous

Student strengths and needs
- Exhibits high energy and zeal
- Seizes opportunities; clever
- Needs hands-on approaches to learning
- Requires variety and flexibility
- Possesses a sense of humor

Teacher strengths and needs
- Provides options and variety
- Promotes creativity and risk-taking
- Maintains a light-hearted, fun classroom
- Responds best to freedom and latitude

Blue

Core need is for harmony and positive, close relationships.

Characteristics
- Friendly and sensitive
- Imaginative and communicative

Student strengths and needs
- Values the feelings of others
- Creates harmony
- Sees various sides of an issue
- Needs to feel emotionally connected with others
- Desires affirmation and encouragement from others

Teacher strengths and needs
- Responds to needs of others with care and compassion
- Promotes and facilitates personal growth and development of others
- Nurtures and encourages others to reach their potential
- Requires an environment that balances individual and group needs

Green

Core need is for mental competency.

Characteristics
- Analytical and conceptual
- Independent, self-motivated and logical

Student strengths and needs
- Possesses problem-solving skills
- Sees relationship of parts to whole
- Requires independence of thought and opportunity to work alone
- Needs to ask questions to satisfy curiosity

Teacher strengths and needs
- Excels at problem solving
- Promotes competence and effectiveness
- Fosters inventiveness, precision and knowledge, and discovery learning
- Prefers direct, thoughtful and logical discussion

Gold

Core need is for structure and service.

Characteristics
- Organized and methodical
- Dependable, loyal and responsible

Student strengths and needs
- Organizes and plans ahead
- Respects authority
- Needs order and sequence
- Responds well to a structured, stable environment

Teacher strengths and needs
- Provides structure and follow-through
- Promotes values of tradition, history, institutions, citizenship
- Follows a schedule and routine
- Responds well to structures, policies and procedures

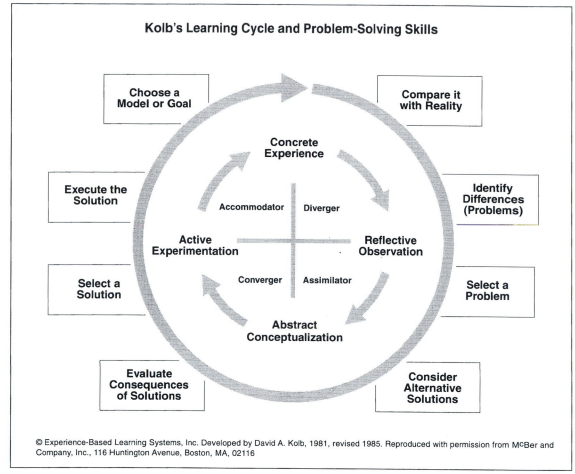

Kolb's Learning Cycle and Problem-Solving Skills

Choose a Model or Goal

Compare it with Reality

Concrete Experience

Accommodator   Diverger

Execute the Solution

Identify Differences (Problems)

Active Experimentation

Reflective Observation

Converger   Assimilator

Select a Solution

Select a Problem

Abstract Conceptualization

Evaluate Consequences of Solutions

Consider Alternative Solutions

The Kolb Learning Style Inventory and True Colors provide common vocabulary based on the strengths that each student brings to the learning community. The Learning Style Inventory and True Colors give language to preferences and explanations regarding various behaviors in learning situations. In addition, the designations of "one, two, three, four," or "assimilator, diverger, converger, accommodator," or "gold, blue, green, orange," lighten the discussion of learning preferences. These designations expand thinking and legitimize differences that are helpful tools. We need, however, to be careful not to use them to label and limit students.

The inventories also help learners identify skills they need to strengthen to take advantage of learning opportunities. The "assimilator" is encouraged to be more aware of the feelings of others and how emotional responses affect a group's efforts. The "accommodator" is challenged to spend more time planning before taking action and to consider the viewpoints of other team members. Kolbs's *Personal Learning Guide* follows the same sequence of steps as it assists the learner in developing new skills.

The True Colors inventory is adaptable to students of all ages, providing children with the awareness of their strengths and areas for development.

The 4MAT® Model

Teachers Roles

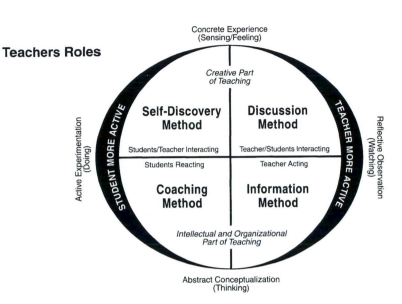

The 4MAT® System Model

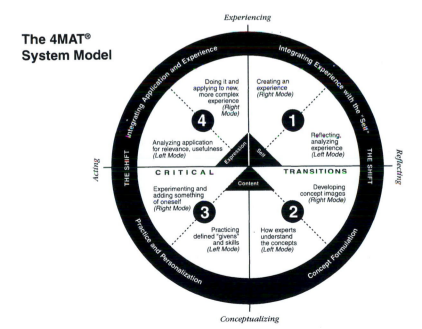

True Colors also gives teachers a framework for considering the effects of teaching style on the different children in their classes. The "orange" teacher, who uses open-ended questions and enjoys the galvanizing effect of spontaneity, is reminded to develop lessons in the classroom that meet the needs of the "green" student, who prefers independent, subject-oriented study, as well as the "blue" student, who avoids confrontation, and the "gold" student, who likes to think through problems before taking action.

The 4MAT System is a teaching model which combines the principles of several long-standing theories of personal development with current research on human brain function to create a practical teaching method for maximizing human learning. Designed and published by Bernice McCarthy, 4MAT is based on the belief that human learning is a personal and continuous process which consists of creating meaning and understanding through the refinement and adaptation of existing levels of knowledge and experience.

Multiple Intelligences

That people have different strengths is a generally accepted fact. Consider the New Testament notion of spiritual gifts, the Greek concept of a pantheon and the variety of modern geniuses. Current study of human intelligence argues convincingly that any attempt at defining intelligence must consider a

---

Summary of Seven Intelligences

Adapted from Armstrong, Thomas. *Multiple Intelligences in the Classroom.* Alexandria, VA. Association for Supervision and Curriculum Development. 1994.

Linguistic Intelligence — The ability to use words effectively, either orally or in writing.

Logical-Mathematical Intelligence — The ability to use numbers and to reason well.

Spatial Intelligence — The ability to perceive the visual-spatial world and to transform those perceptions into other forms.

Bodily-Kinesthetic Intelligence — The ability to use one's body to express ideas and feelings or use one's hands to handle, produce or craft objects.

Musical Intelligence — The ability to perceive, discriminate and compose in musical forms.

Interpersonal Intelligence — The ability to understand other people, and perceive and respond to the differences in moods, motivations and feelings of people.

Intrapersonal Intelligence — Knowledge of self and the ability to adapt according to that knowledge.

range of intelligence, of which linguistic and logical-mathematical reasoning are only two. In fact, current definitions of intelligence generally work with seven categories (see below). Various efforts have adapted this work to address the practicalities of the classroom and prompt educators to think in terms of modalities or ways of learning. Insight from these efforts further substantiates experiential learning theory and practice.

The Experiential Learning Cycle does not directly address each of the intelligences, but it does provide a context whereby all modalities can be incorporated into a lesson. There are obvious connections between the Experiential Learning Cycle and the theory of multiple intelligences. The cooperative and interactive nature of experiential learning involves students linguistically and interpersonally. Logical thinking comes into play in the various discussions students and teachers have, especially in instances where students instruct or tutor each other. In addition, the reflective and generalizing phases of the cycle require logical thinking and learning. The activity, of course, is a kinesthetic experience, which can be musical and spatial learning. Similarly, transfer or application are places that can incorporate musical, spatial and kinesthetic learning. This might be the place in the learning cycle where students apply their new learning and utilize their preferred modality. Just as likely, this phase allows students to apply the new learning in a way that is unfamiliar, thereby encouraging the development of those areas. Finally, the focus on the processing of learning,

which runs throughout the learning cycle, connects to interpersonal and intrapersonal strengths.

The Teacher's Role

The teacher's role in the Experiential Learning Cycle is to design and to facilitate. Each role is demanding, creative and enormously rewarding.

Designer

As a designer, the teacher develops activities that are open-ended and capable of being examined at a variety of levels. The activity must have a discovery nature. Students and teachers might be able to predict the outcome, but the activity prompts discovery and process. The purpose of the activity is not to get to the right answer, but to explore the topic, raise questions and illuminate the process. Experiments from the Motion class illustrate effective, open-ended questions:

- In your group, who has the fastest reaction time? After discussing the problem, write a procedure that will allow you to discover who is the fastest person (Motion curriculum, p. 65).

- Dominoes are placed in line equally spaced from each other. Describe what will happen when the first domino is toppled. Explain how your group would determine the average speed at which the dominoes are toppled after the chain reaction is started (Motion curriculum, p. 87).

The role of designer also requires the teacher to develop activities that are "layered" so that students of different abilities find challenges appropriate to their skills. One student, for example, can delve into extrapolation and interpolation while another student explores the differences between systematic and random error.

Facilitator

The design of the activity encourages different approaches to the problem. This touches on the teacher's second role — that of facilitator. Although the teacher may have in mind an approach known to be most expeditious, he must not impose that on the students. In struggling with various methods, students learn more and with greater understanding. Because students are fresh to the issue, they may come up with a new technique or unique observations. It is important that these new approaches be encouraged. As facilitator, the teacher needs to do broad-based assessment and challenge students to find out why their method did or did not work. The teacher also needs to be open to learning himself and recognize that he may not have the best answer to every question.

The teacher of the Motion class observes and questions, "Tell me what you have found so far. How did you decide on these measurements? What happened when the dominoes were furthest apart? What possibilities for error are in this procedure?" The questions ask for recounting and rationale. In addition, the questions prompt dialogue that is essential to learning. The students reflect on choices made during their investigations, rehearse the steps they have taken, and assess the results of their actions.

As facilitator, the teacher must be able to determine gaps the student has in information or skill and adjust lessons or resources accordingly. The teacher needs to determine the student's thinking processes in order to design lessons that best meet student needs. The teacher also facilitates the student through all phases of the Experiential Learning Cycle, not just one stage.

Summary

Discovery is essential to learning. We learn best what we have uncovered and reconstructed ourselves. Many avenues lead to knowledge. In addition, the process of learning is an act of care and reciprocity between student and material, student and teacher, student and student, student and ideas. The process of experiential learning embodies these aspects of the learning process. The steps of action, reflection, generalizing and transfer, which comprise the Experiential Learning Cycle, tap into the discovery nature of learning as well as support the different ways in which people come to understanding.

While the distinctions between the various stages of experiential learning are sometimes blurred, it is critical to follow the entire process. Activity without reflection remains activity. Reflection without transfer is merely looking backwards. Generalizing and abstracting concepts transforms simple reflection into application.

The teacher's role in the experiential learning classroom is demanding. The teacher must be an active designer of activity, conscientious about the various strengths and needs of the students, and develop activities that challenge the more able student as well as the less able. In addition, the teacher must be a conscientious facilitator, able to step in and out of the processes according to the students' needs. This requires understanding the learning preferences that individual students bring to the classroom, as well as the various intelligences that individuals possess. This knowledge will better enable the teacher to design and facilitate experiential lessons that truly meet students' needs and strengthen their achievements.

Challenge by Choice

All serious daring starts from within.

— *Eudora Welty*

Dark-haired Sally throws open the door of her classroom on Wednesday afternoon to see a half-dozen other children involved in various projects. An intense four-year old, she enjoys the excitement and action at school.

"Hi, Sally," calls out her friend Charlene. "Look what I'm making!"

Sally joins Charlene and her quiet partner, Noah, as they build elaborate towers with blocks, Styrofoam packaging shapes and toothpicks. The children exchange a few words before Sally scans the room to see what other classmates are doing.

She makes her way to the writing table where Nathan, who prefers to work alone, is drawing pictures. Sally finally drifts to where her teacher and another classmate pour and measure colored water into containers of various shapes and sizes. They hold beakers of liquids up to the light, discussing their observations.

Soon Sally settles herself at a computer. She chooses a drawing program and begins creating. She creates one picture, then another, exploring the "paint tools"— lines, patterns and brush strokes.

Fifteen minutes later Sally opens up a memory game on the computer. In spite of the noise around her,

she plays two rounds, thrilled when she beats her electronic opponent.

Other students arrive, hang up their coats, greet friends and move about the room, deciding where to begin their afternoon. Some children make their choices quickly, interested in working with a friend or enticed by certain materials. Others take time to carefully survey the several stations, asking questions of classmates or teachers. The room is busy with conversation, exploration, discovery, excitement, interest and learning.

These preschool children remind us that we learn according to our interests, and that the actions of discovery and challenge fuel those interests. "Free time" during the opening of the preschool session is, in fact, exploration and testing of new skills. Noah manipulates objects to construct shapes he has yet to determine. Sally investigates the intricacies of a computer drawing program. Children build mastery naturally, taking full advantage of their readiness. This is the way of authentic learning and the way of adventure learning.

Sally's interest with the memory game means that she plays with it, tries new commands, attempts new designs. She gains facility and confidence as she uses existing skills and develops new ones. Adventure learning at the upper grades means that students explore areas of study rich with content. They stretch with pride toward new heights. The ownership and commitment that accompany such pursuits encourage even more discovery and risk

taking, which, in turn, strengthens the breadth and depth of learning. This is *Challenge by Choice*— the second building block of the AITC model.

Overview

From its very beginning, the concept of Challenge by Choice has directed all of the Project Adventure's programming models. So important is this concept that virtually all Project Adventure workshops begin with an introduction to this operating principle.

Several perspectives support Challenge by Choice:

- Meeting challenges promotes cognitive, intrapersonal and interpersonal growth.

- Human beings have a basic need for competence and effectence.

- Human beings desire self-efficacy and are able to determine their own potential for success in uncertain or ambiguous situations.

Challenge Promotes Growth

> *"Come to the edge."*
>   *"It's too high."*
> *"Come to the edge."*
>   *"We might fall."*
> *"Come to the edge."*
>   *And they came.*
>   *And he pushed them.*
>   *And they flew.*
>
> — *Apollinaire*

Doing the same thing over and over again might be satisfying or relaxing; but it is unlikely that a repetitive task does much for one's intellectual growth. Reading only romance novels might titillate one's fantasies, but will do little to challenge higher intellectual pursuits. The competitive athlete pushes herself to run faster, jump higher, ski more aggressively in order to improve her skills and competence. Similarly, taking intellectual risks encourages cognitive growth. Such risk taking pushes the intellectual capacities to search for new connections, find new avenues, reach for higher goals. This extension, in turn, enhances the individual's capacities for more complex learning (Vygotsky, 1978; Duckworth, 1987; Caine and Caine, 1991).

Authentic learning requires taking risks. A child learns to ride a two-wheeler by taking the risk to ride without training wheels and, later, without an adult's steadying hand on the bicycle seat. On four wheels, the youngster cannot keep up with neighbor kids who whiz by on two wheels. Curbs, gravel driveways and mud catch training wheels and

Work is an outlawed word in Linda Click's first-grade classroom. The denotations and connotations of the word run counter to the values of this school where reading, spelling, graphing, computing, categorizing and other cognitive skills are treated as exciting "challenges." Each day children are given a variety of reading and math challenges to try. Small group projects are challenges that strengthen the students' developing collaboration skills as well as their understanding of the particular content area under study (solar system, *Charlotte's Web*, animal homes). Instead of homework, these children have "home challenges."

The "No Work" symbol, bold with its red outline and slash mark, is a reminder that classroom learning activities are opportunities for growth. Thoughtful and effective processes, diligent effort, thorough planning, the use of knowledge and skills are far more important here than simply getting the right answer.

drag the rider to a halt. When the youngster longs for speed, the only step to take is to meet the challenge and learn to ride on two wheels. It's a scary time of wobbling and falling, but learning to ride means going to that edge and pushing ahead. Once the child masters two wheels, however, she whizzes past her older companions and bounces joyously over bumps, delighting in new-found skills.

Learning occurs at that edge of new territory. This "zone of proximal development" (Vygotsky, 1978) is the place where the learner has some skill or knowledge base, but needs additional skills to move forward. It's where the youngster on training wheels takes off the training wheels because she is anxious to ride on two wheels. This place often feels uncomfortable, because it is unfamiliar. The new behavior or new subject matter requires new skill or knowledge. This is precisely why there is learning.

Another way to look at the role of challenge in growth and development is the model of disequilibrium (Piaget, 1968), which suggests that growth is a product of the individual's need for equilibrium. The individual constantly works to integrate new experience, knowledge and information into her existing knowledge base so that the disequilibrium or uncertainty is mediated, and equilibrium or balance is once again achieved. The young bicycle rider feels disequilibrium from her desire to ride without training wheels, her knowledge that riding on two wheels is possible, and her own inexperience with riding on two wheels. That need

to feel balance or equilibrium pushes the child to meet the challenge and learn a new skill—riding a bicycle without training wheels.

Academic learning and interpersonal growth come with challenge and risk taking. Each of us knows our own fears, strengths, limits and goals. Each of us knows when we are ready to move ahead— to learn how the computer software works, find out more biographical information on the author, try another sonata. Supportive opportunities to reach for new areas and develop new skills offer the kinds of challenges that promote authentic, meaningful learning—learning that has breadth and depth.

Competence and Effectence

The greatest of human freedoms
is the freedom to choose one's attitude
in a given set of circumstances,
to choose one's own way.

— Viktor Frankl

It is not enough that the learner faces challenge, but that she perceive the challenge as accomplishable. Success in meeting a challenge depends on one's sense of competence-effectence, or ability to have control over a situation and effect some kind of change. In fact, it is suggested that human beings possess a basic desire for competence and effectence and search for opportunities to exercise their abilities and develop new competencies (Ewert, 1989). This sense of control and possible effect is the difference between an experience that produces

eustress, or positive anxiety, and an experience that produces *distress*, or negative anxiety. The perception of a challenge as eustress physiologically enables the brain to function in an open, connecting manner, thereby promoting learning (Caine and Caine, 1991).

When the learner sees herself as "in charge" of the challenge, she manages, commits to and follows through with the challenge in a healthy manner (Glasser, 1993). By providing students with choices, we offer them the opportunity to own their learning and enable them to be self-motivated and connected to the material. This sense of ownership and capability, in turn, enables the learner to push through difficulties and experience that state of "flow," which characterizes engaging and challenging endeavors (Csikszentmihalyi, 1991).

Unfortunately, the pattern of our current educational system slowly starves children of the opportunity to learn about and develop the ability to make choices. At the same time that students develop the intellectual and psychological abilities to make increasingly more sophisticated decisions, schools begin to eliminate the opportunities for students to exercise and refine those skills. As students progress through our educational system, their days become more regimented and segmented. The school day is parceled into fifty-minute blocks orchestrated by bells and entrenched schedules. Curriculum tracks students and restricts options. While this progression continues, students step closer and closer to a world where there will be highly complex decisions to make and fewer structures to their day. No wonder so many nineteen-year-olds flounder during their first years after high school graduation, unable to make decisions about work and often stumbling miserably through the first year after high school graduation. They are unskilled in handling new freedoms of choice in their personal and academic lives.

As teachers, we would do much better service to our students by tapping into their need for competence, their ability to make decisions and their desire to experience education as a meaningful part of their lives.

Self-Efficacy

Human beings rise to the expectations set before them. If we expect mediocrity from our students, then we will get mediocrity. If we expect high achievement, then we will get high achievement. Challenge by Choice accepts the proposition that individuals know their own abilities, their limits, their potential for accomplishment. When an individual is encouraged to meet a challenge and is supported in that effort, she is more likely to meet with success. That success, in turn, leads to additional efforts at taking healthy risks. In other words, success breeds success. This self-efficacy, this ability to evaluate one's potential to meet a challenge in the face of uncertain results (Bandura, 1977; Ewert, 1989), is the crux of Challenge by Choice.

Safety and Challenge

Challenge by Choice does not operate in a vacuum, of course. In order for a student to accept a healthy challenge, there needs to be an atmosphere of safety and support. This feature of the Full Value Contract (see Chapter Six) is a necessary balance to risk taking in the classroom.

Brain research indicates that safety is an essential condition for learning and for intellectual growth. In the presence of perceived danger or threat, the brain downshifts and becomes incapable of the kind of complex operations characteristic of in-depth learning. The brain cannot make new connections to existing patterns of understanding or create new paradigms for constructing knowledge (Caine and Caine, 1991).

A seventh-grade social studies teacher once humiliated a student in front of the class for neglecting to include bibliographic information to support material paraphrased from another source. The child was mortified. The experience was so frightening to the student that she was afraid to ask the teacher for any explanation. Why did paraphrasing need to be credited in the bibliography? How was that different from the footnote? It was in an-

other class a year later that the student understood her mistake and learned why paraphrasing requires citation. For the remainder of her year in seventh-grade social studies, however, pleasing the teacher became this child's primary concern. In the social studies class she never again passed in anything other than what was explicitly required. She rarely asked a questions and avoided answering questions of which she was unsure. Feeling threatened rather than safe, this child learned an interesting lesson about social studies: "Don't ever make a mistake."

Two Arenas of Challenge

There are two types of challenge in the classroom: academic challenges and behavioral challenges.

Academic Challenges and Choice

Academic challenges involve the subject area content and the skills that students use to approach it. In the adventure classroom students establish academic goals (see Chapter Six) that fit within the framework and expectations of the particular class. Students choose their own challenges, such as developing an understanding of the principles to algebraic equations, learning effective methods for persuasive argumentation, or using the experimental method to investigate the effects of color on a human being's level of relaxation.

During an interdisciplinary unit on motion, for example, all students are required to submit reaction papers, lab reports and a final project.

Throughout the unit, students must demonstrate various math and writing skills along with scientific inquiry technique. The content, standards and number of reaction papers are negotiated according to the student's writing and math abilities and goals for improvement. Students choose which labs they will complete. They design their own experiments based on the essential questions guiding their investigation. The standards for quality of work are high, and work that does not meet those standards is assessed accordingly. Students must accomplish a certain number of comprehensive activities as minimums for various grades. On a daily basis they choose which activities to pursue in class and hold each other accountable to individual goals. The students help evaluate the appropriateness of the challenges that classmates have chosen.

Like their older counterparts, first-grade students have daily math, reading and writing challenges. The students choose which activities to complete first, which ones to pursue with a partner and which ones to do alone. As in the high school class, elementary students set goals against which to measure their efforts. The range of choice in other classes is even wider. In some cases students write out a detailed contract for a three-week unit, stipulating their learning goals and the activities they will undertake to meet those goals.

An exciting advantage of operating within the framework of Challenge by Choice is that students are encouraged to go beyond what they can already do or what they already know. Because students identify their own individual and group challenges, they build on existing strengths and develop those areas that need improvement. The student eager to engage in high level literary criticism can move ahead at the same time that her classmate, struggling with historical research on an American novelist, also progresses.

Behavioral Challenges

Challenge by Choice provides an effective framework for the social development of students. A learning environment that is community based demands attention to the intrapersonal growth and interpersonal relations of its members. Learning in the AITC classroom falls or flies on the wings of interpersonal relationships and the health of the adventure learning community. The working relationships of the community members affect students' ability to learn. Students do well academically and interpersonally in a class that attends to the health of its relationships. If the class threatens, stifles, angers or frustrates students, they downshift to self-protective and often obstructive behaviors.

Members of a research team who distrust each other do not share ideas and information. Unable to build on collective knowledge, take risks with ideas and test out hypotheses, they produce work that is mediocre. A hockey team suffering from internal rivalry will never make the play-offs. Players who care only about their individual performance cannot develop the necessary skills for their team to excel. Similarly, unresolved conflicts, confusion

about roles and operating under erroneous and unchecked assumptions impede academic growth in the classroom.

Students in the AITC classroom confront daily the challenges of learning within a community—listening, taking turns, incorporating ideas, sharing materials, being honest with self and others. Just as students know their own academic challenges and risks, they know their behavior and interpersonal risks as well. The best way for someone to develop interpersonal and social skills is to acknowledge those areas that need work and to commit to working on them.

Membership in a community requires responsibility to that community. Students in the AITC classroom set behavior goals (see Chapter Six) in relation to their teamwork or class relations. Inevitably the behavior goals extend to situations outside the classroom, but the initial focus is the classroom. Attention to behavior and interpersonal relations in the classroom is important in a model based on a community of adventure learners. Developing the skills of collaboration, negotiation, feedback and group goal setting enhances the group's work and enables individuals to internalize those skills so that they can become even more effective as co-learners.

The key is choice. Choosing a goal is taking ownership and making a commitment. When teachers relinquish authoritarian goal setting ("You need to listen better and not interrupt") and students identify their own growth areas ("We are going to be more attentive listeners in group today"), learning is transformed and the change is astounding.

Teachers and students at the Cedarwood Elementary School talk about *wise choices* and *other choices*. *Wise choices* are those that are positive, supportive of learning and helpful. When a student's behavior in the lunchroom begins to get out of hand, another student or a teacher is likely to ask, "Are you making a wise choice?" First graders and kindergartners know that any time they complete lessons in class, have extra time or come early to class, they can make wise choices from the various learning activities arranged about the room. The optional wise choices vary with the theme of study so that children are constantly encouraged to try new activities that connect with the particular classroom unit. When students go through the problem-solving steps to figure out how to handle a behavior problem, the last question they answer is, "What is the wise choice for me here?"

"Challenge by Choice is not whether or not I choose to be challenged, but what kind of challenge I will take on!"

Appropriate Choice and Real Challenge

Concern that students set appropriate and challenging goals often troubles teachers unfamiliar with the AITC model. Challenge by Choice occurs in the context of the community of adventure learners and works hand-in-hand with the Full Value Contract (see Chapter Six). The goals one sets are public. The peer group is sounding board and mirror. Students know when their peers are pulling a fast one. They are quick to call each other when a classmate identifies a goal that is either inappropriate or inconsequential. Similarly, a student having difficulty deciding on an appropriate challenge receives suggestions from classmates.

Each member of the learning community makes a commitment to the Full Value Contract. The Full Value Contract nurtures an atmosphere in which students are responsible for setting appropriate and real challenges for themselves. Students have permission to hold each other accountable in setting their own goals to ensure that a student does not set a challenge that is below the level of previous work.

One teacher exclaimed, "Challenge by Choice is not whether or not I choose to be challenged, but what kind of challenge I will take on." Students in the Motion class are expected to learn about Newton's laws of physics, calculation of speed and velocity and statistical prediction; but they make choices about the depth or breadth of knowledge they pursue and the types of experiments they undertake. The students commit to their goals and meet the challenges they set.

Choice occurs in the context of community. Community informs choice. Classmates provide a check for inappropriate goals. Consequently, students learn to make choices appropriate to the classroom.

Improved Learning

How does Challenge by Choice help students learn more and be better citizens? Challenge by Choice strengthens both academic and interpersonal learning by—

- Accelerating cognitive growth through the encouragement of intellectual risk taking
- Modeling the learning and decision making that characterize adult life and work
- Assisting in the provision of a metacognitive framework
- Acknowledging vulnerabilities

Intellectual Risk Taking

Learning is pushing oneself to try new ideas, practice new skills or test new theories. The painter has to dip her brushes into the paint and apply color to canvas in order reveal the image of her mind's eye. Students must use a new language in order to learn it. Challenge by Choice establishes a norm that encourages students to try new skills without fearing ridicule for awkward efforts or mistakes.

Healthy risk taking, in an environment of validation and accountability, accelerates the learning

process. As students identify and commit to meaningful challenges and reach toward high expectations of academic performance and interpersonal growth, they push themselves beyond their previous limits. Cognitive development increases as does social growth. The confidence gained provides momentum for the process of improved learning.

Challenge by Choice encourages students and teachers to operate in areas of new knowledge where there is often a sense of uncertainty. Stumbling around with new material and trying to understand a process are just as important, if not more so, than repeating the right answer. Challenge by Choice establishes a norm of asking for and giving help. It enables students and teachers to develop the ability to identify and assess their own levels of growth. The learner is truly a partner in the process, developing skills necessary for life-long learning.

More capable peers strengthen their learning as they explain, discuss, coach and assist less able peers. They not only rehearse their knowledge, but develop other ways to utilize it, thus creating a more complex framework for supporting more diverse applications. Less capable peers are supported in their struggles and encouraged to develop their own frameworks. They benefit from several "teachers," any of whom may unlock a door to understanding.

Learning and Decision Making

The world is a place of diminishing "yes/no" choices. Learning how to make choices has become the primary need for life-long learners (Fogarty, Bellanca

and Costa, 1992). Adults must constantly prioritize, plan and strategize in their personal and professional lives. Self-directed work teams, dispersed management systems and the growth in work independence via computer networks, satellite office sites and electronic management, mean that individuals need basic skills to make choices necessary to accomplish their work.

Challenge by Choice means students need to make decisions. Should we go ahead and ask someone else to edit this report or rewrite it ourselves? Do we have enough data to make accurate predictions, or do we risk taking more time to gather additional information? What is the best way to approach a comparative analysis of the Armenian genocide and the Bosnian massacres? There is no better place for young people to learn how to make wise choices, follow through on commitments and be accountable than in a challenging and supportive classroom. What better way to connect academic learning with real life and experience the effects of one's decisions than in a setting which provides continuous opportunity to set and refine goals, to act, reflect, generalize and apply learning? The community of adventure learners provides both context and accountability as students work toward their goals in the presence of and with the assistance of their team members.

Metacognitive Framework

When students identify and commit to academic and interpersonal challenges in the context of the community of adventure learners, they also identify the strategies necessary to meet their challenges. Students committed to improving their grades need to think about what changes to make and then outline the steps necessary to accomplish that goal. Students struggling to understand the human digestive system outline the procedures to assist them in learning the material. Conscious planning about how to learn and deliberate reflection during the process of learning, expands the framework upon which new learning can hang, like adding new pieces to a TinkerToy structure. The more slots and holes available, the more intricate and adaptable the structure. As students' metacognitive frameworks grow, the flexibility of their knowledge increases.

Because students take on challenges that they set for themselves, they assume more control over their own learning and become more active in and conscious about the processes of learning. The student struggling to understand the process of human digestion takes action to enlist the help of a classmate or to look for new study techniques. She draws a diagram of a piece of bread traveling through the system, tracing its conversion for use as energy. She conducts a dialogue with a peer or dissects a lab specimen and examines food in various stages of digestion. Making conscious choices about learning techniques and then reflecting on their effectiveness helps the student to understand her own metacognitive processes.

Acknowledging Vulnerabilities

So long as teachers hide the imperfect processes of their thinking, allowing their students to glimpse only the polished products, students will remain convinced that only Einstein—or a professor—could think up a theory.

— *Mary Field Belenky et al.*

Choosing a challenge and publicly identifying an area for growth is admitting a need. This is a first step for learning—acknowledging a growth area. Acknowledging vulnerabilities means letting down defenses, thereby freeing our creative energy to carry us to new heights. Students and teachers open themselves to greater possibilities of accomplishment when they set goals to meet new challenges. A baseball team that identifies its need for a stronger pitching staff is in the position to trade players. A scientist who acknowledges the need to more clearly identify risk factors that potentially lead to diabetes designs a research project. Students and teachers who identify and commit to learning challenges open themselves to the collective strengths of the learning community.

Challenge by Choice encourages teachers to assess their professional needs, set goals, strategize and pursue those goals. By being transparent about this process, teachers model for their students the kind of intellectual growth that they encourage in the classroom. Students see firsthand how adults continue the process of lifelong learning. Students participate in the struggles and joys their teachers experience and see that knowledge is the domain of everyone, not the private estate of the intellectual elite.

Summary

Essential to Project Adventure, Challenge by Choice is a primary operating principle of the Adventure in the Classroom model. The notion of Challenge by Choice is that individuals know their own limits and challenges; and that individuals make significant intellectual, interpersonal and intrapersonal gains when they choose and commit to challenges which they have identified for themselves. This does not mean that curriculum goals or teacher assessment of student educational needs are ignored.

Rather, the adventure classroom is a place where students take responsibility to establish and work toward academic and behavior goals commensurate with those curriculum goals and in conjunction with teacher and peer assessment.

The operating principle of Challenge by Choice rests on the premises that 1) challenge or healthy risk taking promotes growth; 2) the individual's basic need for competence and effectence is a positive motivation for learning; and, 3) individuals possess the ability to determine their potential success in new situations.

A safe environment that supports intellectual, interpersonal and intrapersonal risk taking is critical to the effectiveness of Challenge by Choice. The Full Value Contract must operate hand-in-hand with Challenge by Choice, providing structures for creating and maintaining that environment, and ensuring that students set appropriate and real challenges for themselves.

Full Value Contract

We do not believe in ourselves until someone reveals deep inside us that something is valuable, worth listening to, worthy of our trust, sacred to our touch. Once we believe in ourselves we can risk curiosity, wonder, spontaneous delight or any experience that reveals the human spirit.

— *e.e.cummings*

Fourteen-year-old Manney slumps across the stage with a street-wise indifference that is his statement of emerging manhood. The drama teacher, Ms. Howard, dashes across the stage with a flourish, illustrating to Manney and the rest of the class the movements appropriate to Shakespeare's characterization of a young man energized with new-found love. She is frustrated by Manney's affected lethargy and disregard of her coaching. With obvious contempt, Manney drags himself even more haltingly across the stage.

Visibly irritated, Ms. Howard asks, "Don't you think that was a stupid way to move?"

Manney challenges, "Ms. Howard, you can't say that to me! This is a Project Adventure class."

Lucas, another student adds, "Yeah! That's not Full Value."

Struck by their confrontation, Ms. Howard pauses before responding. "You're absolutely right. I apologize." She continues, "I was referring to the movement, not to you personally. Do you know what I mean about the movement? I can't seem to make myself clear about that." Manney shakes his head.

Ms. Howard appeals to the class. "Who can explain to Romeo what is needed in the movement?"

Lucas, who is playing Mercutio, pipes up. "You need energy, man!" Bowing lavishly, he bounces across the stage in exaggerated flourishes.

Manney laughs and drops his defensive movements. "Okay, I get it." Following Mercutio's example, he leaps into action with grace and agility.

"Excellent!" praises Ms. Howard. "If this were a movie shoot, we'd print this as a final take."

Mercutio rolls his script into a megaphone. "Wrap it up! Put it in the can!"

This is a "final take." A young actor has created a successful characterization of the enamored Romeo. More importantly, the students and teacher have turned conflict and confrontation into a positive learning experience rather than let it degenerate into a battle of wills. This is the essence of the Full Value Contract (FVC)—valuing each other, one's self and the learning experience.

Overview

The Full Value Contract, the third operating norm of the AITC model, is rooted in the notion that an adventure learning group calls for members to respect the integrity, diversity and strengths of the individuals at the same time that they respect and support the group as a whole. When students and teachers respect each other, they agree to work together and to support each other in their learning. The goal is to *fully value*, in an active fashion, individual members and the history, knowledge, skills and experiences each one brings to the group. How the group *values* these aspects of their membership becomes a deliberate activity, so that group members make informed choices about their language, behavior and expectations. This contrasts with other methods of group development where operating norms emerge without the awareness or direct influence of the participants.

The Full Value Contract asks the following five commitments of the members of the adventure learning community:

- Be here
- Be safe
- Set goals
- Be honest
- Let go and move on

Be Here

The Full Value Contract asks students to make a conscious commitment to be present in the learning experience in body, mind and spirit. It asks for more than just attending class. To "be here" is to commit to full participation and to accept and demonstrate responsibility for one's actions.

To be present in body is a commitment to participate physically. Teachers and students need to talk, listen, share and behave in ways appropriate to the learning situation. Physical presence and participation demonstrate membership as well as support for others in the group. Physical presence prompts students to engage in the learning experience.

To be present in mind is a commitment to participate intellectually in the learning experience. In-depth learning requires more than going through empty motions. The challenge to intellectual presence is a challenge to intellectual excellence.

To be present in spirit is a commitment to adopt an attitude that supports participation. Conscious commitment to a spirit of presence reminds students that they have control over their attitudes and a responsibility to "do what I can to help myself and others to learn."

Be Safe

Basic needs of belonging and safety must be met in order for an individual to stretch cognitively, psychologically and emotionally (Maslow, 1962). In fact, the brain can only develop new connections and engage in new thought processes in an atmosphere that is non-threatening (Caine and Caine, 1991). Each learner needs to feel safe regardless of the correctness of his answers. Each learner needs to be confident of his basic human value before stepping out into new areas of self-examination, growth and risk taking (Rogers, 1951). With incremental success in a safe environment, risk taking increases. The experience of success in a given context, such as meeting academic challenges, encourages additional risk taking (Bandura, 1977). In the academic setting this means

reaching for higher academic standards and increased academic achievement. The classroom, then, must be a place which provides basic safety— safety that is a prerequisite for growth.

Physical and emotional safety are both important in the adventure classroom. It's not enough that a classroom has high quality equipment, the best computers and bookcases filled with printed materials. Students need a learning environment that is as emotionally and physically safe as it is intellectually stimulating.

Physical safety

Physical safety sets the stage for emotional safety. Attention to safe play in cooperative games and problem-solving initiatives is basic. Although bumps and bruises do occur when people run and chase and roll on the ground, none of the cooperative games or problem-solving initiatives sets up scenarios where players tackle, yank or pile on top of each other. The emphasis is on friendly contact and safe play—tagging, holding hands, linking elbows, even hugging!

Adventure activities (see Chapter Seven) are the practice grounds for safety. They provide concrete, physical experience for a group to develop its definition of and strategies for maintaining a safe physical environment. If group members can run hard, throw an aerobie with gusto or dash for the rubber chicken while adhering to group norms of physical safety, they are more likely to nurture the emotional safety necessary for intellectual and interpersonal risk taking in the classroom.

Emotional safety

The AITC classroom connects physical safety to emotional safety so that members of the adventure learning community support each other in their academic challenges. Students and teachers in the AITC classroom attend to a healthy, supportive atmosphere and encourage the kind of intellectual risk taking necessary for academic excellence. Students and teachers in the AITC classroom separate "put-downs" from "put-ups," and learn to give the latter rather than resort to the former. Students and teachers learn to give feedback that separates facts from feelings and observations from opinions. Lucas confronts his teacher, "That's not Full Value." He states his observations, but he doesn't attack his teacher. A supportive atmosphere encourages individuals to take risks, ask questions, introduce new ideas, offer explanations and explore options.

Set Goals

Goals are vital for cognitive, psychological, emotional and social development. The process of setting realistic and measurable goals, as monitored by groups of individuals, improves the chances of success and enhances effort. Goals provide direction and structure. They are the reference points against which we make choices about actions and plans, both as individuals and as a team. When students set goals together, test those goals and reevaluate them based on their experiences, they not only set reachable goals, but achieve at a higher rate than those who do not set their own goals (Lewin, 1944).

In other words, when students assume responsibility for their learning and for monitoring their progress, they set high standards for themselves and more consistently meet those standards.

Goals are generally established on the basis of prior experience. Success yields higher goals; failures beget low expectations or unrealistic goals. Youth who have experienced a repeated sense of failure characteristically set goals that are either too low and present little or no challenge, or too high, presenting a challenge obviously beyond reach. Success without risk often accompanies low expectations. Unattainable goals grant permission for failure. A supportive group, however, nurtures appropriate and rigorous goal setting as peers provide a "reality check" and challenge each other to be realistic in their self-evaluations (Johnson and Johnson, 1991).

The Full Value Contract calls for the members of a group to work collectively toward the attainment of group goals and to support each other in meeting individual goals.

Be Honest

You can't talk yourself out of a situation you've behaved yourself into.

— *Stephen Covey*

The notion of honesty in the Full Value Contract refers to honesty with others and honesty with self. When Manney reminds his teacher, "This is a Full Value classroom," he is honest with himself and the other members of the class. Rather than acting out

or "stuffing" his disappointment or anger, he speaks up in an appropriate manner. He acknowledges his feelings openly and fairly. He is honest with his teacher, appropriately giving her feedback, then working constructively with her to solve the problem of characterization.

Honesty towards self and others is crucial for academic risk taking in the AITC classroom. Honesty challenges the student to raise questions, search for clear understanding, demonstrate knowledge. Honesty also challenges members of the adventure learning community to demand the best from each other. This requires the members to be accountable to each other and responsible for their own actions and words.

Accountability

In the classroom that encourages growth and change, individuals hold each other accountable for their work and efforts to learn. Having set goals, students and teachers make a commitment to help each other reach those goals. Without this accountability, goal setting is an empty task.

Responsibility

If group members agree to be accountable to each other, then they must accept the accompanying responsibility for their actions and their words. They must be willing and able to give and receive feedback around attention to their goals. This responsibility empowers them to make a difference in their academic success and their interpersonal growth.

Let Go and Move On

Many times individuals become embroiled in their disagreements, unable to resolve a conflict or find common ground. To proceed with the task at hand, they must acknowledge their disagreement, choose to put aside their differences, and move forward. Agreeing to disagree is not always enough. Letting go suggests three things:

- Acceptance of others and their differences
- Acceptance of self
- Forgiveness

Acceptance of others

Different learning styles, teaching styles and leadership styles lead to different opinions in a school. The Full Value Contract encourages dialogue and permits disagreements but also reminds the community of adventure learners to embrace the differences and see diversity as a collective strength.

If a curriculum team in an elementary school decides in favor of basal readers over a whole language approach, for example, the advocates of alternate reading methods will have to let go of the argument, accept the decision and look for ways to adapt. There may or may not be room within individual classrooms for alternative approaches, but holding onto the argument detracts and even limits other initiatives. Letting go means moving on.

Acceptance of self

Letting go sometimes requires that we accept limitations, as one student learned. As a high school junior, he was intrigued by chemistry and made excellent grades. College chemistry was a different story, however. The student struggled and studied, sought help at every turn, poured hours into the text and class notes just to maintain a passing grade. Chemistry was no longer an exciting intrigue, but a perplexing mystery. The familiar methods of studying alone, studying with other students, rewriting notes, highlighting entire paragraphs were insufficient for the challenge. The student had to let go of previous methods and expectations. He had to rethink, restrategize and redefine expectations in order to overcome the obstacles.

Forgiveness

Forgiveness is the only way one can truly let go of anger, hurt and vengeance. This radical act of grace is uncommon in North American culture, where "getting back" is often the norm. In the AITC classroom, where individuals are held in esteem, the integrity of the group is maintained and learning is a high endeavor, there are times when students and teachers have to forgive each other for the hurtful ways they sometimes treat one another. To forgive honestly and put aside affronts and attacks goes a long way toward effecting change in broader relationships. The challenge is as much to teachers as it is to students to practice graciousness.

Establishing a Full Value Contract

Establishing a Full Value Contract can occur in a variety of ways. Some teachers prefer to devote the opening few days of school to adventure activities focused exclusively on developing a Full Value Contract. Others introduce the concepts of the Contract incrementally. The presentation or shape of the Full Value Contract also varies with the group. Some groups rely on visuals or graphic representations. Metaphors and images help other groups. Still others craft formal statements.

Formal Group Contract

A formal group contract is a document that outlines the specific behaviors and goals that a class agrees to maintain. Behaviors that groups have identified include agreeing to share materials, one person speaks at a time, coming to class on time and being prepared for the day's work. The formal contract also itemizes behaviors that the class will strive to eliminate, such as pushing or shoving, profanity or late homework.

The appearance of the contract depends upon the group. Sometimes a contract is very formal. It looks and reads like a legal agreement. Some contracts are posters that the class members sign. Other groups paint a picture that illustrates their goals and then captions the specific behaviors to which they commit. What is important is that the group contract be collectively determined and publicly displayed so that the members of the adventure classroom can see and refer to it anytime during class.

Play Hard, Play Safe, Play Fair

The maxim, *play hard, play safe, play fair* captures the essence of the Full Value Contract in concrete terms. Play hard, after all, means to "go for it," throw everything you've got into the activity. Play hard means to put an all-out effort into whatever challenge needs to be met—leading a discussion, preparing a speech or creating a sculpture. Play safe is a reminder that physical and emotional safety form the boundary within which all activity occurs. Play safe is about a challenging yet comfortable and safe environment, where a child does not have to worry that the other kids are going to laugh at her awkwardness. Play fair, among other things, is about being honest. Play fair asks everyone to be open to each other's ideas and suggestions. It challenges integrity of effort, hard work, setting high expectations and truly doing one's best.

Beth Acinapura, at Winthrop Elementary School in Ipswich, MA, uses play hard, play safe, play fair with her fifth graders. The school year begins with a couple of days of adventure activities focusing on building the class team. The class plays cooperative games and adventure initiatives and processes the activities around play hard, play safe, play fair. Through playing and processing of the adventure activities, students begin to clarify how they will play hard, play safe and play fair. They decide, for example, that agreeing to play hard is a commitment to "Get work done on time." Play fair means, "Play by the rules," as well as, "If you don't understand something, ask." Play safe means, "No pushing or shoving," as well as "No put-downs, only put-ups."

The Full Value Contract that the class begins to define for itself on the playing field becomes the Full Value Contract for the classroom. As the class works out their Full Value Contract, they write on a mural the specific behaviors they commit to fulfilling. To demonstrate individual commitment to the Full Value Contract, each student signs her or his name to the document. Throughout the year the students point to their own words and examples boldly displayed on the wall to praise or confront each other as they work together.

Totem

Constructing a Totem that personifies a classroom provides students with the kinesthetic, spatial and artistic means to define a Full Value Contract. First the students determine the particulars of their Full Value Contract. They identify the specific ways that they will value self, each other and the learning in their class. Next they design a Totem that symbolizes their adventure learning community. The design includes three or four sections, with a piece of the Full Value Contract or class goals as the subject of each section. The class then constructs the Totem. Wood or papier mâché make good construction materials. Boxes, Styrofoam and other recycled items also work well. After they have built the Totem, the students add words or pictures on each section to specify the behaviors the class previously identified for their Contract.

The Being

The Being is a large picture of some living entity that the group decides symbolizes itself. The Being can be an outline of a person, a garden, an animal, a village, a lake or a stream. In

some cases the teacher chooses and names the Being for the group. In other classes it is more important for the group to come up with its own representation. In any event, the group draws the entity on a large piece of newsprint, an old sheet or large poster board. Inside the Being, the group writes the goals or attributes they will maintain. On the outside of the Being the group writes those factors that hinder them in meeting these goals. For example, inside the Being might be "group consensus" and "criticize ideas, not people," while on the outside might be "time pressure" and "ignoring new ideas." Like the other visual representations, the Being is displayed in a prominent place.

The FVC and Students

Students, teachers, counselors and administrators who operate within the framework of the Full Value Contract attest to its effectiveness. A classroom or an entire school that operates with the Full Value Contract enjoys several advantages:

- The classroom or school is a safe place to be.
- Students are willing to assume greater challenges and intellectual risks.
- Students develop responsibility and become accountable for their education.
- Academic growth increases.
- Personal growth increases.

Safety

Children spend much of their waking hours in school. Schools should be places where children enjoy spending their day. If the school is a safe place emotionally and physically, students will want to be there. Within a physically safe and supportive environment children grow as healthy individuals and contributing members of a community. Within an emotionally safe and supportive environment, students stretch themselves academically. They push themselves to achieve, certain of the support from their peers.

Willingness to Risk

In a safe environment children take the healthy risks that characterize adventure learning. The shy reader more willingly reads to a partner. The beginning writer puts onto paper and shares with peers the fantastic images that he is anxious to describe. Even the class clown, attempting to learn appropriateness with his comedic talents, curbs his joking without fear of losing face.

Responsibility

As students learn skills to manage their activity within the classroom, they begin to apply those skills elsewhere in the school and in their lives. An elementary student who observes a fight on the playground approaches one of the children later and encourages him to spend some time in the "thinking chair" to figure out why he became involved in the fight and what he should do about it.

Two other students in the sixth grade take seriously their responsibility to make arrangements for a guest speaker. Without prompting from their teacher, they call the speaker, set the date and time, check with the office to reserve the auditorium, and distribute announcements to all the teachers in the school. A high school student who has reached the limits of the teacher's knowledge about CD-ROMs figures out how to bring resources into the school so the class can learn more about this expanding technology.

Academic Growth

When a student is involved in the shaping of the curriculum and learning environment, he is more likely to be committed and engaged in the actual learning. "Our students are working harder and doing much more complex work than they were before," states one teacher. "The significant rise in math and reading scores over the past three years is due to the process, the way we teach, and that includes the Full Value Contract," comments Mark Glasbrenner, principal of Cedarwood Elementary School. If students enjoy coming to school, if they feel safe, if they are challenged, if they take responsibility for their learning and their relationships within the school, then it stands to reason that academic achievement will also improve.

Personal Growth

Robin Fellabella, a teacher at Winthrop Elementary School explains, "With the Full Value Contract, students are much more responsive to discipline issues. When I see a child who has been mistreating another child in the hallway and I ask, 'Were you playing safe?' or 'Was that playing fair?' that student clicks into what I'm talking about. He's able to make the connection right away and identify what it was that he did that was inconsiderate or unfair to others."

If the environment in which children spend much of their waking hours is supportive, if those children feel a sense of responsibility and ownership about their work and see that what they are doing is worthy and worthwhile, they will develop more positive self-esteem and more positive attitudes about school and learning in general. The Full Value Contract contributes greatly to a student's personal growth. Students learn about and work on developing interpersonal skills. As they feel good about school and experience academic learning as positive, they also develop positive attitudes about life-long learning.

> The teacher's role is to facilitate the sharing of information and ideas among all members of the community.

The FVC and the Teacher

The culture change brought about by the Full Value Contract invites the teacher into new roles and relationships in the classroom. The teacher—

- Becomes a facilitator
- Shares responsibility
- Acknowledges vulnerability
- Experiences personal and professional growth

Teacher as Facilitator

In contrast to a traditional model of teacher role, where the teacher is a gatekeeper of information, the AITC model asks the teacher to become a facilitator of learning. The Full Value Contract highlights that role as it empowers students to be resources for each other. The teacher's role is to facilitate the sharing of information and ideas among all members of the community.

The Full Value Contract acknowledges up front that relationships and environment are integral to content learning. As a facilitator of educational experience, learning environments and classroom relationships, the teacher becomes a coach.

The effective music teacher or athletic coach participates with the students as both teacher and learner. The coach teaches skills—correct breathing or hand position, diction, defensive play. The effective coach plays the music with the students or demonstrates technique. The music coach feels the music, expresses her own style and helps

students interpret the music. Finally, the coach pays careful attention to the relationships on the team. Good coaches care as much about how individuals interact as they do about how well they perform. An inspiring performance, whether on stage or the playing field, depends as much upon technical expertise as it does upon the relationships within the group.

Shared Responsibility

AITC teachers share responsibility for curriculum and classroom management with the students. This contrasts with traditional, hierarchical education structures, where the administration makes decisions that teachers carry out regardless of teacher and student perspectives.

Shared responsibility develops incrementally. The teacher may begin by introducing the notion of *valuing self and others* and, for perhaps a week or two, the class discusses what this phrase means. Students identify daily examples of ways they value themselves and others. Simultaneously, the teacher begins to use cooperative learning strategies and introduces students to new roles. For example, some students assume the role of manager. Their responsibilities include collecting assignments, checking whether or not group members have completed their work on time, answering questions regarding new assignments, and making sure everyone understands the directions. As students learn to manage themselves, the teacher is freed from the chains of the paper chase in order to focus more on the business of teaching and learning.

When students share responsibilities with each other and their teachers, they see that they can learn from each other. They develop appreciation for the knowledge, the problem-solving approaches and the teaching styles of others. Students learn to share responsibilities for curriculum content. They become resources to one another, coaching each other, sharing material and providing feedback on each other's work.

Vulnerability

Being vulnerable to members of the learning community is a gift of the Full Value Contract. The Full Value Contract permits the teacher to say he doesn't know the derivation of an equation or how the Cultural Revolution in China directly affected the national economy. When students see adults admit their confusion and muddle through problems, the children learn that there is nothing wrong with not having the "right answer." Children learn to ask for and accept assistance. The teacher who says, "I like our thematic units, but I want to incorporate the fine and applied arts into our work," finds students offering suggestions, bringing in materials to use in class and taking an active role in enhancing the curriculum. When students hear their teacher say, "I need to get your journals returned more promptly. I am going to set a goal to return them within three days," they not only have a role model for their own goal setting and growth, but also the privilege of sharing in and learning from the processes of an adult's growth. Students see that learning is a life-long activity.

Personal and Professional Growth

The Full Value Contract both challenges and supports teachers. It holds them accountable and reminds them that they are responsible to themselves, to each other and to their students. Teachers are more likely to pursue professional development and teaching excellence when they share clearly defined goals, outline methods of supporting each other and assist each other in reaching those goals. The gossip of the lunch room and the back-biting in the department office diminish as teachers take action to value each other and their students, and establish, through the Full Value Contract, mechanisms for confronting each other when words and actions discount colleagues or students.

The contract allows teachers to participate in the joy of learning and urges them to continuously look for new ideas and new ways of approaching materials. Personal and professional growth result as the teacher assumes the role of facilitator, shares responsibility and acknowledges personal and professional vulnerabilities. Teachers who live the Full Value Contract model for their students the struggles and the rewards of membership in a community of adventure learners.

Setting and Monitoring Goals

Among the many reasons that individuals partici-pate in groups is the desire to pursue shared inter-ests. At the same time, members bring to a group their own agendas and personal expectations (Johnson and Johnson, 1991). Consequently, it be-comes important to negotiate individual goals within the context of the group process.

Individual and group goals are important for several reasons:

- Goals provide shape and direction for indi-vidual and group learning. A clearly defined goal, with specific steps for achieving it, is necessary for forward motion, development of skills and effective behavior changes.

- Relationships in the classroom demonstrate themselves in the articulation and commit-ment to goals. Acknowledgment of and ac-tive participation in attending to individual and group goals reflect the interdependence of group members. Realizing a collective goal requires the efforts of all the members. Individuals are more likely to reach their own goals if other team members provide support, encouragement and assistance.

- Individuals are more inclined to contribute to a group's efforts when they feel connected to other group members.

Goals play such a significant role in the Full Value Contract that specific attention to establish-ing and monitoring effective goals merits some attention here.

How many? How often?

The "One day at a time/One step at a time" philoso-phy summarizes the goal setting process. While long-term goals and thoughtful plans of action have their place, goals in the adventure classroom ben-efit from simplicity and manageability. A long list of goals overwhelms most people. For students and teachers new to articulating goals in the classroom, it is important to set just a few goals at a time in order to stay focused and maintain a reasonable chance of achieving them. Begin with one goal at a time. More than that and the students will be unable to assist one another. There will be too many goals to keep track.

In the early stages of goal setting, goals should be articulated so that they can be achieved in a rela-tively short time, such as a day or two. New skills need frequent attention and practice. As goal set-ting and monitoring become established in the culture of the class, moving to weekly or monthly goals is appropriate.

Some teachers find it unnecessary to set time frames for goals. One fifth-grade teacher in the early stages of teaching about setting goals, for example, did not stipulate how long goals should remain in place. Students made choices about academic or behavior goals based on what they were comfort-able with and for whatever period of time they felt was appropriate. The students were conscientious about the process and generally made wise choices. When a child made a questionable choice, the class confronted the individual and encouraged more appropriate decisions. The Full Value Contract enabled them to take on this responsibility and help each other as they set and worked toward meeting individual goals.

Academic and Behavior Goals

Academic goals relate to the academic curriculum. Academic goals that are cognitive in nature focus on: 1) skills to be mastered; e.g., setting up a spreadsheet using Excel; 2) concepts; e.g., showing how Curious George made wise choices; 3) products or projects; e.g., making a presentation to the parent advisory board.

Academic goals also focus on metacognitive development. When a student chooses to create a set of analogies to explain a scientific concept, the academic goal is metacognitive in nature.

Behavior goals relate to social skill development. Behavior goals include such things as giving verbal support to others, listening attentively and using positive language—those skills that affect one's ability to be an effective member of the learning community.

Individual and Group Goals

Students in the adventure classroom set complementary individual and group goals. Because students are individually accountable for their learning, it is important for them to establish and commit

to goals specific to their academic work and their interpersonal growth. The fourth grader struggling to master multiplication tables, for example, sets a goal to master the 6's and 7's without any errors by the end of the week. Concurrently, that same child also sets a behavior goal for the week based on interpersonal relationships in class. In some cases the behavior goal directly supports the academic goal. In other instances, the behavior goal weighs more heavily on group development. For the child who hesitates to ask for help, a behavior goal supportive of the academic goal is to ask a team member to review the math tables each day. On the other hand, a goal to share materials does not directly tie into the academic goal, yet supports team development skills.

Members of the adventure learning community collectively establish goals to direct their academic work and assist their group development. The team may have a collaborative project or may be responsible for making sure each member demonstrates weekly improvement in learning multiplication tables. While the individual child may establish a goal to learn the 6's and 7's by Friday, the team sets a goal to make sure that each team member helps two other team members to review.

Sharing and Supporting Goals

Members of the adventure learning community can only assist each other in reaching their individual goals if they know each others' goals and the impediments to reaching them. Individual goals are sometimes displayed visually. Sometimes individuals share goals verbally. If students resist sharing goals, consider the following:

- Is the *trust level* in the group sufficient to encourage this kind of risk taking? More time may be needed to develop a higher level of trust before students are ready to share goals with a group.

- Are students setting goals that are *inappropriate?* In the early stages of learning to set goals, it helps to have examples of goals appropriate to the group's developmental stage.

- Do students understand that *goals can change?* If they are concerned that a goal isn't quite right, they need to know that they can change it.

- Is there an *atmosphere* in the goal setting process that supports input and help in setting goals? Students don't need to come to a goal setting time with all the *i*'s dotted and the *t*'s crossed. Others can help clarify.

- Is the *group size* appropriate for sharing goals? It helps to begin goal setting with partners or in a small group format of three or four students. People who are new to goal setting often find a partner or small group setting safer and more secure.

Follow-through and feedback

Setting goals only to neglect them not only wastes class time but undermines other efforts to encourage students to take responsibility for their learning.

Four Qualities of Feedback

1. **Compassionate** — Feedback considers the feelings of the listener.

2. **Concrete** — Feedback makes specific points, gives detailed suggestions, delineates words and actions.

3. **Constructive** — Feedback builds rather than destroys.

4. **Concise** — Feedback is crisp and to the point.

If you and your students set goals, then follow through and monitor those goals! Feedback around goals is essential. Feedback is observation. It is viewpoint, not vendetta.

Feedback helps in working toward goals in at least three ways:

1. Feedback acknowledges an individual's efforts toward a goal. Positive feedback is far more effective in behavior change than criticism.

2. Feedback provides other perspectives that help individuals round out their own assessment of progress.

3. Feedback is a concrete reminder of the collaborative and supportive atmosphere of the community of learners. This, in turn, further strengthens the learning.

Two common feedback strategies are *I statements* and *feeling statements*. With *I statements*, individuals who are giving feedback refer to themselves as the subject of the feedback; e.g., "I had difficulty understanding your point in the essay," or "I find this metaphor confusing." Manney could have used an I statement when he confronted his teacher by saying, "I thought this was a Full Value class," or "I don't think that anyone should call someone 'stupid' in this class."

Feeling statements emphasize the speaker's feelings in response to the actions of others. A feeling statement from Manney would have been, "I feel devalued when you say what I'm doing is stupid," or "I feel put down when you tell me what I'm doing is stupid."

With both methods the speaker is the subject, stating the situation in such a way as to share responsibility for dialogue.

Appropriate Goals: SMART and STAR Goals

An effective set of guidelines for setting goals that are appropriate and manageable is summarized by the acronym *SMART*. SMART goals (adapted from Blanchard and Sharp and Cox) are goals that are *Specific, Measurable, Achievable, Relevant* and *Trackable*.

Specific — A goal states *exactly* what you want to achieve. When people give themselves an alternative, such as "I will either finish the Spanish project or do my book report by Friday," they seldom get beyond the *or*. Neither goal is reached. Set one goal. If in the process you see a need to change, then go ahead, but make it clear to yourself and to others that you are making a change.

Measurable — A goal is effective to the extent it can be measured in terms of time and quantity. For example, a goal to finish writing a curriculum outline might be stated as, "I am going to complete the outline, including objectives, and write one week's worth of lesson plans by Friday." The goal can be measured. When Friday comes, you know whether or not you have hit the target.

Achievable — A goal should be realistically achievable. Stretch yourself, but do not frustrate yourself with unrealistic goals. The student who has difficulty with spelling should set an incremental goal that allows him to work toward improvement, but shouldn't set the goal that he wants to spell everything perfectly on every paper.

Relevant — A goal is relevant if it addresses behavior that makes a positive difference in overall performance and is in line with the class. A goal may carry over to another portion of one's life. In the classroom, however, goals must be appropriate to the particular learning community and its work. Establishing a goal to keep one's bedroom clean is not relevant to the English class! However, maintaining an organized work area in the classroom or making sure that materials are returned to their proper place may be an appropriate goal that improves the conditions for studying the American novel.

Trackable — To be able to monitor progress toward a goal, you need to be able to measure performance frequently. Setting a goal to complete five interviews by Tuesday, or to finish the second round of editing by the end of class, are goals that can be tracked. If Monday rolls around and Sally has only done one interview, then she knows specifically what she needs to do to reach her Tuesday goal. If class is half over and Chase is done editing his paper, then he knows he has met his goal.

 STAR goals are an adaptation of SMART goals for students. STAR goals (*Specific, Trackable, Achievable* and *Relevant*) combine the concepts of *measurable* and *trackable*, suggesting that in order to track achievement, you must also measure it. Doug MacLeod, fifth-grade teacher at Winthrop Elementary School, has added the visual effect of paper stars. His students write their goals on stars that hang in the room. As they meet their goals, they replace the old stars with new ones.

Strategies for Setting and Monitoring Goals

There are many ways to facilitate goal setting and promote goal sharing within the learning community. The following have been used effectively with students of all ages in adventure classrooms.

Totem and The Being

Both of these Full Value Contract methods work as goal setting activities. Instead of focusing on attributes of the classroom or qualities to be attained, the students write their goals inside the Being or on the Totem. The Totem can be divided into sections based on the type of goal being set. For example, behavior goals are on the bottom and academic goals are written on top. Classes sometimes use different colored ink to identify academic goals from behavior goals in the Being. Both the Totem and Being work for small group goal setting as well as full-class goal setting.

Contract

Developing a contract is a common goal setting activity. Using a document that has a formal yet friendly appearance signals the importance of goals. Students share contracts within a small group, such as a base team of three or four, or post them in the room.

Introducing goal setting as a form of contracting helps to clarify the commitment involved in goal setting. Preparation for this kind of activity includes discussion around the nature of contracts. When do people use contracts? What do they mean? When can contracts be changed? What needs to happen when someone wants to change a contract?

The sample contract from T. C. Motzkus, a teacher from West Bend, WI, itemizes some steps a student can take to meet a goal: "Whom can you count on to assist you in achieving your goal? What things do you need to do to achieve your goal?" It also reminds the student that other people can help him reach his goals. Even the teacher offers assistance: "Share with me one thing I can do to help you reach your goal."

PERSONAL ACTION PLAN FOR THIRD QUARTER

1. On a scale of 1 to 5 (5 being the highest) select a number which represents how you felt about your achievement of your second quarter Full Value Contract.

2. Compare your academic goal 2nd quarter with your academic goal 3rd quarter. Are you making gradual steps towards improvement? YES or NO - What subject do you want to improve in?

3. Using your academic goal for 3rd quarter from #2, choose a letter grade you would be proud of in this area. _____

4. If you were successful in reading your 2nd quarter goal, how did you celebrate?

_____

5. Who can you count on to assist you in achieving your goal?
   1. _____   2. _____

6. What things do you need to do, steps do you need to take, to achieve your goal?
   1. _____
   2. _____
   3. _____

7. What signs or signals will you see when you are getting close to achieving your goal? (example: improving on homework)
   1. _____
   2. _____

8. Share with me one thing I can do to help you reach your goal.

_____

9. List one thing you can do to support a friend's goal.

_____

10. List one person you are going to try to become better friends with this quarter.

_____

11. List one gremlin or whispering phantom you will try to work on this quarter.

· · · · · · · · · · · · · · · **FEEDBACK FOR** · · · · · · · · · · · · · ·
MRS. MOTZKUS

PLEASE OFFER SUGGESTIONS TO ME ABOUT MY TEACHING—SOMETHING I CAN CHANGE OR DO TO MAKE LEARNING BETTER OR EASIER FOR YOU.

T-Chart

The T-Chart is an effective visual method for setting and monitoring goals. The individual student or class writes a goal across the top of the giant T. "Looks like" and "Sounds like" head the columns on either side of the T. Students write sample behaviors under each column heading.

As the day progresses, students make check marks or put stars next to the items that indicate how they have worked toward a goal. The visual markers become a record of progress toward the goal as well as positive reinforcement. Items that do not have stars or check marks need attention.

Taking Turns

Looks Like	Sounds like
Raising Hands	One voice at a time
One person talking at a time	"What is your idea?"
Sharing Materials	Cindy has an idea.

Good Interview Techniques

Looks Like	Sounds like
Interviewer faces the interviewee	Follow-up questions
Good eye contact	"Can you give an example?"
Note taking	"Can you explain more?"
Alert body posture	One person speaks at a time

High five's

High Five's are a variation of STAR goals. Students trace a hand on construction paper and write individual goals on the cut-out. These hands, or High Five's, hang on a bulletin board so that the individuals' names and goals are in clear view. As students achieve a goal, they take down the High Five and put up another one. At the end of a marking period or semester, each student has a collection of High Five's to survey and show to others.

Maps

Students make a map that shows their destination or goal and the steps necessary to get there. As they meet roadblocks along the way, team members add these to the map. To add some whimsy, cut-out vehicles or pedestrians move daily to show the progress.

Mind maps, flowcharts and other cognitive mapping techniques work well in charting goals. The point is for the learner to be able to clearly identify a goal, define the necessary steps to meet that target as well as potential obstacles, and chart progress along the way. Assessment of progress toward goals, after all, occurs during the process, not at the end.

Stickers

Once goals have been set, stickers are great, unobtrusive ways to acknowledge someone's positive steps toward a goal. Some classes add stickers to their Totem or Being. In other classes, students hand stickers to each other or post them on goal sheets. Surprisingly, high school students and adults delight in stickers just as much as primary grade children do.

Green cards

Another method for giving feedback around goals is *green cards*. Kathy Hunt, a Project Adventure trainer, gives workshop participants green and red poster board cards cut to about 2" x 3". During the course of a day, participants acknowledge each other's efforts toward goals by handing green cards to each other. Similarly, a missed opportunity for someone to work on a goal is acknowledged by a red card. The cards are not substitutes for conversation, but place markers, so that having received a card from someone, the recipient can go back later and ask, "Can you tell me why you gave this to me?" The person handing out a card can also take the first step to talk, and offer, "I'd like to tell you why I think you did a good job and why I gave you this green card."

Feedback sheets

Feedback sheets work best in a small group setting of four or five people. Each student in the group writes his name on a piece of paper along with his goal. The students pass the papers one person to the left. Each student now has someone else's paper to write a positive statement on regarding

that person's goal. The group passes the papers around so that each team member has a chance to write a positive comment on everyone's feedback sheet.

The process can go another round, but this time the feedback is regarding a growth area. Each person identifies a place that the individual neglected to work on a goal, or suggests another area to focus on for academic or interpersonal growth.

Put-up's

Put-up's teach students the importance of positive, concrete feedback. Put-up's show support and encouragement. They can be about someone's class work ("I liked your speech.") or behavior. ("You were a good listener during our discussion.") They are positive comments that help students internalize the value of supportive talk and behavior. The more students hear and offer each other put-ups, the more they internalize the value of the attitudes that accompany those words.

Put-ups are such an important part of the school cultures at Devonshire and Cedarwood Elementary Schools that anyone who puts down another person at any time must compensate with three put-ups. Although three put-ups for any put-down may seem contrived to some, the lesson is clear: Positive, supportive behavior is of utmost importance, and words that attack are destructive and unacceptable.

Summary

The Full Value Contract creates a context for learning. It encourages the growth of all members of the adventure learning community and creates an exciting context for that growth. A community that openly supports learning, treats its members with respect, protects each other's safety and sets and monitors goals is a community that promotes optimal learning for all.

The Full Value Contract encourages adults and children to value one another and publicly demonstrate that in their behavior. It urges everyone to take responsibility for their academic work, as well as their behavior, and make positive changes. The Contract calls upon all learners to care enough to help each other meet their goals.

The Full Value Contract creates a context for community. It provides language and guidelines around which the community grows. To live the Full Value Contract requires constant revisiting of its principles and a willingness to be vulnerable and open. Enhanced learning, growth and honest relationships are the rewards for the hard work that the Full Value Contract requires.

SECTION THREE

Strategies for Teaching and Learning

The Adventure in the Classroom model relies upon four primary strategies as vehicles for instruction: adventure activities, processing, team learning and teaching and integrated curriculum. The AITC model has benefited greatly from Project Adventure's work in these areas, as well as the research of others in the field of education.

The rich legacy of adventure activities that Project Adventure continues to nurture is an undeniable asset to the AITC model. There is much in current research literature, including the discussion of learning styles preferences, to validate what Project Adventure has practiced and known. The focus in this section is on the roles that cooperative games and initiatives play in supporting academic and cognitive growth, the development of interpersonal skills, the development of reflective and metacognitive skills and the support of the adventure learning community. Comments regarding logistical considerations are offered as guidelines to practitioners new to this pedagogical method.

Processing, the activity of deriving meaning from experience, is critical for academic learning and for the strengthening of the adventure learning community. The various strategies and guidelines offered here reflect the attention which the AITC model gives to processing academic content and behavior, as well as processing for cognitive, metacognitive, interpersonal and personal growth.

A great deal of research over the past several years validates the efficacy of cooperative learning strategies upon various academic and developmental goals in education, including achievement, intrinsic motivation and attitude toward school and peer relationships. The AITC model incorporates the strategies of several cooperative learning models and also extends the definitions and conditions for effective cooperative learning as team learning and teaching.

Finally, the AITC model is an integrated curriculum model that not only acknowledges the existing paradigms for integration, but also expands the notion of curriculum integration to address three critical but often neglected aspects for integration. These are the integration of the two curricula of schools, the integration of content and process and the integration of needs or goals. While this may be the most challenging aspect of the model for some, integrating curriculum broadly and deeply demonstrates the purpose of education—developing in students the skills and capacities to be life-long learners.

Activity and the Adventure Classroom

In the early formative years, play is almost synonymous with life. It is second only to being nourished, protected and loved. It is a basic ingredient of physical, intellectual, social and emotional growth.

— *Ashley Montagu*

Twenty-six ninth graders huddle together on the football field on a blustery winter day. Bundled in layers of coats, hats and mittens, they pair up to walk a straight line across an open field. In each pair, one student is blindfolded. The sighted partner maintains safety for the "blind" student. After everyone has a chance at both roles, the teacher challenges the entire group to walk to a point on the other side of the field while they are all blindfolded and maintaining physical contact with each other.

Twenty minutes into the challenge the students remove their blindfolds and spend the remainder of class discussing the difficulties they faced. Then they discuss the capacity of migratory animals to find their way across thousands of miles.

In the coming weeks, these students will read about human survival in extreme conditions. They will investigate math and science concepts of measurement, magnetic fields and planetary rotation. They will make calculations and learn principles of geometry along with

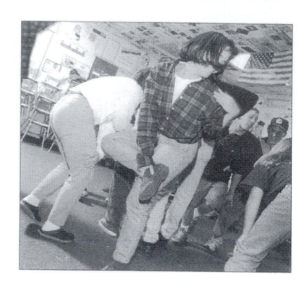

basic navigational astronomy. And in each case, the connections they make to their first-hand experience with the *Blindfold Compass Walk* will help bring to life the concepts, skills, facts and theories that might otherwise remain silent on the page.

Adventure activities, one of the four teaching strategies that comprise the AITC model, are common to all Project Adventure programs. The activity base of Project Adventure is one of the legacies of the organization and no less important to the AITC model than to the Adventure Programming or Adventure Based Counseling models.

In the AITC model, adventure activities follow the experiential learning cycle (see Chapter Four) of activity, reflection, generalizing and transfer. As students participate in adventure activities, they internalize the steps of the cycle and begin to apply this reflective, process-based strategy to all of their learning. When students study calculus or Spanish literature, they know how to reflect on actions, generalize the learning from the experience, and apply that knowledge to the current topic.

In exploring the role adventure activities play in the AITC model, we will look at the following topics:

- A definition of adventure activities
- Theoretical frameworks
- The role of adventure activities in promoting learning and supporting the community of adventure learners

- Logistical considerations
- Having fun and changing pace

Definitions

First of all, just what are adventure activities? How are they like or different from other classroom activities such as reading, math manipulatives or simulations?

There are four basic categories of adventure activities:

1. **Cooperative Games** — These are short games that require minimal props. Cooperative games range from highly active running activities to quiet sit-down games at a desk.

2. **Initiatives** — Initiatives are problem–solving activities that use portable props and can be set up almost anywhere. They explore abstract academic and behavioral concepts in a hands-on way.

3. **Low Challenge Course Elements** —These ropes course activities can be constructed indoors or outdoors. The elements, positioned from one to five feet off the ground,

generally require spotting. Low challenge course elements build on the themes of the initiatives and engage students in exciting learning settings.

4. **High Challenge Course Elements** — The high elements range from twenty to sixty feet in height and are constructed in trees, telephone poles or gymnasium rafters. High challenge course elements require the use of a belay system of ropes, harnesses and hardware to keep the climber safe. These activities provide students with uniquely challenging individual and group learning experiences.

These are the activities in which Project Adventure has its creative roots and energy. Since the scope of most AITC programs may not include access to or funding for a challenge ropes course, discussion here addresses the use of cooperative games and initiative activities.

Theoretical Framework

Various educational and developmental theories support the use of adventure activities in the AITC model:

- Learning styles preferences and multiple intelligences
- Cooperative learning
- Curriculum integration
- Problem solving and critical thinking
- Flow

Learning Styles Preferences and Multiple Intelligences

Research indicates that knowledge becomes significant, is retained and becomes usable when learners truly understand, see and make their own connections, recognize patterns and develop their own meaning. Students need to play with ideas, explore them, test them out, see where they hold up and where they don't in order to develop true understanding. Individuals have different learning styles preferences (Dunn, 1990; McCarthy, 1990), and different intelligences or abilities "to solve problems, or to fashion a product, to make something" (Gardner, 1990). It is imperative, then, that the teaching process open several gateways for students to access the material and construct knowledge.

The use of math manipulatives, unfortunately often limited to the early elementary grades, models this multiple gateway concept. To introduce and develop student skills of logical/mathematical concepts, children count, sort and group beads, wooden dowels, plastic lids and dried beans. Children match piles and paper clips and blocks to see relationships and quantities long before they put pencil to paper. They participate kinesthetically, visually, spatially. They use logical thinking and verbal skills as they problem solve together.

Adventure activities operate in much the same way. Students play with ideas and approach the material from several angles. They are physically involved with the theme, concept, skills or questions. They have first-hand experience with the ideas.

Adventure activities exercise the multiple strengths and styles that students possess.

The *Blindfold Compass Walk,* for example, encourages students to think about how to navigate an uncharted course and question why human beings are unlikely to walk a straight course in the wilderness without a compass. The process of making connections, seeing patterns and recognizing relationships between new information and existing knowledge is the goal of adventure learning.

Another way to look at how adventure activities strengthen learning, regardless of learning preferences, is in light of the three pathways by which people connect new information with existing knowledge

1. **Perceptual:** "Something about the way things look connects to something about how things looked before."

2. **Action:** "Something about what we do calls up what we have done before."

3. **Conceptual:** "An idea, word, or a formula is the link."

"In any given situation, it is the interplay among these three that determines our understanding of it and what we do with it, not our conceptual knowledge alone, and still less our logical structures" (Duckworth, 1987). Adventure activities capture these three possibilities as they engage the emotional, cognitive and physical capacities of students and provide opportunities for each avenue—visual perception, physical action and conceptual understanding.

Activity, the first stage in the Experiential Learning Cycle, is the time "To enter into the experience, to engage the self, to connect personal meaning with experience" (McCarthy, 1992). Adventure activities increase the number of avenues by which students become engaged with the material. In addition, adventure activities bring students together for a shared experience in preparation for in-depth study of the topic at hand.

Cooperative Learning

Research and practice validate the efficacy of cooperative learning structures on academic learning and social skill development (Johnson, Johnson, Holubec, et al., 1984; Johnson, Johnson and Holubec, 1988; Johnson and Johnson, 1992). Adventure activities, by their nature, are cooperative. Cooperative games and problem-solving initiatives require collaboration among team members. As they work together, students talk and listen to each other, articulate ideas, explain and integrate various viewpoints and suggestions. This interaction stimulates cognitive growth (Vygotsky, 1978).

In problem-solving initiatives such as *Blindfold Compass Walk* or *Traffic Jam*, individuals must talk together, share ideas, ask for clarification, articulate possible solutions, integrate ideas, plan and prioritize. One student tries to convince the group to test her solution, for example. She needs to articulate and defend her suggestion and persuasively outline her argument to others. Effective communication skills and an ability to express ideas in

The purposeful integration of subject matter
not only mirrors the real world, but also makes
the interdependence of subjects transparent for students.

different ways transfer to other classroom activities. The student who understands the concept of magnetic north and its relationship to compass and map reading needs to be able to explain what she knows to peers. The more knowledgeable student must think about the information in terms of vocabulary meaningful to her peers. The ability to effectively teach others requires greater in-depth learning than personal understanding often requires.

In addition to verbal interaction, cooperative learning through adventure activities requires students to rely on and develop individual and team strengths. Individually, students need to listen, process directions, manipulate objects, gather data and plan a strategy. They also have to use physical skills to carry out a particular task. The group needs Dasheeda's leadership ability, Hannah's organizational strengths, Sean's flexibility and Gillian's physical stamina to accomplish the activity. Students' self-esteem grows through successful demonstration of their skills. As they witness the contributions of their peers, students become more accepting of each other and willing to take on new challenges themselves. Dasheeda feels encouraged to push herself physically and Sean learns organization strategies from Hannah.

Integrative Approach

Curriculum becomes more relevant to students as they see the connections between subjects rather than experience subject matter in isolation (Jacobs,

1989). The purposeful integration of subject matter not only mirrors the real world, but also makes the interdependence of subjects transparent for students. Subject integration assists the organizing activity of the brain as it looks for and creates connections among the many pieces of information bombarding us daily (Caine and Caine, 1991).

Adventure activities promote cognitive and social growth through their integrative nature. During the *Blindfold Compass Walk,* students rely on spatial, tactile and auditory cues to traverse the course. In order to strategize together, they must listen and negotiate. This interplay of physical, emotional, cognitive and social experiences is critical for the broader and deeper understanding characteristic of authentic learning (Caine and Caine, 1991). The processing of experiences (see Chapters Four and Eight) cultivates students' skills of analysis, assimilation, evaluation and application.

It is critical that as teachers we design instruction in such a way as to reveal the interrelationships between areas of study. Adventure activities assist this process by initiating and promoting these "active linkages between fields of knowledge" (Jacobs, 1989). From the *Blindfold Compass Walk,* for example, students generate topics for writing assignments. They read short stories and biographies of 18th century adventurers. They study the history of navigation and map-making at the same time they learn geometry. The disciplines of literature, math, science, geography and writing step out of their isolation and weave a rich tapestry from the theme of survival.

Problem Solving and Critical Thinking

The emerging world is a place where there are no easy answers and even fewer directives to one's work and life. Skills associated with "learning how to relate," "learning how to learn," and "learning how to choose" dominate educational goals (Fogarty and Bellanca, 1992). Adventure activities demand the kind of intellectual and interpersonal struggles that push problem solving and critical thinking. Negotiating, re-negotiating, building on ideas, compromising, adapting and evaluating are among the higher order thinking skills required by adventure activities. Students exercise "aggressive thinking" (Perkins, 1993) as they turn obstacles into opportunities and create solutions.

Flow

Adventure activities blur the distinction between work and play as they draw participants into an unselfconscious immersion. The result is a state of flow (Czikszentmihalyi, 1991), as play galvanizes experience and maximizes learning. With the use of adventure activities, teachers facilitate the "relaxed alertness" (Caine and Caine, 1991) necessary for effective learning.

Adventure activities engage participants. Students immersed in the *Blindfold Compass Walk* become engrossed in maintaining a straight course. The unusual nature of the activity adds to their fun. Exclamations of "I was sure I could do it!" "Boy, was I surprised!" and "Is that how people get lost in the woods?" indicate that students draw significant

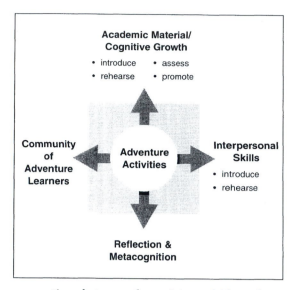

connections between the activity and ideas about navigation. As they play with compasses, practice taking readings, set a course, challenge themselves to get from point A to B to C with only a compass, students develop facility with the instrument, skill in observation and taking measurements, and confidence in computation and estimation of distances. The nature and use of angles, accurate measurement and various geometry principles come alive.

Adventure Activities Promote Learning and Support the Community

Adventure activities address three mutually supportive instructional goals:

- Teaching academic material and promoting cognitive growth

- Teaching collaborative and interpersonal skills

- Teaching skills of processing and metacognition

In addition, adventure activities nurture and support the community of adventure learners, the context for learning in the AITC classroom.

**Adventure Activities
that Introduce Subject-oriented Concepts**

Activity*	Theme
Monarch	Life cycle of butterflies
	Social systems in a monarchy
	Effects of changing group membership
Impulse	Reaction time and the process of stimulus/response
All Toss	The effects of goals on one's efforts
	Qualities of effective goals
Object Retrieval	The role of checks and balances in government
Human Camera	Observation skills
	Descriptive writing
	Perspective (both literal and figurative)

* See Appendix I for instructions to these and other adventure activities.

Academic Material and Cognitive Growth

Adventure activities are interactive, intellectually challenging, exploratory in nature and dependent on discourse and dialogue. As a method for academic instruction, adventure activities —

- Introduce concepts, themes and topics
- Rehearse and practice skills and concepts
- Review, evaluate and assess skills and conceptual understanding
- Promote in-depth learning

Introducing concepts

Adventure activities effectively engage students in a new topic of study. They provide students with a first-hand experience to prompt discussion. Adventure activities can also generate questions about new material. In *Quail Shooter's Delight*, for example, one or two students stand in the center of a circle. The students in the outer ring have a collection of soft throwables that they simultaneously toss into the air. The individuals standing in the center catch as many objects as possible. After a few attempts, with different catching techniques and different people in the center, the group begins to make generalizations about loft, speed, arcs and the weight of the objects. Soon the group looks at how these factors affect someone's chances of catching objects. They generate a list of questions regarding probability factors of catching and holding onto various objects. From here the students begin a unit of study on probability and statistics.

Rehearsing skills and concepts

Incorporating adventure activities into a unit provides an opportunity for students to practice and develop skills and concepts that are new to them. The application of new skills in adventure activities aids in the internalization process that may not always be achievable through rote memorization, workbooks and paper and pencil drills.

**Adventure Activities
to Practice Skills and Develop Mastery**

Activity	Theme
Name Game	Renamed *Memory Circle* or *True/False Toss,* this game is used to review factual information.
Rob the Nest	To review spelling words, vocabulary, components of a set, balls are labeled with letters or words. For a group to win, they must amass the appropriate letters or words.
People to People	To review scientific names for physiological features ("Patella to tibia").

Learning styles theories highlight the different ways individuals prefer to learn. Some individuals learn new material by reading and reflecting, while others need to be physically active with the material in order to understand it. Adventure activities help in attending to the variety of learning styles preferences of students. Adventure activities are physical experiences, certainly, but as part of the Experiential Learning Cycle (see Chapter Four) they provide opportunity for reflection and generating concepts and applications. Participating in various learning experiences also enables teachers and students to broaden their repertoire by increasing their own experiences and strategies to learn and teach (Hand, 1990; Marshall, 1990).

The ninth graders studying survival embark on an orienteering course with their compasses and new knowledge. Working in cooperative task teams, they follow compass readings and pace off prescribed distances in an attempt to find specific locations. They calculate distances, take averages and find ratios. They process their work in order to assess their learning and their interactions. All of this occurs in an adventurous and supportive environment that engages students with the material and with each other.

Assessing skills

Games to review material and factual information are not new to the teacher's bag of tricks. *History baseball, hangman, literature charades* and a host of math, science and spelling games fill the methods files. The cooperative games that are part of Project Adventure's activity base provide another resource. Adaptable to various content areas and physical in nature, they involve students intellectually, emotionally and physically and enhance the individual's ability to process information effectively. The activities adapt to various skill and content goals. *Memory Circle* for example, can be used to check on spelling words, test students' factual knowledge about a compass, and assess mastery of new vocabulary.

After the ninth-grade students complete their reading and finish their orienteering initiative, they gather in the classroom to review basic facts about compasses, compass reading and celestial navigation with the *Memory Circle* game. Each student comes to class with three or four short-answer, factual questions about the material. The class stands in a circle. Possession of a soft throwable—fleece ball, softie, rubber chicken—designates the questioner. That student asks a question, calls on

Traffic Jam

A group of eight students stands on a line of nine carpet squares, each student in possession of a single square. The students face the empty square, thereby forming two teams of four (see right). The goal is for the two teams to switch sides. Students may not move around someone whose back they are facing. They may move into an empty spot around someone they are facing, however; and they may move forward into an empty spot.

The students work together to find a sequence of moves to complete the task. Once they finish, the teacher asks them to determine how many steps a group of two, four, six or eight will take to complete the task. The students develop a table and give their predictions a try.

The teacher poses another question: How many steps will it take a group of one million? The students soon discover the need for an algebraic equation to solve the problem. Next the students study the solution from another angle. Using paper and pencil, they try to diagram the sequence of steps a group of six (three on each side) will have to take to complete the activity. They try to figure out the sequence for a

group of ten (five on each side). Soon they arrive at a sequential solution.

The algebraic equation comes alive. Rather than dealing with arbitrary numbers and a set of rules in a book, the students play with and describe actual experience. The rules they have learned; e.g., "Whatever you do to the left side, you have to do to the right," take on real meaning. The students realize that the same equation reveals the sequence for groups of four, eight, sixty-four, *ad infinitum*. They have another reason for mastering the process of handling equations.

someone in the circle, then tosses the object to the designee who must answer the question, then ask another question, and call on someone else in the group. Students build on previous questions by asking for further examples, clarification or reasons. Since questions are posed before anyone is called to answer, everyone is individually accountable and attentive. At the same time, the supportive environment encourages students to answer questions.

Promoting in-depth learning

Perhaps the greatest value that adventure activities add to the learning process is their potential

to open pathways for connection and aid in the development of in-depth learning. In *Traffic Jam* students find themselves lured into an intriguing exploration of several science and math concepts—scientific method, tabulating data, graphing, pattern recognition and algebraic equations.

Adventure activities pull students into the material and allow groups to study concepts to varying degrees of complexity. Students unfamiliar with algebra stop the *Traffic Jam* activity at the tabulation and pattern recognition phase, while others proceed into more complex graphing theory.

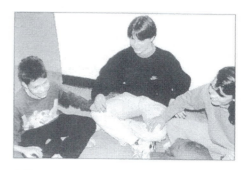

Collaborative and Interpersonal Skills

Students and teachers in the AITC model need to be able to work collaboratively. They need to attend to cooperative, interpersonal and process skills to benefit their work together. Adventure activities aid in this process because they provide opportunities to put these skills into immediate action.

Adventure activities teach cooperative skills—those skills necessary to carry out a collaborative task. Cooperative skills include sharing resources, sharing information, extending ideas and planning collaboratively. As they work through the *Blindfold Compass Walk,* the students have to listen to each other and combine and negotiate the various ideas that group members suggest. They determine how best to use their resources—who seems to have a good sense of direction, who has figured out a method to complete a task, what cues can assist them when they cannot depend on sight.

The AITC classroom is a community of adventure learners who teach, coach and support each other. Such an environment demands a high degree of interpersonal skills that often need to be explicitly taught and rehearsed. Jose may do a good job mediating a conflict between his younger siblings, but may not possess the strategies to manage conflicts with a peer. Lois may be able to empathize and listen intently to a friend's worries, but may need to learn how to be a better listener in a group discussion. Physical involvement and

Twenty-three sixth-grade students sit in a circle holding hands. Their science teacher, Ms. Motzkus, joins them. "Morning," she says, glancing around the room at the faces of the twelve- and thirteen-year-olds. "Let's say 'hi' with the squeeze. If there is anything you want to share when you get the squeeze, we'd like to hear that." She gently but firmly squeezes Robin's hand. Robin says, "I am glad that I got my science project done a day early." The next student is Jack, red-headed and pudgy. He gives a sheepish grin and nods his head almost imperceptibly as Robin squeezes his hand. He passes the impulse on to Paul, a popular boy—the sixth-grade jock with dark hair and a child's face. "I hope I get a *B* on my math test tomorrow." The students continue in the circle, offering bits and pieces of their lives, naming their hopes, telling of their accomplishments and acknowledging their anxieties.

Ms. Motzkus begins her sixth-grade class this way each week. The short activity brings the class back together after a weekend of family outings, sports, overnights and friends. It is a simple activity that reminds students and teacher that this class is a community of adventure learners, working together to support and encourage each other.

Mr. Hall closes each week in his American Studies Seminar with a feedback session. He finds that the *Yarn Ball Web* works well to teach feedback and attentive listening skills. The class sits in a circle and Mr. Hall holds a ball of yarn in his hand. "Before we begin, look around the room and identify three or four people that did a good job somewhere along the line this week. These are people you want to give positive feedback to about their class work. Think about specifics. 'You were great,' isn't specific! When you speak, you'll throw this ball of yarn to the person you're talking to. Then that person will talk next to someone else and throw the yarn. Remember to hold onto the yarn before you throw the ball so we can see where the yarn's been. That will make a kind of spider web."

Mr. Hall gives the class a few minutes to think before he offers the first comment. "Tony," he says, "your presentation yesterday was very entertaining. Your graphics really illustrated the points you were making." Mr. Hall throws the ball to Tony, holding onto the end of the yarn.

Tony speaks, "Hey, Jim, thanks for helping me out last night. I sure was gonna be in hot water with my dad!"

Mr. Hall interrupts, "Hmm… That sounds interesting! It's great that Jim came to your aid, Tony, but right now you need to focus on Jim's class work. What feedback can you give him about what he did in class this week?"

"Oh, well, he got all his reading done. That's a pretty good thing for him."

"Speak to Jim," Mr. Hall prompts.

"OK. Ah, Jim. Hey, it was great you did all the reading this week." Tony looks back at Mr. Hall.

"Yup, that's right. Talk right to the person you're giving the feedback to. Now hold onto the yarn and toss the ball to Jim."

Jim looks across the circle to Margie and says, "Margie, I liked that newspaper article you brought the other day about that tissue regeneration thing. It really fits with this medical ethics stuff we've been talking about." Pointing out the various contributions of their classmates, and listening to each other's feedback, these kids learn just what it means to give and receive positive feedback and discriminate the various contributions classmates have made over the week.

Jim tosses the ball to Margie, and the sequence continues.

---

emotional support are as important for the learning of interpersonal skills as they are for cognitive growth. The interactive and playful characteristics of adventure activities nurture a supportive context for building and practicing new behaviors and social skills.

One advantage of adventure activities as a means for teaching and learning cooperative and interpersonal skills is their immediacy. Direct instruction about any social skill must be followed up with direct experience. Role playing, while a common teaching tool of "affective curricula," is not real playing. The roles are contrived. On the other hand, in order to solve *Traffic Jam* or *Quail Shooter's Delight*, students have to communicate effectively. Students need to look at and listen attentively to each other. Having tried out new interpersonal behaviors with adventure activities, students are better able to apply those skills in a collaborative astronomy project or writing assignment.

Processing and Metacognition

As part of the Experiential Learning Cycle, adventure activities initiate the exploration of new ideas, analysis of strategies, formulation of metacognitive frameworks and expression of feelings. Because they encourage different types of thinking and problem solving, adventure activities encourage the examination of one's learning. Processing (see Chapter Eight) brings an understanding of these different types of learning to the conscious level. With facilitation by the teacher, students transfer their new learning to other contexts and other settings (Perkins and Salomon, 1992).

Reflecting on the process involved in pursuing a problem-solving event—such as a lab experiment, a math equation or a writing project—is critical to the long-term gains and understanding of that activity. The higher level thinking skills of analysis and synthesis rely heavily on an individual's ability to see patterns, make connections with past experiences and develop new methods and patterns for new situations. Metacognition, thinking about thinking, is the "active processing" of learning events that "allows students to review how and what they learned so that they begin to take charge of learning and the development of personal meanings" (Caine and Caine, 1991). The time spent in facilitating problem-solving initiatives and processing those initiatives is well spent in preparing students to engage in purposeful reflection on all their academic work.

When students identify the steps of their learning and articulate strategies they employ, they strengthen their cognitive abilities. If a student understands, for example, that she needs to grasp the whole picture before mastering the pieces that make up that whole, she can try to provide that framework for herself or ask other members of the learning team to help in the process.

Processing interpersonal skills enhances students' abilities to negotiate, cooperate, communicate and manage their working relationships with each other. Just as reflection on how one learns deepens and promotes long-term understanding and mastery of material, so reflection on group dynamics provides a richer opportunity for learning about those relationships. The student has knowledge that he can immediately apply to other group work—a cooperative task team, lab experiment with a partner or a reading group.

Adventure Activities and The Learning Community

The community of adventure learners, as the context for learning, must be healthy, educationally rich and stable to create the most effective educational environment possible for its members (see Chapter Three). Adventure activities nurture the community's health through the development of group processes and support of the principles that make up the foundation of the AITC model—Experiential Learning Cycle, Challenge by Choice, Full Value Contract.

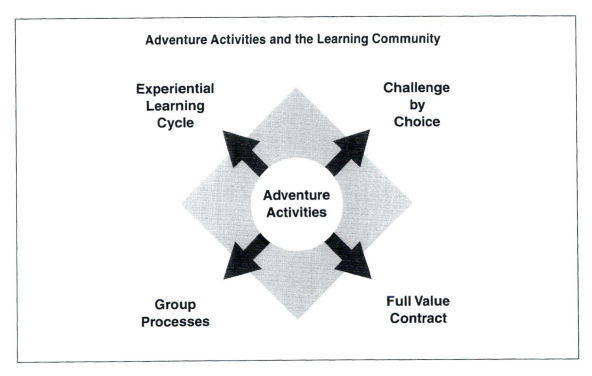

Adventure Activities and the Learning Community

Experiential Learning Cycle

Challenge by Choice

Adventure Activities

Group Processes

Full Value Contract

Experiential Learning Cycle

In the AITC model, adventure activities follow the Experiential Learning Cycle (see Chapter Four) of activity, reflection, generalizing and transfer. Students learn these steps and eventually internalize the cycle and apply it to their academic material. As activities and lessons follow the cycle, students get their hands on the sequence in a very tangible way. They not only do an activity, but they process it by reflecting, then generalizing and abstracting. Finally, they address how to transfer the learning to other situations.

Challenge by Choice

A middle school teacher from New Hampshire shared a significant insight with her team during a workshop when she explained, "I see now that Challenge by Choice means that the students identify the ways that they can challenge themselves in the work they have to do. It's not that they choose whether or not they are going to work." Challenge by Choice (see Chapter Five) is not a matter of working or not working, but what to work on and how.

Early attention to establishing a supportive, challenging classroom climate is critical. Students need to experience what challenge is, to recognize its qualities, to identify what they need in order to face challenges, and to establish ways of assessing challenges and their response to them. Only then can students recognize and grow with the challenges available in their classroom. Adventure activities enable students to experience challenge, reflect on that experience, generalize about personal challenges, then apply their new knowledge to new challenges.

Full Value Contract

In the classroom, cooperative games and problem-solving initiatives serve the same function that they do in an adult training workshop—to establish and nurture an atmosphere that values individuals, the group and the learning experience. Adventure activities accelerate the process of developing a Full Value Contract as students and teachers play and maneuver through problem solving together. They see first-hand the various strengths each member brings to the community of adventure learners. The hands-on experience of adventure activities jump starts the group development process of negotiating norms and establishing goals.

Group processes

Because learning in the AITC model occurs within the context of the community of adventure learners, attention to group process and the health of the learning community are as important as attention to task and content. Process and task are mutually supportive.

Adventure activities nurture the health of the learning community by providing the opportunity to establish—

- Affiliation
- Identity
- Trust
- Safety

Affiliation

Being engaged in activities with other people to an extent that one is completely involved and in a state of flow elicits a sense of affiliation that carries over into other shared endeavors. The connection experienced by members of a basketball team is a result

Thirty-two strangers wait expectantly in a large meeting room during the first hour of a five-day Adventure in the Classroom workshop. They have completed the registration process and gathered necessary materials. There are studious perusals of the training manual and silent nods of greetings. The mood is one of cautious curiosity.

Thirty minutes later these strangers laugh and share personal stories during *Partner Stretches*, where participants do various simple stretches and stunts in pairs, changing partners with each new activity. The group then gathers in a circle to toss a rubber chicken and learn each other's names. Rubber chickens tossed and caught or tossed and missed meet with jokes and laughter. An occasional, "What's your name, again?" or "I need some help here," are easy requests for assistance to which someone quickly responds with a helpful answer. There is no such thing as a "stupid" question. The group plays a couple of tag games next, and the teachers begin to show increased ease with each other. When it comes time to sit and talk about the activities, the group closes into a circle of easy comfort. There are a few complimentary pats on the back, a handshake or two and warm smiles of emerging camaraderie.

of play, practice and a commitment to shared goals. Participation in adventure activities promotes a similar level of bonding which leads to a trust level that permits healthy discussion, disagreement, sharing and criticizing of ideas and shared responsibility. This team sense carries a group to a higher level of functioning that results in quality work.

Identity

With a growing sense of team, a group develops its own identity. Stories about its efforts at the *Spider's Web* become oral history for the class. As part of their emerging culture, a group will often create a tag for itself—a cheer, gesture, rallying call or name. This tag follows the students into their class work and helps students feel that they are part of a team. "Remember the *Wall!*" is a shout of encouragement to one class, reminding everyone that during a day of frustration, hard work and exhaustion, the group experienced a boost of energy at the *Wall*. When someone says, "Remember the *Wall!*" to another classmate, it's a way of saying, "Hey, you can do it!"

For a group of sixth graders, the phrase "on belay" is more than a climbing command. It's a shorthand way of asking for or offering support to someone in class. Rita asks Jill, a member of her small group, to be "on belay" as she prepares for a make-up test following a long absence from school. Asking Jill to be "on belay" really means, "Will you help me review and make sure I'm ready for the test?" and, "Will you give me the encouragement I need to do all the work?" This sense of belonging encourages the kind of risk taking and creative intelligence that are hallmarks of the adventure classroom.

Trust

Trust is essential to the adventure classroom. In order to make an oral presentation or enter an experiment in a local science fair, a student needs the confidence that her attempts, rough or polished, will be respected, valued and supported. The learning community needs a level of communication that encourages students to offer and receive feedback. Adventure activities allow learners to explore and practice communication skills and to develop a level of trust that permits them to take new steps in learning.

Students in a sophomore biology class, engaged in research on a local landfill, practice delegating and sharing responsibilities. They negotiate who will take which turn, who will be responsible for giving nonverbal signals to the group, and what safety precautions need to be met. Through these efforts they develop a level of trust that enables them to ask each other for support, encouragement and feedback. They practice saying to each other, "I don't feel comfortable doing this by myself," or "I'm uncomfortable with your procedure, because I don't think it is organized."

The science teacher who begins the first class of the week with the passing of a *Hand Squeeze* or *Impulse*, the kindergarten teacher who begins the school day with *Partner Stretches*, and the English teacher who devotes the first week of a semester-long creative writing class to *Willow in the Wind* share similar goals—to help members of the adventure learning community develop trust and trustworthiness with each other.

Safety

Research demonstrates the deleterious effects of threatening environments on the brain's capacity to engage in higher level thinking (Caine and Caine, 1991). Studies on school climate, student motivation and achievement argue for the establishment and maintenance of an environment that is safe, enjoyable and fun. Students need to feel physically and emotionally safe in their schools and classrooms. They need to experience learning as fun, enjoyable and intrinsically rewarding.

Students take on risks daily and meet personal challenges constantly—getting to class on time, negotiating friendships, taking a test or giving a speech. Teachers and administrators may acknowledge this fact in their rhetoric, but they do not always acknowledge it in a tangible, experiential way. As a result, students continue to experience life in school as a world alien to everything outside the school grounds. To encourage positive behavior changes, teachers need to establish a climate within the classroom that says and lives, "Hey, give it a try. It's safe here. We know this is hard and you're doing your best. That's what is important."

The experience of physical and emotional safety during cooperative participation in adventure activities has profound carryover to a student's willingness to participate in academic initiatives, especially for those students who otherwise find school threatening. Cooperative games, communication and trust-building activities used in the early phases of a class are more than ways to initiate a particular climate and culture. They build a collective history that affirms the class as a safe place to be. Such experiences encourage individual members to support each other, grow together and take on the kind of challenges that promote intellectual growth and creativity.

Logistical Considerations

Incorporating adventure activities into the curriculum can be confusing. After all, adventure activities can be used in many ways. Is there an academic or social skill to teach? An operating norm to explore? A concept to introduce?

While we cannot explore all the considerations regarding activity development, choice and implementation here, we can examine a few basic points.

Goals

Choices around adventure activities should begin with identified goals. What does the class need? Where is the class headed? What skills do students need to develop? What material do they need to learn? Be clear about instructional objectives as you choose appropriate adventure activities. Isolate the content, interpersonal or group process goal. Do you want to introduce the topic through the adventure activity? Do you want to use the activity to develop skills? Is review the purpose of the activity?

Clarity around goals assists in choosing or developing an activity. By keeping the goal in clear focus, you avoid a potpourri syndrome, where any adventure activity goes. In the early stages of a class, the focus may be on dismantling the boundaries between students. "De-Inhibitizing Activities" (Schoel, Prouty and Radcliffe, 1988) are best suited to such a goal. If a teacher wants to encourage students to criticize ideas rather than people, communication and problem-solving initiatives fit the bill.

Clarity around goals also guides the adaptation and framing of activities. *Traffic Jam*, for instance, introduces algebraic equations, pushes deeper application of math concepts, explores the sources of communication breakdown or addresses leadership skills. The difference in framing, facilitating and processing the activity depends upon the instructional goal.

Scheduling

In planning activities, consider both long-term and short-term schedules. How long will the group or class be together? What specific issues does the group need to address at a particular time, whether it be for one class period or a three-week unit?

Again, begin with goals. What is the goal for the designated time period?

The long-term schedule is generally determined by the school calendar, while short-term schedule is a function of curriculum and class schedule. The first weeks of a high school creative writing class may be spent establishing the writing process and encouraging students to share their written work with each other. Establishing a baseline of trust and acceptance are the goals for those weeks. Later in the semester the focus may be on the collaborative writing process, when a greater emphasis on teamwork and cooperation is appropriate.

There is no hard and fast rule to designate the time and frequency for including adventure activities in the curriculum. One teacher spends the first half of class for the first two weeks of school in activities. He then shifts to activities that take only ten or fifteen minutes and includes them twice a week for the duration of class. Another teacher allocates one class period each week for adventure activities.

Two things are important, however: 1) Establish a time schedule that fits the class goals and is appropriate for the group, and; 2) maintain consistency. When activities are interspersed without rhyme or reason, and the timing of those activities is irregular, the class begins to feel off-balance or even chaotic. Determining a schedule, informing the students of that schedule and even involving them in setting up the schedule helps to ensure that everyone understands the approach. In addition, clear goals and sensible scheduling will

Simple, flexible and *manageable* are the key words to remember when choosing adventure activities to incorporate into a curriculum.

help to mediate any criticism that a skeptical administrator, parent or colleague directs your way.

Scheduling also needs to respond to the changing events and dynamics of a group. Good teaching requires the ability to adjust plans in the best interests of the students. The class sometimes needs to revisit certain types of activities because other events have intervened and affected group dynamics. For example, de-inhibitizing activities help to bring the students back together after a week-long school vacation.

Simplicity

Simple, flexible and *manageable* are the key words to remember when choosing adventure activities to incorporate into a curriculum. Any new approach to curriculum or classroom management elicits some anxiety for the instructor. Begin with something simple and begin small. Keep these four criteria in mind:

- Space
- Time
- Props
- Disruption to others

Space

Can you stay in your classroom? If not, what space is easily accessible? The gym may be ideal because you want to have a lot of room. But the headaches of checking with other classes, getting permission from the physical education teacher, and making sure kids don't wear shoes that will damage the floor may require more energy than the curricular goals merit. Plenty of activities can be done right in the classroom—*Human Camera*, *Toss-a-Name Game* and *Traffic Jam*—to name a few. In the early stages, stick to activities that are not restricted to one type of setting. If you plan to go outdoors, have a back-up plan in case the weather doesn't cooperate. If you are going to use the gym, have another place or other activities ready in case the basketball coach decides to hold an unscheduled practice session. If you have easy access to an outdoor play area or an all-purpose room, then use it. Remember, though, much can be accomplished in a limited space.

Time

Consider the schedule of events for the class. Moving to another location may be appropriate if you have planned to spend the entire 50-minute period in an activity. If you want to spend only ten minutes in a group warm-up, then time spent moving between two locations and getting everyone settled and focused at each place will reduce class time. Remember to factor in travel and transition time as well as time for the activity.

Anticipate the unexpected. What happens, for example, if the activity takes more time than you had planned? Or what happens if the students complete it in half the time you had anticipated? In either case, return to the goal of the activity. Choosing to adjust the time depends on whether or not the group has met the instructional goal. Since processing the experience is part of the sequence,

It's a bright spring Monday morning when the sophomore students walk into Mr. Alvarez's classroom and are handed balloons. "Before you blow up your balloons, we need to move the desks and chairs to the sides of the room and clear the floor," instructs their teacher. A colorful game of *Boop* is soon underway and quickly concludes with *Fire in the Hole*. The shenanigans, twisting bodies, smiling faces and laughter settle down after the remains of the exploded balloons have been collected. Everyone gathers in a circle, cross-legged on the floor, to begin the business of class.

addressing changes or surprises will be a natural part of the learning cycle. Look to the group as you make time decisions. A well-functioning group often recognizes what is best for its needs.

Props

Here, too, simplicity is important. You have enough to keep track of in a day—attendance slips, homework papers, mid-semester reports, grade books, class notes and a coffee cup—without worrying whether you have five paper cups, twelve balloons, two Frisbees, a half dozen fleece balls and four spot markers for a 20-minute activity. The toys may be great fun and the goal may be clear, but if the purpose of the adventure activity is to nurture climate, this scene is more likely to seed a hurricane than to encourage a gentle rain.

Disruption

A boisterous game of *Ah-So* will probably do little to nurture relations with a colleague who thinks the best class is a quiet class. Students in the next room will not be particularly appreciative either if they hear desks banging and loud applause every Tuesday during third period. Being a good neighbor goes a long way to building support for an adventure approach to learning in your school.

Having Fun and Changing Pace

Adventure activities support the adventure classroom in numerous ways. Adventure activities meet a host of needs and concerns in the classroom. I cannot emphasize enough the importance of clearly defined curriculum goals in choosing and implementing adventure activities. There is another side to the coin, however, that merits some attention here. It's OK to step out of the rigors of planning and design once in a while to have some fun together.

Having fun

Mr. Alvarez's students have just completed a two-month, intensive study of local history. The unit culminated in an open house for school and community members the previous Friday night. The open house included foods representing the town's ethnic composition, displays of the town's major employers and presentations of demographic changes in the community over the last twenty years. During this integrated, interdisciplinary unit, the tenth graders lived and breathed the history of their town—researching, interviewing, writing, reading and studying about their community. The open house was both final project and celebration of the work and the learning.

So why the balloons and a silly game of *Boop* to start the class? Why not? The students worked diligently on a complex project, gained insight into the history of their community, learned basic skills of ethnography, became experts on the economic and social factors that have shaped their community, and engaged in the struggles of team effort. Celebration is in order. The students will spend a good portion of their class talking about the open house and reflecting on the entire project. Celebration during the open house and celebration on this day bring closure to the unit.

Research on effects of class atmosphere, conditions for brain receptivity and deep meaning notwithstanding, it is good to have some fun once in awhile. Teachers often lock themselves into a prescription of holidays and vacations and maintain a classroom that acknowledges the lighter side of life only when the calendar allows—Valentine's Day, the last day of school, Christmas break. What restricts classes to having parties only when the student teacher's stint is over or the classroom teacher takes a childbirth leave? As teachers, we will do ourselves and our students a greater favor if we remind each other that people are spontaneous, creative creatures who can share the gifts of play regardless of the calendar.

Changing Pace

Ms. Thomkins and Mr. Jenks, well aware of the needs of their students and able to read the subtle and not-so-subtle messages, recognize that before

It's fifth period of the day. Ms. Thomkins and Mr. Jenks are beginning a lesson on decision making with their Co-op Class, an alternative program in a high school for at-risk students. Two girls in the back of the room argue about a mutual friend. Another girl chats across the aisle to her boyfriend. Along the side of the room, another student gazes intently out the window. Aware of the undercurrents of issues elicited by the previous weekend's block party, Ms. Thomkins and Mr. Jenks suddenly call out, "OK, clear the desks, get the chairs out of the way. Everybody on the floor in a circle!" Within minutes, students and teachers match concentration and cunning in a lively round of *Ah-So!*

any content can be addressed today, time needs to be spent getting at the unspoken but volcanic issues bubbling just below the surface. Before opening the discussion about an alleged break-in, the teachers take dramatic action and shift the direction of the class. The game encourages energetic, whole-hearted participation and quickly becomes a loud match of wits and concentration. Afterward, students are poised emotionally and physically to discuss the serious issues that are on their minds, and that affect their ability and willingness to concentrate on the academic content of the class.

Teachers must attend to the intricate weave of emotion, physical state and cognition. Too often, a reliance on detailed curriculum and the security of a well planned lesson binds classes into frustrating corners. Teachers need to be willing and able to acknowledge their students' needs and to respond to those needs in an appropriate manner. Cooperative games, communication and trust activities, and problem-solving initiatives are often appropriate tools to utilize when the pace or the atmosphere of the class needs altering or there is a need to refocus the group on its process, the academic material or other issues.

Summary

Adventure activities strengthen learning for a number of reasons. Adventure activities are cooperative. They engage students in various learning styles and intelligences. Adventure activities strengthen cognitive development and interpersonal skills. In addition, they foster integration of curriculum and enhance problem-solving and critical-thinking skills. The balance of challenge and support encouraged by adventure activities prompts the sense of flow characteristic of effective learning and deep concentration.

Adventure activities enhance learning in the AITC model by providing an engaging way to teach academic material and support cognitive growth. They provide opportunity for developing cooperative and interpersonal skills and metacognition. Adventure activities also play an important role in nurturing the community of adventure learners by enhancing the Full Value Contract and Challenge by Choice. Adventure activities also strengthen the development of group process.

Focusing on curricular goals, scheduling and simplicity helps teachers as they design and implement adventure activities into their curriculum. Beginning simply and building on small successes goes a long way toward building a teacher's confidence in utilizing adventure activities and encouraging students to participate.

Processing in the Adventure Classroom

All our lives are a marvelous, rich,
incredible jumble of pure incident, with one
mindless thing after another happening—
mindless, that is, until we have a vantage point.

— Carol Bly

A cold, gray February wind blows across the playground of the Essex Elementary School. The students in Mr. Joseph's fourth-grade class cluster in cooperative groups of four and five. One group completes a series of math papers, making sure that everyone understands the word problems. Students in another team read and finish a writing assignment. Another group sits with their teacher processing the week's work.

"Well, how do you think you did this week?" Mr. Joseph asks the students.

"We got all our work done," offers Jenna, a perky child with soft red curls.

"Who was the checker this week?"

"I was," nods Nick, opening up a manila folder that contains the group's assignments for the week.

"Did everyone get their things to you on time?" Mr. Joseph asks Nick.

"Yeah, except Toby didn't get her math papers in until yesterday." Nick shuffles through the papers to find the weekly record of assignments.

"I had a hard time figuring out the math assignment Monday. Then I forgot to take it home, so it was late." Toby sounds apologetic.

The teacher asks, "Do you know why you got stuck?"

"Yeah. I couldn't figure out what to do with the left-over numbers on the division problems."

"What do you mean?" Mr. Joseph queries.

Raoul offers an explanation. "You know, Mr. Joseph, the difference when you multiply the divisor with the number on top, and then you subtract it—when you draw the line and subtract, like this." Raoul pulls out Toby's paper and points to one of the problems. "Here. She didn't know what to do after this part."

"Oh, I see. Here, where you subtract this multiplication product from the numbers you're dividing. Is this where you were confused?"

"Yeah. But Raoul helped me figure it out, and I think I get it now."

"How was your work together as a group? How was the cooperation and sharing?" The teacher moves on with his questions.

"We did okay. We got confused with our interview project a little bit. Jenna thought she was supposed to interview Mr. Brackman, and Raoul had already interviewed him, so they got mad at each other." Toby looks back and forth between Jenna and Raoul.

"How come that happened?" Mr. Joseph questions the students.

"Well, when we got the assignment, Jenna just read through the instructions and wasn't listening while we were figuring out how to divide up the interviews," explains Nick.

"Yeah, but you didn't ask me if I knew how we were going to do it, either!" defends Jenna.

"So what do you need to do about it?"

"Well, we decided that when we get our weekly projects, we should let everyone read the stuff by themselves first. Then after that, we'll talk about it and figure out together how we're going to do the project," Raoul explains. "See, some of us just started reading and figuring out what we wanted to do, and the rest of them were talking about it, but they didn't ask us if we understood."

"Sounds like that's the making of a good group goal for next week. What do you think?" asks Mr. Joseph.

"Yeah, we already wrote that down here in our folder. See?" Nick opens the folder again to the group's goal-setting sheet. "Read assignments by ourselves first, then talk about them. Make sure everyone knows what to do," he reads from the sheet.

Before concluding this processing time, the teacher spends a few more minutes with the group and asks some review questions on their math and reading assignments. He puts the team folder on his desk and nods. "Good job. You're on your way."

Student-centered curriculum, thematic teaching, experiential lessons and cooperative learning strategies characterize effective teaching; but adventure learning requires processing in order to construct knowledge from experience. Processing—the activity of deriving meaning from experience—is the heart of the AITC model.

Overview

Processing in the AITC model is an essential teaching strategy that enables students to make sense of the lessons and experiences to which they are exposed. Processing is a broad spectrum of reflective and analytical activities through which an individual or group reviews a set of events to gain understanding and learning that can be transferred and applied to new situations. Processing is "the having of wonderful ideas" (Duckworth, 1987). Processing transforms learning at the memory level into knowledge that is "personally meaningful and conceptually coherent" (Caine and Caine, 1991).

Through the activity of processing, knowledge becomes reorganized and shaped so that the individual can purposefully integrate it into the larger system of understanding. Processing enables a learner to connect new skills, concepts, information and ideas with those already internalized. Processing integrates new frames onto existing scaffolds.

While much of the brain's processing activity occurs at an unconscious level (autonomic system, organ functions, emotional responses), conscious and deliberate processing is the catalyst of learning. A football team reviews videotapes of a game to analyze and evaluate their plays. They process past experience to improve future performance. The debate student tests her case in order to polish her arguments. The computer student revisits the design steps of a new program during a trouble-shooting session before choosing a course of action. The writer struggles to put words to ideas and discovers voice and vocabulary. In each case, the goal is to make sense of the experience, transform the learning and apply it to a new situation.

Several vantage points help to explain the complexion and role of processing as it relates to the AITC model:

- Theoretical framework
- Processing and the adventure learning community
- The processing sequence
- Content of processing
- Reflection, processing or debriefing
- Strategies for managing processing in the classroom
- The teacher's roles

Theoretical Framework

Learning takes place through experiencing and processing (Dewey, 1938). Processing facilitates cognitive, metacognitive, personal and interpersonal growth and teaches students to be active managers of their learning. To thoroughly immerse oneself in an activity or lesson does not, by itself, promote growth. Processing asks us to think about that immersion, to take from it new ways of thinking, new ways of thinking about our thinking (metacognition), and new understandings of the world and its descriptors.

Processing —

- Nurtures discovery and the construction of knowledge

- Enables connections so that content and skills become accessible to the learner

- Aids the transfer of learning

- Promotes the development of higher order thinking skills

Discovery and the Construction of Knowledge

People will believe more in knowledge they have discovered themselves than in knowledge presented by others.

— *David Johnson and Roger Johnson*

Discovery is essential to the learning process. Discovery is what happens in true intellectual pursuit. When we don't know the answer, we are challenged to move ahead and figure out what to do. "What you do about what you don't know is, in the final analysis, what determines what you will ultimately know" (Duckworth, 1987). Discovery happens through processing, through the steps of reflecting on the situation or the problem, then analyzing, generalizing, choosing a course of action and, finally, trying out that course.

With the discovery process comes "felt meaning" (Caine and Caine, 1991) that accompanies authentic learning and creates the meaningfulness that opens our understanding to depth and breadth. Meaningfulness—the pit-in-the-stomach sensation of "I get it!"—is rooted in personal recognition and understanding. The information itself and in isolation may not be meaningful, but one's perception of the connection between that information and the larger context of information and experience marks the discovery process. Piaget's theories, for example, are meaningful inasmuch as they inform a teacher's understanding of cognitive development, regardless of whether that teacher accepts his theories in total or can accurately name and define the stages of development.

In looking at the teaching strategy of processing, we should remind ourselves that the goal of learning is *understanding*—the construction of knowledge, the making of meaning (Belenky, et al., 1986; Caine and Caine, 1989; Brooks and Brooks, 1993). It is not until we have explored how we have learned that we can understand how what we have learned affects what we already know and what we have yet to learn (Bellanca and Fogarty, 1991).

What you do about what you don't know is,
in the final analysis, what determines
what you will ultimately know.

— Eleanor Duckworth

Connections

*In most lives insight has been accidental.
We wait for it as primitive man waited
lightning for a fire. But making mental
connections is our most crucial learning
tool, the essence of human intelligence;
to forge links; to go beyond the given;
to see patterns, relationships, context.*

— Marilyn Ferguson

Discovery and construction of knowledge mean that the student is able to make relevant connections between new knowledge and existing knowledge. These connections allow the student to re-arrange, reapply and recombine concepts and skills, like rearranging hooks on a pegboard. Without this conscious activity, the information is simply what someone else says the student should know.

"It's not only that you feel good that you came up with this idea; it's also that you don't *have* the idea unless you've created it. All else is just words…you have to put the idea together yourself, or you don't have it at all. Otherwise it's just words" (Meek, 1991). Processing enables the putting together of ideas. Processing enables us to construct and reconstruct the scaffold upon which we organize our knowledge and allows us to actively pursue new connections and new patterns.

Most of us prefer to organize our own desks, clean up our own files, put our tools away so that we know where things are. Similarly, the act of processing, of engaging in conversation with self or others, enables the student to consciously organize, file and store knowledge in ways that make the knowledge accessible. The interpersonal and intrapersonal discourse of processing build connections between what would otherwise be isolated bits of information. The connections give substance to ideas and meaning to experience.

Transfer of Learning

Construction of knowledge and the internalization of concepts are meaningful to the extent that the individual can apply that knowledge. Making connections between previous knowledge and new knowledge is a first step to that application. The next step is to transfer that learning. It's not enough to teach spelling rules without helping the student learn to edit his own writing and employ correct spelling. What good is a student's ability to define a list of vocabulary words if he cannot recognize the power of those same words woven into a controversial editorial?

Transfer "requires the mindful abstraction of a principle, the effortful search in one's memory, the selection of the appropriate principle, and, finally, its application to a new instance." The activity of transfer is not easy, and requires a certain amount of help (Perkins and Salomon, 1992). That help comes in the form of facilitated or structured processing. The activities of thinking through, analyzing, drawing generalizations, forming new constructs must be actively facilitated either by the student himself, by the more able peer (Vygotsky, 1978) or by the adult teacher.

Development of Higher Order Thinking Skills

Processing utilizes higher order thinking skills critical to one's success as a life-long learner. The skills of assessment and evaluation, analysis and synthesis, integration and transfer can only be strengthened through their use in the activity of processing. In addition, the activity of processing learning on a consistent basis validates those skills in the real life experience of classroom learning. The development of those skills is integrated into the content of math or English or social studies. By emphasizing the activity of processing in the AITC model, we consistently strengthen thinking skills and demonstrate to students the interdependency of thinking skills and content. After all, thinking skills and what have been isolated as study skills are, in fact, the skills of life-long learning.

Processing and The Adventure Learning Community

The purpose of group processing is to clarify and improve the effectiveness of the members in contributing to the collaborative efforts to learn.

— Pete Yager

Whether it is a private or public activity, processing is discourse. During those private moments of thought, for example, the individual carries on conversation with himself. An interior dialogue ensues which may take the form of writing as well as thinking. As a public activity, processing requires dialogue.

When members of an adventure learning community process, they communicate. They speak and listen, write and read, argue and defend, compromise and integrate. These processing activities, in turn, strengthen the community and its members in a number of ways:

- Communication facilitates an exchange of ideas and the construction of knowledge.
- Processing develops cognitive and interpersonal skills.
- Communication nurtures the Full Value Contract.

Exchange of Ideas and Construction of Knowledge

Dialogue is open-ended;... in a genuine dialogue, neither party knows at the outset what the outcome or decision will be.... Dialogue is a common search for understanding, empathy, or appreciation.... It is always a genuine quest for something undetermined at the beginning.

— Nel Noddings

Community growth relies on the interchange of ideas and the development of shared knowledge. The more lively the interactions, the greater the opportunity for growth. Conversation generates ideas, connections and context. When information is exchanged between a teacher on one hand and the students as an entity on the other, the communication is limited to two directions (see Fig. 8.1).

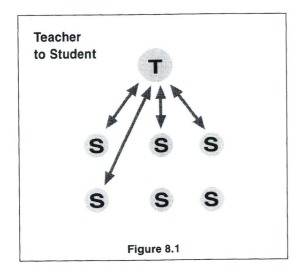

Figure 8.1

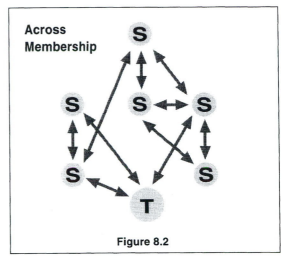

Figure 8.2

When the learning community exchanges ideas across its membership, the richness of communication increases significantly. More dialogue, discussion and argument occur. Out of this emerges better understanding of the content, stronger cognitive skills, insight about self and knowledge about the community (see Fig. 8.2).

When members of an adventure learning community process their learning, they share at four levels—cognitive, metacognitive, interpersonal and personal. Intellectual exchange, characterized by cognitive and metacognitive processing, fosters intellectual growth. Discussing a lesson design or a writing topic with a colleague, for example, opens new insights and designs. Out of the sharing come new ideas that neither person had previously considered, but that are even more pertinent to the topic at hand.

Personal experience and interpersonal relationships are the contexts within which intellectual development occurs. Paying attention to personal exchanges supports the cognitive learning as well as the growth of the learning community. It may be difficult, for example, for team members to effectively pursue a research project while an unresolved argument from the previous day stands in the way.

Students need structures and opportunities in the classroom to learn how to manage their relationships and talk about their class work. Processing cognitive, metacognitive, interpersonal and personal learning in the classroom teaches students how to balance these interdependent facets of growth.

Developing Skills

Processing develops cognitive and interpersonal skills. Accidental skill development happens regularly in schools. Students learn how to study for a teacher's exam, how to approach the principal about altering the school dress code, and how to stay out of or get into trouble.

Intentional skill development also occurs. A senior seminar focuses on political issues and responsible personal action. A unit on nutrition encourages students to improve their eating habits. Learners process regularly on a conscious and a subconscious level. From an experience emerges personal understanding that students apply to their daily lives.

Teachers must be explicit about teaching processing skills and facilitate the activities of processing so that students can apply and internalize these new skills. By conscientious and active facilitation

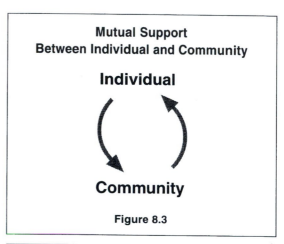

Mutual Support
Between Individual and Community

Individual

Community

Figure 8.3

of processing, teachers invite students to become partners in their own learning and help them develop a life-long love of learning.

The cognitive and interpersonal skills that intentional processing develops support individual students, who then become supportive members of the learning community. The strengthened community, in turn, continues to support the growth of the individual. The cycle is ongoing, enriching itself with greater texture and color (see Fig. 8.3).

Living the Full Value Contract

There can be no Full Value Contract without processing and communication. Communication is necessary to establish safety. Goal-setting requires communication. Feedback is communication. Letting go of disagreements or hard feelings occurs only after individuals have processed their difficulty and reached consensus about what can and what cannot be done.

The Full Value Contract supports individual students and the adventure learning community as a whole in their educational endeavors (see Fig 8.4). The experiences of academic growth and personal success sustained by the Full Value Contract strengthen the adventure learning community which, in turn, promotes individual growth. Willing to be in school, students work harder, improve academically and feed the system in a positive way. The experiences of the learning community and its individual members inform and refine the Full Value Contract. This exchange refuels the individuals and the learning community.

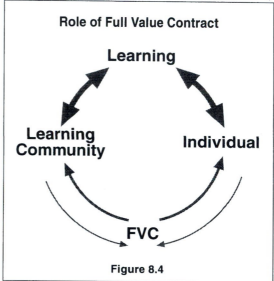

Role of Full Value Contract

Learning

Learning Community

Individual

FVC

Figure 8.4

The Processing Sequence

To make meaning out of an experience, people need to reflect on the event. They need to identify and acknowledge feelings and draw out cognitive understanding to bring personal significance to the experience and to carry learning beyond the present. In the language of Project Adventure's Adventure Based Counseling model, the processing experience is captured by three questions: What? So what? Now what? (Schoel, Prouty, Radcliffe, 1988). (See Fig. 8.5)

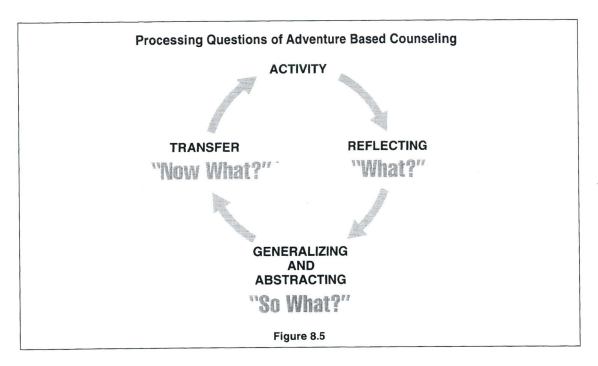

Processing Questions of Adventure Based Counseling

ACTIVITY

TRANSFER
"Now What?"

REFLECTING
"What?"

GENERALIZING
AND
ABSTRACTING
"So What?"

Figure 8.5

What? So what? Now what?

What? is a way to identify the specific and clarify the observable. Answering What? identifies words spoken and actions taken. Jenna, Raoul, Toby and Nick, in the beginning of this chapter, reflect on the activities and initiatives of the week. The students talk about what they have done, how they approached their problem solving, the ideas they tested, the attempts that appeared to go smoothly and those that did not. They try to answer "What?" Toby, for example, "couldn't figure out what to do with the leftover numbers on the division problems."

So What? asks for interpretation and analysis. Students determine the next steps. Toby figures out what to do with the remainder in the division problem. The team looks at group decision making. From here students question, "Where has this happened before?"

The last step is to pull out those principles, decisions and changes that need to be made for the future. *Now what?* asks for prioritizing and

decision making. If a lab report is incomplete because of poor time management and misunderstanding about directions, *Now what?* prompts the student to strategize around better time management. Jenna, Toby and Raoul decide to "Let everyone read the stuff by themselves first," when they receive team projects. They have identified a group goal to which they then apply their new learning.

In the AITC model *What? So What? Now What?* become: *What did I do? Why did I do it? What did I learn?*

What did I do?

Again, the first step is to clarify what just occurred, and make sure everyone is on the same page.

A fourth-grade class concluding a three-week unit on *Charlie and the Chocolate Factory* begins a large group processing session with the question, *What did we do?* The students review the chronology of the unit to lay the groundwork for their analysis, generalization and further strategizing.

Students establish the history and validate individual experiences. Discussing just what *did* happen helps to get the facts straight and resolve differences of perception. One student insists, "The substitute told us to rewrite our descriptive paragraphs," while a classmate maintains, "The substitute didn't say anything about our paragraphs!" Time spent on this disagreement moves the discussion to the point that "It doesn't matter what the substitute said. Some kids had two days to rewrite and others had only one class period."

Even in individual processing, asking *What did I do?* is the necessary first step, whether the student struggles to learn a new computer program, processes an argument or reviews a writing assignment.

Why did I do it?

In answering *Why did I do it?* the fourth graders studying *Charlie and the Chocolate Factory* review the reasons for developing story maps that require rereading the story, reviewing the order of events, introducing various characters and developing plot and character. This analysis enables students to identify the strategies they used and assess how well they met stated goals. They share their methods with each other and learn new ways to approach a piece of literature.

Why did I do it? also helps students pinpoint difficulties and strategize next steps. When the learning team at the opening of this chapter discusses the problems they have had, they realize that Toby "couldn't figure out what to do with the leftover

numbers on the division problems." Then Toby and her teammates identify the real reason that the paper was handed in late. She didn't understand an important step in the division process. Toby picks up this missing piece, and the team learns to separate real reasons from assumptions.

What did I learn?

The next step for Toby and the group is to look at *What did I learn?* With Raoul's help, Toby learns what to do with the remainders in the division problems. Through the conversation in the group, other teammates review the steps of division and understand the reasons for Toby's apparent irresponsibility.

In a similar way, the students share with their teacher what they learned regarding the miscommunication about their group interview project. They explain how behaviors affected their teamwork and identify ways to improve as a group.

Processing Before, During and After the Experience

The tendency to think of processing as subsequent to experience is a restrictive view that ignores the cognitive, metacognitive, interpersonal and personal learning that both precedes and accompanies a learning situation. In fact, the activities of processing occur before, during *and* after the experience (Baud, 1985). Most hikers, for example, don't wait until after their hike to think about and process the activity. Planning for the trek requires thoughtful anticipation. Depending on the length of the hike, the terrain, the number of people going, the weather and safety considerations, preparation for the journey requires varying degrees of reflection, generalizing, abstracting, synthesizing, analyzing and applying. The hike itself is seldom a mindless activity; and in keeping with effective practice, the hiker processes the experience at its conclusion.

Similarly, academic activities find the learner engaged in the various processing activities before, during and after the experience. Some activities, such as giving a speech, taking a test and carrying out a lab experiment require more thoughtful anticipation and preplanning than other classroom experiences. The point is that effective teaching does not confine processing to the conclusion of learning, but consciously weaves the activities of processing throughout the academic endeavor.

Content of Processing

Historically, adventure education has applied processing to outdoor activities. More traditional methods of instruction—lecture, note taking, library research, memorization—have often been divorced from processing. The various aspects of an experience have often been lumped together, so that students reflect on their individual feelings about an activity at the same time they examine teamwork skills. Often neglected have been reflection and analysis of thinking skills exercised during the activity or in-depth understanding of the content itself. The AITC model advocates a comprehensive approach to processing, and applies the Experiential Learning Cycle to *all* strategies of teaching and learning and to the interpersonal relationships and skills that build the adventure learning community.

Processing Academic Content and Behavior

Learning is shaped by the interplay between emotion and cognition (Caine and Caine, 1991; Beane, 1990). Focusing on cognitive outcomes without regard to the social milieu, physical well-being and emotional development of a student severely limits the student's learning and cognitive growth. In the same way, exclusive focus on emotional life limits the child's growth if the cognitive and academic components are left to chance. Processing in the classroom must reflect a balance of cognitive growth and interpersonal development.

Regardless of whether the activity portion of the Experiential Learning Cycle is a small group discussion or reading a short story, reflection asks the students to review their steps, procedures and methods. As they generalize from the experience and their reflection, students may pose questions to test out a hypothesis or read various resource materials for further information. They then apply their new learning, skills and understanding. Students might

do another set of calculus problems or write a critique of a story. What is important is that they put into practice the knowledge they have constructed from the previous steps.

The AITC classroom also devotes processing time to working relationships and interpersonal skills. To maintain a healthy learning environment, students need to be able to give feedback to each other on their behavior, primarily in the context of effects of behavior on the learning environment. When a student tells a member of his project team that her loud talking and constant questioning make it difficult for him to concentrate on the writing assignment, this is not to hurt the girl's feelings, but to inform her of the negative effects of her behavior on someone else's work.

The Full Value Contract (see Chapter Six) and a classroom climate that actively values individuals, the group and the learning experience, help to ensure that the processing of interpersonal relationships remains healthy and positive and does not degenerate into attacks on individuals. The commitment to the Full Value Contract not only gives permission but also offers a way to manage the processing of interpersonal relationships.

Four Areas for Processing

Another way to look at just *what* is processed is in terms of the *cognitive, metacognitive, affective* (personal) and *social skills* (interpersonal) areas for learning (Bellanca and Fogarty, 1991).

Cognitive processing, of course, addresses intellectual activity and growth. The focus is on the content of the lesson. The kind of discussion that often occurs in classrooms around what students read, write and learn from a lecture is cognitive.

Metacognitive processing focuses on *how* one learns. This is the thinking about thinking that enhances students' learning and provides them with skills to adapt to all learning situations. Metacognitive processing is "like stepping outside the situation and looking in at what's going on" (Bellanca and Fogarty, 1991).

Processing around *social skills,* or interpersonal interactions, strengthens students' collaborative skills. Social skills processing pays deliberate attention to interpersonal interactions and provides direct instruction and feedback. Setting goals, trying out new behaviors and getting feedback is just as important in the development of interpersonal skills as it is in the development of cognitive and metacognitive skills.

Finally, processing at the *affective* level focuses on feelings. Attention to personal experience in the classroom helps students recognize the ways that emotions affect learning. Processing the personal experience must be accompanied by instruction, goal setting and feedback around one's expression of feelings and strategies to learn from and with one's emotions

These four categories help to structure processing activities in the classroom as well as maintain a focus during processing activities. While the AITC classroom may not always sequence through all four types of processing with each activity, a balance of these areas exists in the AITC classroom.

Reflection, Processing or Debriefing?

The adventure world often substitutes *reflection*, *debriefing* and *processing* for each other, implying that these words are interchangeable. I propose, however, that they are interdependent concepts, and, like members of a family, share characteristics, yet maintain individuality.

Reflection

Reflection is often used to capture the processing stages of generalizing, or pulling out, analyzing and reconstructing learning. In other words, it is used to encompass the entire range of processing activities. I use *reflection* to denote only the second phase of the Experiential Learning Cycle, and the first step of processing. Reflection is the holding up of a mirror to the activity and is only one phase of the complete processing experience. Just as a mirror sends back to us an observable image, reflection is

identifying the *What?* of the experience. A mirror doesn't analyze or transform. It shows the details of our face that we are otherwise unable to see. In much the same way reflection repeats the facts of an event and presents the details.

Processing

Processing goes farther and deeper than reflection. Processing *includes* reflection. The writing student reflects on his essay when a student editor returns it with comments. He processes when he evaluates the comments and chooses how to go about making changes in the paper. Similarly, the second grader reflects when she laments, "I'm mad at Kim." She identifies the *What*, but processing takes her back to look at what happened to make her mad, inward to identify why she feels mad, and forward to what she can do about the situation. In other words, processing links the reflection to generalizing and abstracting in order to reach the transfer stage (see Fig. 8.6).

Debriefing

Debriefing, like processing, is a comprehensive set of tasks. It encompasses the steps of reflection and generalizing. It's origin is in military use, and both denotations and connotations reflect that origin. To *debrief* is to "question or interrogate to obtain knowledge or intelligence gathered on a mission," or "to instruct not to reveal classified or secret information" (*American Heritage Dictionary*, 1970). Education should not be conducted as a military activity, so I avoid using the term debriefing.

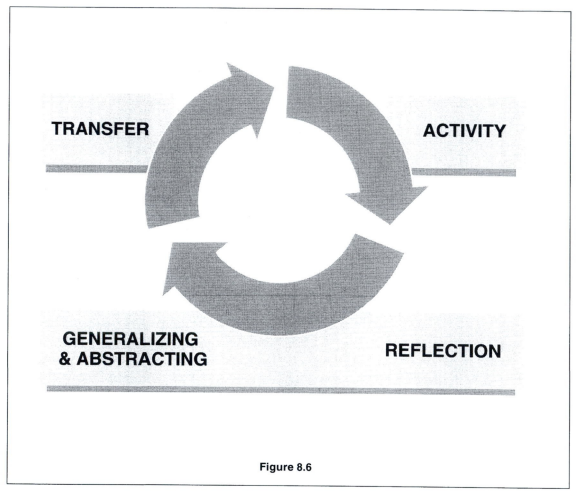

Figure 8.6

Another reason I find processing is preferable to debriefing is in regards to time. *Debrief* connotes a finite time. A debrief occurs at a specific time and comes to a conclusion. *Processing*, on the other hand, suggests a continuation of time. The activity of processing is ongoing. Even if the time for processing a lesson is over, students continue to mull over questions raised and comments made during the structured processing time. New thoughts may emerge later in the day. Processing more accurately reflects that collection of mental, intrapersonal and interpersonal activities that, together with activity, forms the learning processes.

Processing Strategies

There is no one way to process. Decisions regarding how and when to process are based upon the teacher's observations, goals, skill, comfort level, craft, intuition and knowledge. In addition, the collection of learning preferences within a classroom, along with the vicissitudes of the school year and interest levels of students, demand that teachers vary the processing strategies they use.

We have looked at processing from four vantage points: cognitive, metacognitive, interpersonal/social skills and personal/affective, and the sequence of processing: What did I do? Why did I do it? What did I learn? Another way to look at processing is in the context in which processing occurs:

- Large group or whole class
- Cooperative group or small learning team
- Individual basis

Large Group

In the early stages of teaching the skill of processing, it is important to model processing with the whole class to help students learn how to maintain focus and consistency. Other factors to be considered regarding group size include —

- *Goal of the activity or lesson.* If the goal has been set for the full class—designing a story map for *Charlie and the Chocolate Factory* or a large-group issue such as valuing differences among characters—then the processing should be done in the large group. Similarly, if the goal has been for a small group, and cooperative task teams have been working together on a collaborative project, then processing should occur within those groups.

- *Context within which the lesson or activity has been facilitated.* When the entire class has collaborated on a problem-solving initiative, then it is appropriate to process in the large group. Individual lessons might best be reflected upon individually.

If sharing of individual learning is important, and the group is in the early stages of sharing individual goals, then sharing personal learnings will teach students the importance of communicating learning.

- *Time available for processing.* If there will not be enough time for everyone in the class to express their thoughts and share insights, then consider using a small group or individual method that will permit everyone to participate.

- *Appropriate grouping to facilitate the type or quality of reflection.* A large group "go-around" opens the door for everyone to share brief answers to the processing questions. If students need more time to discuss the lesson, then a smaller group is a better choice.

The following suggestions illustrate different groupings and various methods for processing. Although these examples include strategies for cognitive, metacognitive, personal/affective and interpersonal/social skills processing, it is important to identify the area of focus for a processing session.

Processing With the Whole Class

When a group is larger than fifteen members, it is impossible for discussion to actively and consistently engage everyone. If a class numbers more than fifteen, students can exchange ideas, but true dialogue is impossible. If everyone has even one minute of "air time," it will take fifteen minutes just to hear each person offer one thought. Processing with a large group (more than fifteen people), then, is more likely to be a sharing of ideas rather than conversation. To manage a large group session, remember the following:

- Use a structure that provides equal opportunity for everyone's input.

- Maintain the focus of the processing time. If the subject of the reflection is content, then redirect unrelated comments to that issue. If the processing focus is on a behavior issue, then keep the group centered on that.

The following strategies will get you started with larger group processing.

■ *Process around a particular theme.* For cognitive or metacognitive processing, focus on one aspect of the topic under study by using one of the following questions:

- What was something new that you learned about this topic?

- What is the next step you need to take as you proceed on this project?

- What do you need to find out or locate in order to proceed on this topic, project, lesson or experiment?

If the group has been working on a particular behavior goal, such as "one person speaks at a time," then process specifically around that theme.

One of the following questions can get you started:

- Where did you see someone work on this behavior?

- On a scale of one to five, how well did you do on this goal?

- Give an affirmation, put-up or thank-you to someone who contributed positively to this goal.

■ *Go–arounds* are quick check-ins on a group's progress, needs or questions. Go-arounds check the pulse of the group and open doors for everyone's input. They are less threatening than other forms of processing, because people only have to share one word or phrase and can pass if they wish. Keep the following guidelines in mind:

- Once you have asked the go-around question, give the entire group 3-5 seconds of "think time" before anyone begins to speak.

- Answers should be short (one word, brief phrase).

- Go around the entire circle, giving everyone a chance to answer.

- Everyone has a right to pass.

- Everyone has a chance to give a one-word response before anyone asks a question or offers explanations.

- Begin the sharing wherever anyone wants to be the first to speak, then go either clockwise or counterclockwise from there. Random answers lead to confusion about who has answered, who hasn't, who has chosen to pass. An orderly sequence helps assure that each person gets the entire group's attention for her or his minute.

The following are effective go-around strategies:

- Thumbs up/thumbs down. Give a thumbs up, thumbs down or thumbs sideways to indicate what you think or feel about…

- Share one word that expresses a new idea/insight/feeling you had during this lesson.

- What is something new that you learned about…?

- What one question do you want to pursue as we proceed with this topic?

- Strike a pose to illustrate a question or insight you had during this lesson.

- What was the hardest/easiest/most challenging/most interesting part of this lesson?

■ *Snapshots* is a technique I learned from T. C. Motzkus. Pantomime distributing packages of photographs, explaining that you have just picked up these pictures from the photography studio. Remind the class that everyone had a roll of film from the week and these are the prints. Ask the students to look through the prints to find one picture that they want to throw away and one that they want to enlarge to poster size. The picture to discard may be out of focus or unflattering. It may be of an event they don't want to remember. The picture

slated for poster prominence, on the other hand, is something they are proud of, something they want to share. It's a great shot. Students then describe their imaginary snapshots in the group or write about them in a journal.

■ *Pictures or postcards* are effective visual aids to processing in a group of any size. You can create your own library of pictures from magazines or photographs. A collection of black-and-white postcards—everything from sculpture to portraits to industrial scenes—makes a great visual prompt to processing. The pictures are useful in a large group because they help to focus and contain the processing time. Any of these items can be offered to a group in various ways.

- Choose three pictures that show a progression of your learning/feelings/place in the group, or that depict changes in the group during the lesson.

- Choose a picture that shows where you want to be in relationship to this material/the group/your goals by the end of the week/semester/day/unit.

- Choose two pictures that illustrate how or where you can apply your new knowledge to another subject or project.

- Randomly distribute pictures. The group's task is to use the pictures to tell the story of its progress on the unit, project or lesson. Each person takes a turn and adds to the story as her or his picture fits.

■ *Affirmations, thank-you's or feedback* can be done in a go-around fashion or as sharing across the group. Processing with a focus on affirmations, thank-you's or feedback concentrates on students' specific behaviors during the lesson. Frame this type of processing clearly and provide students with appropriate instruction. The following guidelines may help:

- Provide specific examples to illustrate the behavior you are affirming. "Lisa, I appreciated that you took time during study hall to help me study for the vocabulary quiz."

- Speak directly to the person to whom you are giving feedback. "Thank you, Jim," not "I'd like to thank Jim."

- Accept thank you's simply and graciously.

■ *Processing around the Full Value Contract.* A group that has identified qualities of behavior and specific guidelines for a Full Value Contract needs to reflect on those guidelines. Processing with a focus on a group's Full Value Contract reminds students that they are accountable to each other. In the early phases of a community's development, you will need to step back and ask one or two of the following questions:

- What parts of our Full Value Contract have you relied upon this week?

- Where are we neglecting something in our Full Value Contract?

- How did the Full Value Contract assist you/ your group in carrying out this assignment?

- What additions or changes do we need to make in our Full Value Contract as we approach the next unit of study?

- When did you call upon something in the Full Value Contract to deal with a problem in class this week?

■ *Murals* are a length of art paper, shelf paper or newsprint hung along one or two walls in the room. As the week or unit progresses, students chronicle their learning, regarding either cognitive, meta-cognitive or interpersonal learning. A smaller version can be a scroll that each cooperative team keeps to share with the whole class at the conclusion of the unit, include in their portfolio or use as a review tool at the end of the unit.

■ *Classroom totem* is an idea adapted by teachers at Cedarwood Elementary School from Jeannie Gibbs' *Tribes* curriculum. A class draws a totem on large paper. Students write in four sections:

1. Things we are good at

2. Greatest achievements to date

3. Three things we would like to improve

4. Words we like people to use when they describe us

Each section is either a shared response or a collection of individual student responses. In other words, "Things we are good at" could be the entire class defining what they do well together or each student recording something he is good at doing.

A totem can also be a three-dimensional structure that groups construct with boxes, paper tubes and found objects. As the unit progresses, students add to the totem to show their story and processes.

Processing in a Small Group

Processing in the AITC model also occurs within the various cooperative groups or small learning teams. These groups of three, four or five students are manageable for the students to develop their own skills for cognitive, metacognitive, interpersonal/social skills and personal/affective processing. But even in small group settings, students need direction and coaching. Small group processing is not coffee break time for the teacher, but an opportunity to listen, get a handle on what's happening and facilitate as needed.

The following strategies will get you started with small group processing.

■ *Processing around goals.* Goal setting around academics and behavior is on-going in the AITC classroom. Processing around goals reminds students that goals are important to learning. A weekly or daily check-in with two or three of the following questions helps students focus on goals:

- In what place or at what time did you see someone in the group work on her or his goal?

- In what place or at what time did you work on your goal?

- When did you have an opportunity to work on your goal that you neglected to take advantage of?

- What about another person?

- What do you need from this group to help you work toward your goal?

■ *Charts* aid processing around individual and group goals:

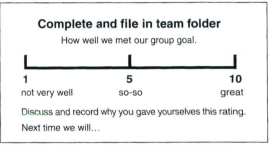

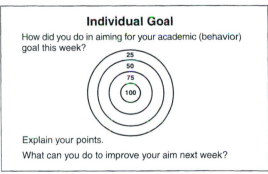

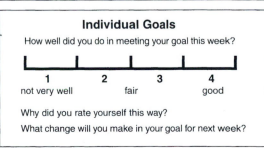

■ *Group art work.* Art forms are very effective ways to help students learn how to process. Strengths otherwise hidden in the group reveal themselves through art. Visual approaches also push students to express their understanding of a particular concept, skill or idea in forms other than the oral or written word.

The group can work collectively on one piece— a drawing or sculpture like the whole-class totem— or they can begin the piece as individual contributions that they pull together into one final product. Here are some suggestions:

• Each student uses clay, pipe cleaners or popsicle sticks to create a representation of his individual goal. After students work on their own pieces, they bring them together and make one sculpture that incorporates the individual creations.

• The group draws a collective mind map of the topic just completed.

• Each student identifies four specific events during the lesson that stand out, and draws, paints or sketches each event. Together they assemble the different scenes to tell the story of the group's process during the lesson.

■ *Feedback* (see Chapter Six) is a difficult but important skill for students to learn. Structured processing time with the focus on giving and receiving feedback challenges students to practice these skills. Feedback processing is generally centered on

interpersonal skills or personal goals. Feedback also aids in metacognitive and cognitive growth as it requires thoughtful review and analysis of the work, product, actions or words under consideration.

Feedback sessions can be short and very focused. For example, the group might be instructed to "Give each person two points of feedback regarding her or his goal today." Longer feedback sessions can be structured so that each person in the group has four minutes to receive feedback from the rest of the group regarding personal goals.

For longer feedback periods, assigning roles to students helps to facilitate time and task management. Common roles for this type of processing are *time keeper, recorder* (who records the feedback for an individual) and *process manager* (who makes sure that the group stays on task).

Structure feedback sessions so that everyone is clear about what needs to happen, and no one gets shortchanged. The discomfort level of feedback nudges students off track. Setting time limits (four minutes per person) or quantity (three comments, or two pieces of positive feedback and two pieces regarding growth areas) helps to maintain equity among the group.

■ *Pass the paper, Roundtable* (Bennett, Rolheiser-Bennett, Stevahn, 1991) and *Storytelling* are different names for an activity in which a piece of paper begins with one person who comments on the processing question posed by the teacher. After a one-or two-sentence response, that student passes the paper to the next person who responds to or builds upon the previous comment. After one or two rounds, the paper goes into the group's folder or to the teacher.

In a variation of this, each student writes a response to a processing question that the teacher poses. After a designated time period or at a signal, students pass their papers to the right (or left), and each student then responds to the comments on the paper she now holds. Again, one or two rounds suffice.

■ *Partner feedback* is an alternative to written forms of reflection and assessment. At the end of the day or the week, students meet for six or seven minutes with a partner and share their reflections about their participation for that time. In some cases it helps to provide one or two sentence starters. These can be as direct as "I liked it when I…" or "A time when I could have worked on my goal but didn't, was…"

■ *Aha!* is another small group activity. The directions are simply to share an Aha! you had during the lesson.

■ *Thank–you's* and *affirmations* are important in the learning community. Offering thank–you's to members in a cooperative task team is a good way to conclude a lesson or activity. A variation is to have students write thank–you notes to each other in their small group. Each note should be one paragraph long and should include specific actions or words for which the writer is thanking the note's recipient.

Processing at the Individual Level

Teachers must instruct and facilitate students to process their learning experiences as individuals. After all, this is what education is about—nurturing innate curiosity, teaching basic skills for inquiry, evaluation and assimilation, and assisting intellectual growth. Students who are not experienced with a teaching methodology that develops reflection and processing need particular guidance and encouragement to learn how to process effectively at an individual level.

■ *Journals* are effective means for individual processing. Students may be asked to respond to specific, open-ended questions following an assignment, activity or lesson.

- What was the easiest/hardest/most challenging/most enjoyable part of the lesson? Why?

- What were two surprises for you during this lesson?

- What strength/ability/talent did you use to complete this project?

- What are two or three new things you learned from the reading assignment/project/homework?

- What steps did you take to complete this essay/worksheet/lab project?

- How can you apply your new skill or knowledge to another project or subject?

Second graders in Melissa Weber's class at the Devonshire Elementary School write in their journals at the end of each day about their participation in the day's activities. They make specific reference to ways in which they have worked on their goals, then refine their goals for the next day based on their self-assessment. The teacher uses various techniques to respond to the entries, sometimes randomly selecting journals, reading a particular set of journals for a week, and then reading another group's journals the next week. At other times students share their journals with a partner who comments on the entry.

■ *Artwork* encourages students to think about their work from other perspectives. Keep a collection of art materials—clay, pipe cleaners, chalk, balloons, craft sticks and recyclables such as boxes, Styrofoam trays, egg cartons, bags and juice cans—handy for student use. Encourage various art forms, such as drawing, sculpture and finger painting. Numerous responses can be represented visually.

- Show your understanding of the concept or topic.

- How do you feel about your participation and your group's work on this project?

- What strength did you rely on to meet this task?

- Use the art materials to demonstrate the principle/concept/skill that you have been studying.

- Use the art materials to demonstrate the principle/concept/skill to someone who doesn't speak your language.

■ *Individual assessment forms* are designed to meet the age, subject area, and skills you are focusing on in a particular lesson. These include such things as—

- Smile sheets for young students that have three to six smile faces representing different feelings (happy, contented, frustrated, angry, confused, excited) for students to circle how they feel about their work, the lesson, their attention to a behavior goal.

- A drawing of a hand mirror in which students write their reflections on their work for the lesson or the week.

- A form with four or five basic questions that students answer focuses processing. Questions can include: "What is something new that I learned? What was a surprise to me? How did I help my team? How did I hinder my team? Something else I would like to learn is…

■ *Personal interviews* with students are effective but more time-consuming. In a setting where students have significant responsibility for managing their own learning process, a teacher who

removes himself from personal contact with students is remiss. It is important to manage processing in such a way that it strengthens the students' skills and understanding and helps both student and teacher assess the educational needs of the student. Occasional one-on-one interviews with students remind teachers and students of their responsibility to each other and provide another opportunity for individual exchange and feedback. Personal interviews can be spread over the course of several days. Sometimes students rotate through a schedule over the course of the semester.

Guidelines for Teachers

The role of the teacher during processing merits substantial examination. For our purposes here, however, the following guidelines outline some of the basics.

Stay Focused

Be specific in your processing goals and remain focused. Don't let a content process bleed into processing personal experiences or feelings without direct acknowledgment of that change. Otherwise questions remain unanswered and confusion reigns. If a group cannot focus on processing the day's work because the students are caught in their feelings,

you may need to shift gears and allow time for the group to talk about their personal experiences. This will allow the group to move on to content discussions. In all cases the teacher's job is to maintain the focus and help students stay on task.

Listen and Wait

You have a unique opportunity to listen to the workings of your students' minds as you facilitate processing. Listen. Listen. Listen. When you want to speak, count to ten. The goals of processing are to make connections and construct knowledge from experience. Questions you ask or comments you make should be made with that in mind. By listening attentively, you can see how a student's understanding of the material is developing and what changes in a lesson are necessary to effect the learning.

When there is discussion among group members, listen for themes and recurring issues. Does one student repeat the same point? Why? Are others listening and responding?

Don't rush to fill the silent spaces. A pause in the discussion is not an invitation for the teacher to speak. During the quiet time a student who has been reluctant to speak may be formulating thoughts. Other students may be drawing new analogies. Don't let the temptation to talk override your discomfort with a little silence. This is another good time to count to ten!

Identify Goals

The messy business of processing will become even fuzzier if you and your group are not clear about goals for a processing session. Whether students are engaged in individual, small group or large group processing, whether the focus is on content or the process itself, be clear about your goals. If you are processing content to evaluate how well students understand the material or how easily they can apply the learning, choose an appropriate method such as a flow chart or journal entry specific to the topic. If the goal for processing is to see how students feel about the material, then a go-around or art work might be more appropriate. Identifying goals will help to maintain focus for you and the students.

Vary Processing Methods

Good teaching taps a variety of instructional strategies. Effective processing involves a variety of strategies, too. It is also important to vary the intensity or length of processing. Modulate the methods you use to meet the developmental needs of your students as well as their interest levels and experience.

Affirm Experiences and Feelings

Such feedback as, "That sounds like an exciting idea," "You make a good point," and "I understand you were frustrated by that," go miles in encouraging students to discuss, share, question each other and risk self-disclosure. If students get nothing else out of school, they should come away with a sense that who they are and what they have to offer has value. If schools are to be safe places where students can take intellectual risks, try out new ideas, test out their hypotheses and explore unfamiliar concepts, then teachers must make certain that

students experience affirmation of their intellectual endeavors. Teachers who model this type of support teach their students to encourage each other.

Seize Teachable Moments

Processing time is teaching and learning time. When processing is at the small group or individual level, circulate to see and hear the learning taking place. Use this opportunity to ask your own questions and check out your own perceptions. The excited planning of one group that sees how to rewrite the opening scene of their play opens the door to sharing guidelines about editing or character development or whatever is applicable to their situation.

Take notes as individuals raise questions in their small groups that are applicable to the entire class. Also, note conversations or behaviors that you want to address at a later time. Much is happening. There is much to seize.

Summary

The activity of processing is critical to the development of cognitive, interpersonal and personal skills. Processing facilitates the discovery nature of learning and the building of connections between previous knowledge and newly constructed knowledge. Processing improves the individual's ability to access and implement new knowledge and skills. As a result, processing aids in the transfer of learning to new situations and content. Processing follows a sequence of *What did we do? Why did we do it?* and *What did we learn?* and requires the individual to reflect, analyze, generalize, evaluate and apply. As a result, these more complex thinking skills improve.

Integral to the Experiential Learning Cycle, processing is vital to all learning situations. While it typically follows the particular learning experience, the activities of processing occur before, during and after the prescribed learning event. For students to learn through any teaching strategy, processing must be integral to the lesson. The power of a lecture, a hands-on science activity, an essay writing assignment and a cooperative problem-solving initiative depend on whether or not students process the experience and distill the learning from it.

The life of the adventure learning community depends upon the healthy and consistent attention to processing. This strengthens interpersonal skills, enriches the exchange of ideas and supports the Full Value Contract. Processing must address both academic and behavioral domains of the classroom. To ignore one shortchanges both. In addition, there must be balance among processing the cognitive learning, metacognitive growth, social or interpersonal skills and personal or affective experience.

There are as many strategies to facilitate the various types of processing as there are teachers and classrooms. The teacher orchestrates structures based upon the curriculum goals, developmental needs and abilities of the students. Variety helps to maintain balance and push each member of the adventure learning community to grow academically and personally.

Team Learning and Teaching

*For the body does not consist of one member
but of many. If the foot should say,
"Because I am not a hand, I do not belong
to the body," that would not make it
any less a part of the body.*

— *St. Paul's First Letter to the Corinthians
(Revised Standard Version)*

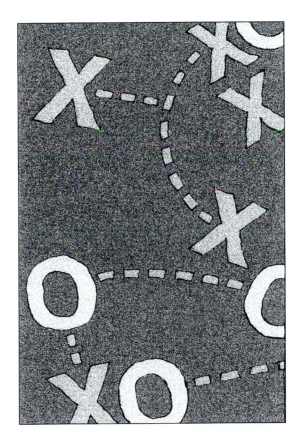

"**H**ey Mike, can I see your social studies homework?" Jim whispers across the desks to his classmate. He shares a table with Mike and two other students. The four of them are working on a class project to follow up a unit on *The Glass Menagerie.*

"Come on. You're supposed to be doing these questions with us," complains Lou, glaring at Jim.

"Ah, get a life! They're almost done, and besides I have to get this social studies thing done or Jacobs will have my head."

Across the room Suzanne, Cheri, Willie and Tina discuss a scene from the Tennessee Williams play. With their books open, Cheri writes a list of props and costumes while Willie jots notes about the characters.

It's E block, middle of the day in this suburban high school. Twenty-six sophomore students in English class sit in groups of four or five, preparing their *Glass Menagerie* projects. Mr. Lindall, an energetic young teacher, squats on the floor next to Benny and Kalisha. "What project are you doing?" he asks.

Benny, slumped in his chair, arms folded across his chest, stares out the window. Kalisha drops her eyes to a piece of paper in front of her where she has been doodling for the last twenty minutes. Sandy pleads with the teacher, "Can't I just do something by myself? They won't help, and I'm tired of trying to get them to work."

Put kids in small groups, give them a project that requires them to share materials and information and make collaborative decisions, and all will be well. Right? Wrong! Mr. Lindall has good intentions. He is aware that good teaching utilizes a variety of techniques and strategies. He knows that students need a supportive atmosphere and options for students to demonstrate their creativity and talents in areas other than writing and speaking. His desires are noble. His reasons are legitimate. His aims are good. His understanding of process, cooperative learning strategies and conditions for effective collaboration are lacking, however.

Team learning is much more than group work. Team learning is students teaching each other, learning collaboratively and meeting high academic standards. Team learning and teaching requires direct instruction in the social skills necessary for healthy group development and cooperative problem solving. Team learning and teaching also demands interdependence between team members so that students mutually support each others' efforts. An exciting, challenging and effective strategy, team learning and teaching offers rich opportunities for academic, professional and personal growth.

Overview and Definitions

A broad base of research, development and curriculum work in cooperative learning informs the AITC model. A brief look at some fundamental vocabulary illustrates how Project Adventure builds on the research in cooperative learning and adapts language to meet the scope of the AITC model.

Goal Structures: Individualistic, Competitive and Cooperative

The best answer to the question, "What is the most effective method of teaching?" is that it depends on the goal, the student, the content and the teacher. But the next best answer is, "Students teaching other students." There is a wealth of evidence that peer teaching is extremely effective for a wide range of goals, content, and students of different levels and personalities.

— *Wilbert McKeachie*

There are basically three ways to structure lessons in a classroom. Lessons can have *individual* goals and tasks so that students work independently. In a ninth-grade biology class, for example, one student studies ants, compiles a notebook of articles, constructs and observes an ant farm. Another student carries out a similar project on honey bees and assists a beekeeper once a week. A third student pursues a composting project by maintaining a compost pile with waste from the cooking classes. She compares the effectiveness of two types of compost bins and builds one of her own design. Each student's progress is independent of the other. These students do not need to share information or resources with each other, and their classroom interaction is limited to social conversation.

Competitive classroom structures pit students against each other in a race for points, grades and even information. Scavenger hunts of historical facts, grading on a bell curve, presetting the number of students eligible for particular grades, and limiting time and resources necessary to complete a laboratory experiment pit students against each other in this win-lose setting. Someone wins at the expense of another.

In *cooperative* lessons students work together toward a common goal. They assist each other and are responsible for learning material individually *and* collectively. In the biology class three students collaborate on a project on ants. They compile a group notebook and maintain observations about the ant farm. With the aid of their collective resources, one student develops a workbook for elementary children, another student designs an experiment to test the ants' tracking abilities, and the third student develops an exhibit for the library on the life cycle and social structure of ants. The students are evaluated on the quality of their individual projects as well as on their group project. In addition, they evaluate themselves on their individual and group process, including time management, decision making and role assignment.

Each of these three goal structures has its place. It is the teacher's responsibility to assess the students, the material and the goals of the class to determine the most effective structure at each step in the curriculum. Generally 80–93 % of classroom time is devoted to competitive or individualistic structures. Students rarely have the opportunity to practice skills appropriate to cooperative ventures or gain the advantages that cooperative settings provide (Johnson, Johnson & Holubec, 1988). This is astounding, given the need for collaborative skills in the workplace. In addition, schools, colleges of education, business leaders, human resource organizations, parents and teachers continue to call for students of all ages to be able to work together.

The AITC model recognizes that individualistic and competitive structures serve particular instructional and learning needs. An advanced math student in a heterogeneous algebra class needs instruction that challenges her, while another student requires individual lessons to learn the basics of equations. To best meet the needs and abilities of such students, a certain amount of individual instruction is necessary. The AITC model does not exclude individual and competitive instruction, but places them within a collaborative setting.

A common strategy in self-contained classrooms is to devote the morning session to what one Devonshire Elementary School teacher calls *challenges*. These are cooperative lessons that everyone must complete before lunch. Challenges are sometimes discipline- or skill-related lessons. At other times they are small projects connected to a larger unit. Challenges are student managed, and the children are responsible for teaching each other.

As students do their challenges, the teacher works with individuals or small groups to provide remedial, skill-specific or advanced instruction. For example, during one challenge time, a fourth-grade teacher rotates short lessons with reading groups one day, then tutors two children on decimals. There is a constant flow of students from cooperative lessons to individual instruction. Students receive necessary instruction to meet their particular strengths and weaknesses. Team members check up on and assist each other as they return to their challenge groups, making sure that no one misses out on the activity of the small group.

Team Learning versus Cooperative Learning

There are several approaches to cooperative learning today. Specifically designed cooperative lessons and pre-packaged curricula are available for particular subject areas. Teachers attend workshops on cooperative teaching strategies and learn how to infuse them into existing curriculum. The "structures" approach to cooperative learning (Kagan, 1992), for example, provides dozens of ways to organize and facilitate student cooperative groups. The jigsaw method (Aronson, 1978), and the group project method (Sharan and Sharan, 1976), are more involved methods appropriate for long-term projects and study. Still another approach, the conceptual approach to cooperative learning, grounds itself in theory and general principles that teachers utilize as they develop their own cooperative lessons (Johnson, Johnson, Holubec, et al., 1984; Johnson, Johnson

and Holubec, 1988; Cohen, 1986). Each of these approaches adds dimensions to the general conversation of cooperative learning by strengthening the research and paving many avenues to improve classroom instruction.

Team learning, as embraced by the AITC model, is an amalgam of cooperative learning strategies. *Team* refers to a collective body of learners, and *team learning* conveys the notion of a community of learners. As an inclusive term, *team learning* combines the principles, strategies and theory of cooperative learning with the principles, strategies and theory of adventure learning communities.

Learning and Teaching

Team learning and team teaching operate together as one strategy in the AITC model in order to emphasize two underlying values of the model: 1) all members of the adventure classroom are partners in the shared activities of learning *and* teaching, and 2) teachers must model collaboration in order to more honestly teach collaboration.

Team learning and teaching affirms that students and teachers come to the classroom with knowledge and experience. In the process of sharing this knowledge, students and teachers teach each other and learn from one another. In other words, teachers are teachers and learners, and students are teachers and learners.

The AITC model also joins the notions of team learning and team teaching to emphasize the importance of modeling. Students need to see us, their teachers, as team learners and team teachers. As teachers,

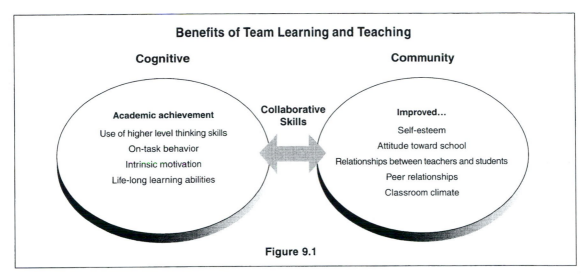

Benefits of Team Learning and Teaching

Cognitive

Community

Academic achievement

Use of higher level thinking skills

On-task behavior

Intrinsic motivation

Life-long learning abilities

Collaborative Skills

Improved...

Self-esteem

Attitude toward school

Relationships between teachers and students

Peer relationships

Classroom climate

Figure 9.1

we ask our students to struggle with different learning preferences, cooperative problem solving, interdependence and interpersonal skills. Without participating ourselves in collaborative teaching and learning efforts, we limit our appreciation of the challenges that this type of learning presents and neglect to develop our own team skills. Without struggling and learning to collaborate with our peers, we cannot honestly teach students how to work collaboratively. Unless we engage in team teaching, we say to our students, "Do what I say, not what I do." To be honest and authentic in our teaching, to truly have an effect on students' perceptions of education and learning, we must model those behaviors that we expect our students to demonstrate. Until we, as teachers, struggle with our own boundary and style issues through team teaching ("I am the English teacher. My lesson on characterization is really great. What do you mean it won't fit in this unit on 'Inventors'?"), we cannot be authentic teachers and coaches to our students in their cooperative learning groups.

Adventure in the Classroom is a culture built upon the ideal of collaboration in learning and teaching, work and play. Educators embrace that culture only if they live the principles and behaviors that characterize it.

Benefits of Team Learning and Teaching

Practice and theory over the last twenty years demonstrate the efficacy of collaboration in the school. Various benefits of cooperative learning for students and teachers have been researched, identified and categorized (Johnson and Johnson 1984, 1988; Slavin, 1970; Sharan and Sharan, 1976; Kagan, 1992). Positive correlation exists between cognitive gains and interpersonal gains. After all, it only makes sense that a child who enjoys going to school is likely to learn more and better. A youngster who feels good about school is unlikely to do things to interfere with learning. Positive attitudes about school lead to on-task behavior, which strengthens achievement. Higher achievement that is recognized and rewarded, in turn, promotes self-esteem; and this results in a more positive attitude toward school, teachers and peers.

While the following summary uses the vocabulary of *team* learning and teaching, it is adapted from the work of Johnson and Johnson, Slavin and Kagan on *cooperative* learning.

Team Learning and Teaching Promotes Cognitive Growth

Team learning and teaching promotes cognitive growth and in-depth learning in several ways. Team learning and teaching strengthen —

- Academic achievement
- Use of higher level thinking skills
- On-task behavior
- Intrinsic motivation
- Life-long learning

Academic achievement

Team learning and teaching strategies promote higher achievement, greater retention and greater cognitive growth among students and teachers than do individual or competitive structures. In cooperative learning models, age level, ability, subject matter or gender do not appear to affect the academic achievement outcomes. As students share information and explain ideas and facts to each other, their own understanding increases. Team learning and teaching requires participants to discuss, share information and explain ideas—the kind of oral rehearsal necessary for the storage of information into memory and the promoting of long-term retention of the information (Johnson, Johnson and Holubec, 1988).

Teachers, teaching and learning as team members, gain the same advantages as their students. As teachers build on each others' ideas, offer rationales, synthesize and evaluate information together, they develop their own cognitive skills. They learn the material in richer and deeper ways. In situations where they team teach across disciplines, they experience an increased appreciation and knowledge of other subject areas.

Use of higher level thinking skills

The nature of team learning requires team members to discuss, negotiate, persuade others and defend ideas. Often in team learning students must develop one product (one paper, one presentation, one lab) or come to consensus. In order to do so, group members need to think more broadly and deeply, especially because individuals are accountable for their own contributions. In other words, for team members to be involved in the dialogue or in creating the required product, they must actively engage their various skills and enlist those higher level thinking skills of analysis, synthesis, evaluation, assessment and negotiation. This consistent and varied use improves these skills and increases the students' facility with them.

On-task behavior

Fully functioning teams hold each other accountable and make certain that group members participate positively to further the common good. Learning and teaching teams foster positive, on-task behavior through encouragement, feedback, interdependence and accountability. Each member of the group has a stake in what everyone else in the group is or is not doing. Therefore, it is to everyone's advantage to assist each other in accomplishing the task before them.

Practically speaking, there are more eyes and ears on everyone's work. The teacher is not the only one who monitors student work. Likewise, the principal or department head shares the support and administrative roles with the staff. One principal recounted, "Now that the teachers themselves plan and implement in-service for new faculty, it's much more comprehensive. The teachers have a better understanding of what new faculty need. They're attuned to each other, and they expect more of each other."

The Full Value Contract further supports on-task behavior in a team learning and teaching setting. Members of an adventure learning community have the responsibility and the permission to encourage each other as they work toward their goals. They have the responsibility and permission to confront each other when they are not attentive to tasks.

Intrinsic motivation

Adventure learning and teaching teams set their own individual and group goals as well as their own plans to meet those goals. Whether or not they meet established criteria is up to them. Achievement and success are in the hands of group members. One important outcome of this empowered ownership is increased intrinsic motivation. The more students cooperate, the more they recognize their intrinsic motivation. In team learning and teaching settings, students persevere in pursuit of their learning goals and believe that their own efforts determine their school success. They "want to be good students and get good grades; and believe that ideas, feelings, and learning new ideas are important and enjoyable" (Johnson, Johnson and Holubec, 1988).

Life-long learning

If you look at the new economy, it's an economy of ceaseless change....Jobs are created. Jobs are destroyed. Companies are created. Companies are destroyed.... The bottom is dropping out of our economy for people who lack the education and skills to participate. ...in this new economy, life-long learning is not just a nice thing. It's a necessity.

— *William A. Galston*

Self-management, intrinsic motivation and responsibility for learning are essential for adult learning. If a student experiences academic success and feels that she is learning; if that student develops more consistent on-task behaviors and is rewarded for them; if she enjoys the new ideas, connections and creativity that spring from use of higher level thinking skills; and if that student develops an increased sense of ownership and commitment for her learning as a result of increased intrinsic motivation, it follows that this same student develops the skills of a life-long learner.

Team Learning and Teaching Supports the Learning Community

While team learning and teaching improve academic accomplishment, it also supports the learning community by positively affecting —

- Self-esteem
- Attitudes toward school
- Relationships between teachers and students
- Peer relationships
- Classroom climate

Self-esteem

The ownership, motivation, peer support, goal setting and monitoring that accompany team learning and teaching boost self confidence for students and teachers. Members of team learning and teaching groups enjoy the significance of their work and the fruits of excellence. Members are mutual beneficiaries of each others' contributions. Like community members who come together for a barn-raising, team learners and teachers accomplish far more collectively than any one person alone, and nurture relationships at the same time they construct a building. One significant result is that self-esteem blossoms, because team members actively value each other, the learning and the community itself.

A teacher in Columbus, Ohio, once said about her adventure learning community and its commitment to team learning and teaching, "You can't help but feel good about teaching here. Your self-esteem grows when you keep hearing from other teachers, 'That's a great idea.'" This teacher enjoyed the fruits of membership in a community of adventure learners. Her grade-level team and cross-grade team worked together to develop curriculum, devise new student assessment methods, plan thematic units and address administrative and policy matters. Learning and teaching were cooperative endeavors for both students and teachers.

Attitudes toward school

Students exercise direct input and control over the learning situation in cooperative settings. This, in turn, directly effects motivation. Students recognize that their choices and contributions directly influence the classroom and their own work. As a result, attitudes toward school, the material and learning in general improve. Instead of, "Why do we need to know this?" teachers hear, "Hey, I want to find out more. This is really interesting!"

Similarly, teachers' attitudes toward their workplace and their colleagues improve with the increase of effective team work. In team teaching situations, teachers have control over the curriculum, influence over the structure of the day and shared responsibility for student outcomes. Because they support each other in these endeavors, teachers take the kinds of professional risks that strengthen positive attitudes toward their work, colleagues and administrators.

Relationships between teachers and students

Relationships between teachers and students are affected by their respective attitudes toward school. The shared responsibility of team learning and teaching places teachers and students in a more equitable relationship. Students grow in their abilities to effectively manage their responsibilities. As a result, both students and teachers develop confidence and trust in the students' abilities to manage those responsibilities.

The assumption of accountability improves relationships between teachers and students. The teacher isn't the only one overseeing students and their work. Students monitor each other. This takes the heat off the teacher for always being "the bad guy." Grades are no longer the sole responsibility of the teacher. Students share in the evaluation and assessment of each other's work and uphold high standards for themselves.

Peer relationships

As students learn to work cooperatively, experience the contributions, perspectives and skills of their peers, and learn the processing and group skills necessary to manage the collaborative relationship, they more readily accept the ability, cultural and ethnic differences of their classmates. Students experience first hand the benefits of different perspectives and strengths in meeting academic challenges. The result is improved peer relationships both inside and outside the classroom.

Peer relationships also improve as students transfer their collaborative skills to situations beyond their academic studies. A teacher at one elementary school noted that students carry their cooperative problem-solving strategies from the classroom to the playground to handle their own arguments.

The students have learned to go to each other for help and advice, and they advise each other about how to handle disagreements.

Classroom climate

Classroom climate improves as students feel positively about themselves, each other, their class and school. At the same time that the atmosphere grows more supportive, students take responsibility for their own and each other's learning. The role of the teacher becomes facilitative and pro-active. Students see a reason to be in class and recognize the positive effects of their contributions. There is less need for the teacher to be the authoritarian voice and punitive presence. "The kids really do it all themselves," remarked a second-grade teacher. "They even take care of their own discipline." In cooperative classrooms, where students have or are learning the interpersonal skills to effectively manage their process, students say, "Yeah, I like coming to class. I wish we could do this more often." Rasheeda, a third grader who has attended a Project Adventure school since kindergarten, responds to a question about what she likes about school with, "We get to work in groups and help each other. I like coming to school."

Teachers enjoy similar benefits. It's great to work in a setting where the members of that learning community, the teachers and students, are happy to be there. Attitudes, expectations and behaviors are generally more positive. Disagreements are opportunities for growth rather than fuel for the fires of discontent.

Necessary Conditions for Effective Team Learning and Teaching

Effective team learning and teaching is not just a matter of putting students in groups. Academic achievement and cognitive growth are not the results of students simply talking to each other. And group projects, in and of themselves, do not ensure positive attitudes toward learning or improved peer relationships. Effective team learning requires five basic conditions (Johnson and Johnson, 1988):

1. Interpersonal skills
2. Processing
3. Positive interdependence
4. Individual accountability
5. Face-to-face interaction

The AITC model and its emphasis on team learning and teaching modifies these conditions and expands them to seven:

1. Consistent and conscientious development of interpersonal skills
2. Consistent and conscientious development of processing skills
3. Goal setting and positive interdependence
4. Individual accountability
5. Face-to-face interaction
6. Full Value Contract
7. Challenge by Choice

Development of Interpersonal Skills

Without skills to negotiate differences, plan together, support, challenge and encourage each other, students risk breakdowns in their cooperative activities from which they will be unable to recover. Effective team learning and teaching demands conscientious instruction and direct application of necessary social and interpersonal skills (see box). "It takes time. Initially it's hard for parents to understand why we're doing this, but they begin to see how important it is for kids to learn how to talk to each other and really listen to each other," explains one middle school teacher.

The focus on consistent and conscientious attention to interpersonal skills must align with the academic curriculum and needs (see Chapter Ten). This means occasional backtracking or review. Children need to learn how to be attentive listeners, how to incorporate other people's ideas, how to give positive feedback and how to manage conflict within the group. To ignore direct instruction of these skills is to undermine the learning.

Development of Processing Skills

To be effective group members and to develop competence in their collaborative efforts, students must process both their individual work and their group experiences. Students do not develop processing skills as a result of membership alone. Processing skills must be taught incrementally and in age appropriate ways.

Direct instruction around such things as feedback, goal setting, attentive listening and eye

Interpersonal Skills

- taking turns
- sharing materials
- asking for clarification
- encouraging
- using quiet voices
- staying on task
- moving quietly to groups
- checking for understanding
- using names
- saying "please" and "thank you"
- pacing group work
- extending another's answer
- ignoring distractions
- negotiating
- active listening
- resolving conflicts
- reaching agreement/consensus
- following through
- following directions
- including everyone
- managing materials
- celebrating success
- sitting in the group
- staying with the group
- looking at each other within the group
- criticize ideas, not people
- describing feelings when appropriate
- energizing the group
- disagreeing in an agreeable way

— *adapted from Bennett,*
Rolheiser-Bennett and Stevahn, 1991

contact, as well as the immediate application and experience with these skills is critical. Learning how to process cognitive learning also requires direct instruction. The various metacognitive and critical thinking skills, such as analyzing cognitive approaches, formulating questions and developing a hypothesis, are as important to the academic curriculum as learning multiplication tables and how to write an argumentative essay.

Positive Interdependence and Goal Setting

Positive interdependence is the nature of working relationships within the classroom. The phrase, *We sink or swim together* (Johnson, Johnson and Holubec, 1988) captures the essence of positive interdependence. Orchestrated by the teacher through the use of many techniques, including group rewards and restricting resources to necessitate sharing, positive interdependence is the reason people work together at all.

Goals, on the other hand, provide direction for learning in the adventure classroom. With goals in place, students and teacher can make decisions about time and resources. The group can identify strengths, needs for growth and strategies for goal attainment. Goals help the learning community assess and evaluate progress and adjust instruction. In addition, group goals provide focus and purpose. Group goals create group incentive.

Individual and group goals need to be aligned so that individual learning, group learning and curriculum goals support each other and foster

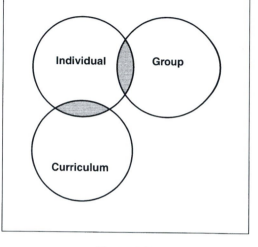

Goal Alignment

Figure 9.2

Figure 9.3

effective learning. When either one is out of alignment with the others, the intersection is unbalanced, and individual learning is negatively affected.

When a cooperative group is clear about its focus and purpose, the members more accurately identify necessary tasks. The goal provides them with a mark against which to measure their activities. This is critical in a classroom that is student directed and where groups of students work simultaneously on different activities. It is impossible for a teacher to monitor everyone's contributions. As students understand their group and individual goals, they monitor each other. It is to each team member's benefit to make sure that the other group members are doing their part.

A group goal gives the members incentive to do the work and to do it well. Team members are more likely to encourage each other if their final product and evaluation reflect the cumulative efforts of everyone. This is a by-product of positive peer pressure.

Positive peer pressure, and the learning of interpersonal and processing skills, promotes more positive working relationships among students. Students in an adventure classroom say things like, "Here, I can help you with that," and "Maybe we should check with Jim to see if he got this problem figured out."

In a first-grade classroom where each student has a role in the cooperative group, the "tutor" takes seriously the responsibility to answer other students' questions. When someone has a question, the student writes her name in a designated place on the board. Tutors are responsible to keep an eye out and to find the classmates who wrote their names and to help them find answers to their questions. Tutors know that if someone has a question they cannot personally answer, they can direct the inquiry to someone who might be able to help. The teacher coaches, "If it's a math question, and you don't know the answer, who in the class is good at math? Who can help with math?"

Types of Positive Interdependence

Outcome Interdependence

Goals and/or rewards are linked so that if one person achieves the goal, the other members benefit.

Positive goal interdependence exists when students achieve learning goals only if all members of the group achieve their learning goals.

Positive goal interdependence can be maintained through the following means:

- Single product from group
- Random selection of one individual's work for which everyone in group receives credit
- Group progress chart to show total accomplishments of group
- Individual levels of mastery that each one must achieve for group to receive credit
- Minimal criteria that all members must achieve for group to receive credit

Positive reward interdependence exists when everyone is rewarded or no one is rewarded. Each group member receives the same reward for completing the class work. Two common ways to create positive reward interdependence are:

- Bonus points added to each team member's scores when everyone in group achieves specified level
- Non-academic rewards given when everyone in group achieves specified standards

Mean Interdependence

Specific actions are required of all group members.

Positive resource interdependence exists when students need to share information, materials, ideas, people or responsibilities in order to complete the task.

Positive task interdependence exists when a lesson or activity is divided into separate steps, each of which is the responsibility of one person in the group. For example, one person reads the requirements for an experiment. Another person assembles the equipment. Another student takes notes for the lab report. A fourth group member records the data.

Positive role interdependence exists when different roles are identified for each person in the group. The emphasis is on roles, regardless of task. Roles can be working roles—*reader, recorder* and *runner*—or social skill roles—*tutor, complimenter* and *problem solver.*

Situation or Identity Interdependence

Interdependence is maintained via external circumstances.

Positive identity interdependence exists when group membership is enhanced or symbolized in a group name, motto, cheer or song. Students may choose group names or mottoes that are completely unrelated to each other or anything else in the class. Their identifications may be tied into larger unit themes. In a second-grade classroom doing a month-long space unit, the learning teams chose such names as "rock-eteers," "star-shooters," "comets" and "planeteers."

Positive competitor interdependence exists when the group unites in an effort to compete against another group for points, reward or problem solution.

Fantasy interdependence exists when fictional settings or fantasy events are used to unite a group's efforts. In the *Spider Web* activity, for example, the group is challenged to pass all its members through a giant spider web before the spider returns.

Environmental interdependence exists when group members are bound together by their physical environment. This can be accomplished by placing chairs together, putting students in a specific place in the room, on the playground, or school lawn. In some adventure activities, such as *Human Knot,* participants are literally bound together by tangled handholds.

— adapted from Johnson, Johnson and Holubec, 1988

Individual Accountability

Many of us who attempted group work in our classrooms twenty years ago fell into the black hole of no accountability. Intent on creating collaborative classrooms and building relationships among our students, we had great group activities, but didn't know what to do with those students who saw their chance to grab a free ride. Jackie, Stan, Rikki and Vinnie did all the work while Ashley sat back and wrote notes to her boyfriend. If there is one thing that the last fifteen years of research in cooperative learning have taught us, it's the need for individual accountability. Individual accountability does not circumvent or negate the advantages of cooperative learning; it supports it.

Face-to-Face Interaction

Cooperation without eye contact is like delivering a speech with your back to the audience. A fair exchange of ideas, effective feedback and working relationships suffer when team members do not look at each other. Many times, if students are put into cooperative groups and have not learned the importance of eye contact, they settle into static unresponsiveness toward each other. They speak in monologues. Mini-conversations surface as people talk to their neighbors. Anyone who tries to make a point is lost in the emptiness of mismatched conversation.

To accomplish goals in a learning team, participants need to look at each other and talk directly to each other. Sitting in a circle or with desks face-to-face brings everyone up to the table, literally and figuratively. Only then can the group plunge ahead together.

Full Value Contract

The Full Value Contract (see Chapter Six) is Project Adventure's major contribution to cooperative learning. The Full Value Contract ushers cooperative learning and teaching into the realm of true team learning and teaching. The Full Value Contract embraces the whole of the academic setting as a complete, organic being.

The Contract reminds teachers and students to pay as much attention to the processes of learning as they do to the content of learning. The Full Value Contract asks each member of the learning community to support the other conditions of cooperative learning: individual accountability, positive interdependence, processing and group skills. The Full Value Contract brings reality to these conditions as learners commit to the relationships of the learning community.

Challenge by Choice

Challenge by Choice (see Chapter Five) puts *challenge* up front. In team learning and teaching, each member should be challenging herself. Team members should also be challenging each other in a supportive manner. *Choice* permits latitude and reminds members of the learning community that members bring different abilities and needs to the class. Challenge by Choice encourages high expectations and responsibility in the collaborative setting. The free ride is a cop-out. Railroading ideas ignores the input, individual challenge and choice making of other members. Challenge by Choice keeps members of the learning community honest with themselves and with each other.

Practical Considerations

In the early phases of team learning and teaching, many practical and logistical questions loom— What about grades? How do I find the time? Will I be able to cover all that I need to cover? What is the best way to group students?

Those who specifically teach collaborative classroom approaches offer a wealth of ideas and strategies to address these questions. Practitioners in the field share tried-and-true "this-works-for-me" answers. A few comments regarding basic concerns are appropriate here, particularly for those who may be new to team learning and teaching.

Will I be able to cover all the material?

Covering material is not the same as teaching material. I can *cover* the American expatriates of the 1930's, but that doesn't guarantee that the students have *learned* anything about those writers.

Covering World War II does not mean that students understand the economic and political factors that influenced the United States to enter the war, or that students can explain the changing role of the United States in world politics from 1944 to 1996.

The worry about covering material really is often a worry about time. Team learning does take time. It takes time for teachers to learn how to organize and manage new structures for teaching and learning that may be unfamiliar. It takes time for students to learn how to be effective learning community members. However, the investment of time and energy to help students learn, thoroughly understand and develop cognitive skills pays enormous dividends both in the short term and in the long term.

A good lecture effectively imparts information to a large number of people; and there are times when a lecture is an appropriate strategy. But a lecture does not stimulate problem solving. A classroom based on the premise that learning is the making of connections between events, facts, experiences, information and processes; that learning is understanding facts, concepts, events, experiences and information, and making them one's own; and that learning is applying knowledge and skills to new and unfamiliar settings, calls for strategies that teach and require those cognitive activities.

"Yes, I spend more time teaching the processes and skills for cooperative learning than I did when my teaching style was more teacher centered, but my kids learn better. They know the material better. But better than that, they understand what they are doing and why," remarked one elementary teacher of fifteen years experience. "Once they learn *how to learn* collaboratively, they learn more. They learn faster. I'm convinced of that," she affirmed.

Where do I begin?

Don't expect students to change their study habits overnight. Don't expect yourself to overhaul curriculum and teaching style in one week, one semester or even one year. Set reasonable goals and expectations. Take incremental steps.

Begin somewhere

Advocates of a structure approach to cooperative learning suggest that focusing on one cooperative lesson, as separate from any other classroom lesson, indicates that very little cooperative learning is occurring. The structured approach emphasizes the application of a variety of formats for all classroom work. Proponents of a conceptual approach to cooperative learning, on the other hand, tend to focus on designing specific lessons that incorporate cooperative strategies.

Regardless of one's preference, it is important to begin somewhere. Incorporate team learning and teaching at whatever entry point makes most sense. This might mean, initially, that the easiest way to initiate team learning and teaching is through adventure activities. In fact, this is a natural jumping off point for many teachers. In other circumstances it might be appropriate to very quickly take steps to weave one or two cooperative structures in other areas of classroom

learning. For someone else, beginning with one short cooperative lesson or activity at a regular interval—every C block on Tuesday or Thursday, or Monday morning's first lesson—is the place to start. This way, you can begin with subject matter that lends itself to a cooperative strategy. A vocabulary lesson, math review or a structured writing assignment might be an easy fit.

Whatever the starting point, maintain some discipline around it. As you gain comfort and begin to internalize the change of schedule or the new structure or the development of adventure activities, take another step. Try another lesson. Introduce a new structure. Use another means of maintaining individual accountability or positive interdependence. Begin somewhere.

Build on incremental successes

Remember the qualifier, *incremental*. Change brought about in small steps increases the potential number of successes that have positive, cumulative effects. For example, breaking down a tennis serve into manageable pieces allows a novice player to focus on and improve one move at a time. Once the player has the stance down, she can focus on grip. Then comes shoulder position or arm movement. The rewards of improvement encourage the next steps.

The same is true in behavior changes, such as altering your teaching style and strategy. If cooperative structures are new to you, don't load up a beginning lesson with two types of group goals, jigsaw methods, three social skills and new

grouping methods. You will find it difficult to evaluate the individual parts of the lesson and will soon be overwhelmed with all the changes.

Be honest with the class

Let students know that you are introducing new teaching strategies. Be clear with them and with yourself about why you think these changes are necessary. Share with them your questions, your hopes, your expectations. Involve them in the planning and evaluation of cooperative lessons. Students are not consumers of education. They are participants in their education. Their perspective is invaluable in the assessment process. The lesson you thought failed may have been a success for your students. Your enthusiasm over another lesson may not match up with what the students actually learned!

Be reflective, honest and gentle with yourself

Good teaching is reflective teaching. After each cooperative lesson, ask yourself the following questions:

- What worked? Why did it work?
- What didn't work? Why didn't it?
- What will I do the same again?
- What will I change for the next time?

Be honest as you answer. If a group size of four students was too large too soon and the students still need to operate in pairs, admit it. If your articulation of group and individual responsibilities was clear and students demonstrated individual accountability, acknowledge the success. Honest answers pave the way to effective practice.

Remember to be gentle with yourself. Team learning puts responsibility in the hands of the students. You are turning over the management of learning to the students. There will be as many paths to the destination as there are students in the class. You are responsible for providing resources, guidelines and expectations, but the product and the process belong to the students.

Be proactive and inform

Whenever teachers make substantial changes in the classroom, students, parents, supervisors and the principal should be informed. A proactive position is more powerful than a reactive one. A parent with information at the outset becomes a supporter at best, and a benign presence in the least. A parent who gets information after the fact becomes an embittered enemy, distrustful of the teacher and capable of obstructing the best educational practices. As the structure of classrooms and schools changes from private domains of autonomous, authoritative educators to communities of adventure learners, connected to and supportive of the community beyond the school walls, then teachers must continue to build relationships throughout and around the school. Relationships require communication.

If at first it doesn't work, try again

Don't let an occasional mishap throw you off course. If things don't work, don't worry. Reflect and review. Try to determine what happened and why. Was the lesson too complicated? Was there poor sequencing? Were groups too large for the task? Were expectations unclear? Was this an inappropriate strategy for this lesson? Take advantage of the learning experience.

What about grouping?

Practitioners, researchers and theorists have different suggestions about how to handle grouping. Elizabeth Cohen (1986), David and Frank Johnson (1991), David Johnson, Roger Johnson and Edythe Johnson Holubec (1988), Jeanne Gibbs (1987) and Spencer Kagan (1992) are members of a large community of researchers and practitioners who have developed strategies for formulating group membership. They are excellent resources on the topic.

Some questions teachers have as they explore cooperative learning are—

- What are some easy ways to get started grouping students?
- Can students form their own groups?
- What kinds of groups are there, and how do you know the kind of grouping to use?
- How often do you change groups?

Guidelines

Think short and small is the best advice about starting cooperative groups. Begin with students working in pairs. This is generally a comfortable number for students and keeps the dynamics simple. The larger the group, the more complicated the interpersonal management.

Begin with short activities or assignments. If students have been accustomed to competitive or individualist settings, they need to learn how to work in a cooperative group. Students are more likely to meet success with short activities and uncomplicated assignments that also allow for clearer assessment of the process.

Some partner approaches include those in the following list, adapted from David and Roger Johnson and Edythe Holubec (Johnson, Johnson and Holubec, 1988):

- **Turn to a neighbor** — For five or six minutes students engage in a short assignment based on the lesson just completed. Appropriate tasks for this structure include explaining to each other the concept just learned, restating the assignment, formulating one or two questions for class discussion, or summarizing main points.

- **Drill partners** — Students quiz each other on factual information that applies to the lesson. Math facts, vocabulary, spelling and material for mastery in any subject area are well served by this approach. The teacher can award bonus points for each partner if each member scores above a predetermined goal on the quiz or test.

- **Reading buddies** — Students read or summarize to each other material they have read.

Partners ask clarifying questions or explain words, concepts or ideas that are unfamiliar to the other.

- **Homework checkers** — Students compare homework assignments. Where answers differ, students discuss and decide together on an answer. They also provide a rationale for their new answer, describing each other's original response and explaining how they came to the new answer. The teacher collects both papers, but grades only one of them.

- **Worksheet checkers** — Two students work on one worksheet. One student is the *reader,* who reads the question and suggests an answer. The other student is the *writer,* who either accepts the answer or provides another one. The partners must agree on an answer before the writer records it.

- **Book report partners** — Students interview each other about the books they have read. The partners do the book report on each other's book.

- **Summary partners** — Students alternate reading and orally summarizing paragraphs. They alternate the roles of reading and summarizing, then check the oral summary with the written paragraph.

- **Partners review** — One partner reads the other's paper. She marks what she likes with a star or exclamation point, and what she doesn't understand or finds weak with a question mark. The reading partner also marks specific grammar, punctuation, usage or spelling errors and discusses those marks with the writer. Finally, the partner proofreads the final draft. All three steps, or any one, can be the focus of a partners review.

Spencer Kagan offers several dozen structures appropriate for various cognitive, social or team building purposes. Among them are the following (adapted from Kagan, 1992):

- **Roundtable** — This is a two-step structure appropriate for the beginning of a lesson and is done in teams of four. First the teacher poses a question or problem with multiple answers, such as "How many things in the classroom require electricity?" or "How many states can you name along with their capital cities?" Next the students create a single list to answer the question by passing one piece of paper around the group, always in the same direction. Each student contributes one answer when the paper comes to her.

- **Round robin** — In this verbal version of Roundtable, students take turns offering answers to the question, going around the team of four in sequence.

- **Rallytable** — Similar to Roundtable, students offer answers to a question, one at a time. However, in rallytable, each team of four works as two partner teams. The answer sheet goes back and forth between two people in the group. After the time is called, the two partner teams compare with each other. This allows for quicker individual response time as well as a chance to see that "two *teams* are better than one."

- **Mix-freeze-group** — This structure fits when the answers are numbers. Students mill around until the question is called, for example, "What is 45 divided by 9?" Students form groups the size of the answer. In this case, students form groups of 5. If not everyone can be in a group, those people go to "lost and found" or "remainders" until the next problem. No one can go to "lost and found" or "remainders" two times in a row. This assures that students need to include those folks first in the next round.

- **Think-pair-share** — In this structure the students have a problem or question that they first *think* about quietly and individually for a specified amount of time. Then the students meet in *pairs* to discuss their ideas. Finally each pair *shares* their collective answer with the class.

- **Think-pair-square** — This structure concludes with the pairs sharing in a team of four, rather in the whole class. The result is that more students are involved simultaneously.

- **Three Stray, One Stay** — In their teams of four members, students work on a task that is either a product or a solution to a problem that has multiple solutions; e.g., a poster campaign against smoking or drug use, an analysis of a poem's imagery or the plan for a school garden. Three members from each group go to another team's table or product where the remaining team member, Student One, explains what her team has done. Students return to their own station, share and discuss what they saw or heard. Then Student Two stays behind while the other three teammates move onto still another location to hear about another group's work.

Each student has had a chance, by the end of the sequence, to talk about her group's product at least once, and has seen the products of three or four other groups and explained them "back at home."

- **One stray, three stay** — Similar to Three stray, one stay, this structure stresses individual observation and reporting skills. In this design, one student moves to another group each turn to learn about that team's work, then returns to her group to report.

- **Spend-a-buck** — This structure fits situations where students need to make quick decisions. Each student has four quarters to "spend" on the various choices; e.g., "To solve his problem, the character in the short story could…" or "To reduce the national deficit, we should…" Students must spend their quarters on more than one item or answer. Someone can, for example, put three quarters on one answer and one quarter on another, or spread the quarters evenly between four solutions. The team tallies results to figure out their group decision.

Student-formed groups

The best way to determine whether students should form their own groups is to identify the goals for the particular class and assess the students' abilities at that stage. Be clear about the purpose of the lesson and the grouping. In many cases informal tasks are appropriate for self-selection. The lessons are short and include such things as homework checking, fifteen-minute review sessions, a half-hour of reading and summarizing exercise, drill work on math facts or science vocabulary. Membership in formal task groups can be effective if students choose their own groups and have the skills and understanding to choose wisely. Students must understand what makes a good work team. Such principles should be explicit in the classroom as part of the early development of cooperative groups. A class that has previously identified the characteristics of a good team and come up with norms for cooperative group operation will have a checklist against which to compare their group selection as they form.

Also consider how long it has been since students chose their own groups. If they have been in structured groups for several weeks and haven't had the opportunity to establish their own, it might be a good opportunity to give them a choice.

Types of groups

The Johnson, Johnson and Holubec team has developed a helpful graph to understand different kinds of groupings for cooperative learning settings (Fig. 9.4).

Although there are other ways to look at grouping students for cooperative learning, this summary describes the essential characteristics of each type of grouping and provides guidelines for which type of grouping to use in different situations.

Changing groups

Group membership changes depending on the learning goals. It is generally advisable to keep base teams together for the duration of the class, or at least for a semester. Informal task teams change with the task, while formal task teams remain in place for the duration of their stated goal.

Don't let interpersonal difficulties in a group prompt you to change the group's composition right away. Let students struggle and learn from their difficulties. You may need to facilitate their conflict management; but if students are learning skills to deal with their group process, they will eventually be able to address the issues that arise. This is especially true as students develop their Full Value Contract and engage in goal setting and feedback. Only if the working relationships are destructive to the learning environment or hurtful to any one member should you change the membership of a team.

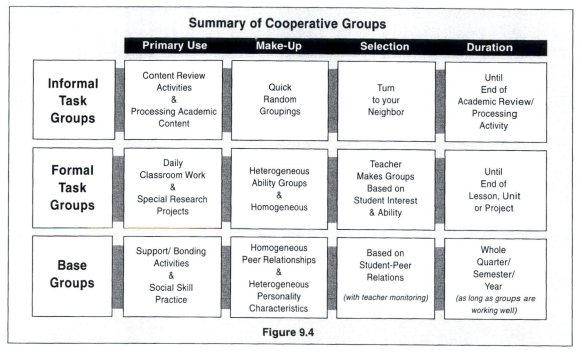

Figure 9.4

Summary of Cooperative Groups				
	Primary Use	**Make-Up**	**Selection**	**Duration**
Informal Task Groups	Content Review Activities & Processing Academic Content	Quick Random Groupings	Turn to your Neighbor	Until End of Academic Review/ Processing Activity
Formal Task Groups	Daily Classroom Work & Special Research Projects	Heterogeneous Ability Groups & Homogeneous	Teacher Makes Groups Based on Student Interest & Ability	Until End of Lesson, Unit or Project
Base Groups	Support/ Bonding Activities & Social Skill Practice	Homogeneous Peer Relationships & Heterogeneous Personality Characteristics	Based on Student-Peer Relations *(with teacher monitoring)*	Whole Quarter/ Semester/ Year *(as long as groups are working well)*

Summary

Individualistic, competitive and cooperative teaching strategies have their place in the classroom, depending upon the instructional goals of the class. Unfortunately, a huge disparity often exists between the need for students and teachers to develop collaborative skills and the amount of time spent in class utilizing those strategies. In the AITC model team learning and teaching are the umbrella over individual and competitive learning. Collaboration is the context of learning. The AITC model uses the term *team learning and teaching* to emphasize the community nature of learning and to recognize the variety of cooperative teaching strategies available to educators.

Documentation on the benefits of team learning and teaching sounds a clear call for this strategy. In the very least, students respond more positively to their academic studies, to the school environment and to each other in correlation to the extent of effective collaboration they enjoy in the classroom. Teachers also benefit professionally and personally as they experience significant gains in their learning efforts with each other. Yet merely putting people into groups does not ensure cooperative learning. Students must develop interpersonal skills and processing skills. They must be positively interdependent. They must have face-to-face interaction and be held individually accountable for their work. In the AITC classroom, there must also be consistent attention to maintaining the Full Value Contract and upholding Challenge by Choice.

A teacher faces many obstacles and concerns in the beginning phases of implementing team learning and teaching. Worries about time and amount of material will only be ameliorated as the teacher begins to weave structures into the day's work, builds on small successes, involves students in the reflective evaluation of the strategies and assumes a proactive stance. While the work is hard, the rewards are many.

Integrated Curriculum

*When we try to pick out anything
by itself we find it hitches to everything
in the universe.*

— *John Muir*

The halls of Central High School's east wing display the process and plans for a proposed garden at a local retirement home, the culminating project of a semester-long interdisciplinary course entitled, "Changing Faces." Flow charts outline the work schedule. A draft of the presentation to the town planning board hangs on one wall next to spread sheets that itemize project costs and anticipated benefits. A scale model, complete with miniature plants, stands proudly in the display case. Framed copies of newspaper articles chronicle the undertaking.

The town planning commission has approved the project and allocated funds to purchase plant material for the garden. Recently, the students faced a problem due to a brick wall abutting the property. The approved landscape design neglected to take into account the effects the wall would have on temperature and moisture retention for the plantings in front of it. To relocate benches and alter plant materials meant an expenditure of more money than the budget allowed. To increase spending for materials, the students would have to reduce the maintenance budget. Neglecting to address just one

Studying a topic within an integrated curriculum carries the advantage and richness of multiple lenses.

feature of the lot led to several rounds of negotiations, budget adjustments and design changes. Addressing this problem reminded students that the lattice work of tasks and resources changes design if any one aspect changes.

Operating with the philosophy that people learn best when they see the interrelationships between disciplines, the teachers of this class have brought their particular skills and subject areas together in a comprehensive, interdisciplinary approach. English, math, science, art, social studies and computers have been interdependent partners in this course on "Changing Faces" rather than fifty-minute parcels of content. Students have learned and put into practice knowledge and skills traditionally isolated by discipline-based learning. Students have analyzed statistical data, written essays and interviewed local politicians and area residents. They have written letters and newspaper articles, solicited funds from local foundations and made multi-media presentations to the planning board. They have spent time with residents of the retirement home, assessing needs, documenting personal histories, participating in strategy sessions. The work has been demanding, but the results have exceeded expected outcomes. The rewards have been incalculable.

It's All Connected, After All!

Each discipline has an integrity of skills and methods specific to that subject area. Species classification is rooted in the earth sciences. Formal style grammar and expository writing are matters of language. Algebraic equations are mathematical statements. But the disciplines of mathematics, physical science, earth science, social science, art, literature and so forth, serve primarily to organize information and itemize knowledge bases. Beyond that, they are artificial boundaries which blur as we get down to the real stuff of life. Parenting, for example, requires some sociology, a little history, a dose of math, a fair amount of language and substantial experience with home economics. The youth soccer coach brings physical education, psychology and philosophy to bear as she works with her team. The technologically sophisticated specialty of tissue engineering requires training in biology, human physiology, chemistry, biomedical engineering, ethics and physics. The software systems marketing expert, who maneuvers the intricacies of computer software through the mazes of marketing, must be able to meet the varied and complex needs of many clients.

Integrated curriculum is just common sense. It is how we live. We "do" math *throughout* the day, not just for forty minutes in the morning. We "do" math for a variety of purposes: estimating if there is enough cash to fill the gas tank and buy milk, balancing a checkbook, figuring out the number of grams of fat consumed at lunch, deciding if there is enough time to go to the YMCA for a workout, and helping a ten-year-old understand how fractions, decimals and percentages are three different ways to express the same idea.

Studying a topic within an integrated curriculum carries the advantage and richness of multiple

lenses. In a workshop on integrating curriculum, Heidi Hayes Jacobs shows a set of keys and asks the participants to imagine themselves an assembly of specialists from various fields. The sociologist, mathematician, musician, writer, historian, economist and anthropologist each uses his specialty as a lens to study and generate questions about the keys.

The sociologist asks, "Who owns these keys? What kind of work does this person do? How do keys and locks influence behavior?" The mathematician counts the keys. The musician picks up the keys and jingles them, listening for a melodic line. The writer jots down word pictures or writes a poem. The anthropologist takes the keys and tries to find what doors they unlock, what they might reveal.

Each discipline offers its own perspective. Each discipline generates questions and embarks on a particular path of inquiry. Alone, each discipline provides a one-dimensional snapshot. The snapshot shows good detail, but the snapshot is just one picture. The collection of several disciplines, however, reveals more possibilities and captures nuances otherwise lost. This interplay creates different angles, like a Picasso painting that looks into,

outside, around, underneath, on top of the object. Studying the French Revolution with the lenses of history, social studies, music, art, economics, literature, science and math is like the CAD/CAM programs that produce multi-dimensional graphic representations that rotate and telescope, turning objects inside-out and upside-down to expose the many surfaces from numerous angles.

Overview

Early childhood educators know the importance of play, imagination and verbal communication to human growth and development. Teachers of young children connect play with cognitive and social learning. They know that the best way to teach categorizing or shapes or predicting is by using a variety of toys or materials in a variety of settings and subject areas. Children count and sort blocks, collect and sort items from a nature walk, read several books on a theme, even have snacks that match a theme—goldfish crackers for an aquarium field trip and gelatin blocks in different geometric shapes to reinforce the vocabulary of squares, rectangles, triangles and ovals.

Something happens in the process, however, and by the time children reach second or third grade, educational practice acts as if children no longer see or need to see how new ideas and skills connect to each other. Reading becomes something separate from math, distinct from science, unrelated to physical education and different from social studies.

As teachers, we must teach in ways that open windows to knowledge and help students develop the skills necessary to traverse, live in and cultivate that rich landscape. If we want students to see, experience and know the interrelation between algebra, logic, expression of thought and writing, then we must teach in a way that models and reveals the interrelations.

Human Need for Integration

Brain research (Caine and Caine, 1991), human development (Heath, 1991) and organizational development (Wheatley, 1993; Senge, 1990) remind us that human beings are driven by a basic need to integrate the many experiences of life. The brain searches for and creates new patterns. Individuals and organizations constantly shift and reform to adapt to change. Particles of energy vibrate in constant tension to maintain balance and adjust to the slightest variables in their environment. That same need reflects itself in the human processes of learning new material, incorporating new information and constructing knowledge. It only makes sense, then, that approaches to teaching and learning integrate subject and approach, the processes of learning and the metacurriculum of interpersonal relationships. To do otherwise stifles the learning process.

Integration of Curriculum Fosters Relevancy

Conscientious integration of curriculum widens the avenues of relevancy for the learner. When students see that their own questioning of authority echo those of the American colonists in 1773, the material comes alive for them. They want to learn, to explore, to search deeper and higher. This integration should not be limited to subject areas. Curriculum integration must include integration of the processes and relationships that shape learning. "No topic—not the Boston Tea Party nor the bombing of a clinic nor the Pythagorean Theorem —can assume rich significance without probing questions that make connections to higher principles and other contexts....Students need the technique and creative reach to find the music in the relationships of things. And while curriculum content alone may give them some notes and tunes as points of departure, it is the metacurriculum that cultivates their art with the instruments of their minds" (Ackerman and Perkins, 1989).

Extensions

Previous chapters detail the ways in which particular strategies (adventure activities, processing, team learning and teaching) promote learning and support the community of adventure learners. The supporting theories of brain research, the efficacy of experiential learning and contextual learning apply here as they do to the other strategies.

This chapter focuses instead on the following three issues:

1. Definitions and existing paradigms of curriculum integration
2. A broader and deeper meaning of curriculum integration
3. Getting started

Existing Paradigms

Science, social studies and physical education formed the core of the original Hamilton-Wenham Regional High School model (see Chapter Two). Students analyzed water samples from a local lake and graphed results. They studied the ecological and social history of the area and designed a plan for site use and management. They participated in cooperative games and struggled with problem-solving initiatives to enhance their peer relationships. The teachers of this early model knew instinctively that effective learning required two conditions: 1) active involvement with the material; and 2) exposure to a range of skills and perspectives.

Unfortunately the arid winds of educational reform blew across the landscape of public education and swept away the rich soil of integrated approaches to learning. Schools reverted to the practice of compartmentalizing teaching skills without regard to context. A focus on "the basics" of reading, writing and computation wrapped itself in the assumption that skill development occurred without context and independent of content.

Curriculum isolated reading from grammar and spelling from literature, as if so many separate blocks merely needed to be stacked, one on top of the other, to build a literate human being.

Teachers of the AITC model, however, continued to teach their disciplines as the lenses through which to view the world. These teachers found like-minded colleagues who were willing to link units of study, team teach an occasional lesson and connect their subject curriculum to students' own experiences. What these educators knew instinctively soon received validation from consistent practice and research in such areas as the human brain and effective teaching, and the recognition by back-to-basics proponents that isolated skill building is questionable practice graced with questionable results. At the observable levels, isolated skill building quells student motivation, thereby limiting, rather than promoting, achievement.

Traditionally, the options for curriculum integration have been viewed from two vantage points: 1) options for curriculum integration; and 2) options for student structures

The options for curriculum integration are like the organization of books in the library according to subject. Options for student structures are like the floor plan of the library. There are books throughout the building, in the conference rooms, along the stairway, in the children's room, in the adult reading room and in the reference room. The curriculum is accessible to all. Decisions just need to be made regarding which rooms and which books best belong together.

	9th gr.	10th gr.	11th gr.	12th gr.
English	Survey of Am. literature	Survey of Eng. literature	Mod. European fiction	electives
Social studies	Survey of world history	American history	Civics	Senior seminar
Math	Algebra	Geometry	Pre-calculus	Calculus
Science	Earth science	Biology	Chemistry	Physics

Options for Curriculum Integration

Consider a not unfamiliar course arrangement for Average Public High School, USA represented in the graphic above.

The wisdom of this organization is suspect. Each department has a well-developed rationale for its sequence, but there is no flow to the overall order of this curriculum. It does not make sense to cross match American literature and world cultures in the ninth grade, then teach American history in tenth grade alongside English literature. Why not teach American literature the same year as American history? Why not coordinate earth science with geometry? While simply aligning related courses does not equal integration, it at least creates a logical order of instruction for the whole school curriculum.

When a curriculum moves toward integration, themes and genre in English class parallel events and themes of the history class. Math and science are two approaches to the same topic. Integration pushes us to identify themes that form the hub of the curriculum. Skills are taught in context along the spokes that are the content.

There are several strategies to design integrated curriculum. "Curriculum mapping" is a first step staff can take to see what is being taught across the curriculum at which time. Next teachers make common sense rearrangements that more consciously and conscientiously connect material.

When integration becomes more aggressive, teachers generally begin the design process by determining an organizing theme or question. From there they brainstorm possible connections. This leads to a webbing procedure where teachers cluster lessons and activities according to skill or content area. Teachers write guiding questions that help maintain focus throughout the unit of study by providing guidelines against which to choose appropriate activities and lessons.

The models of curriculum designed by Heidi Hayes Jacobs (1989) and Robin Fogarty (1991) give language to two particular styles of integration .

Continuum of options for content design

Heidi Hayes Jacobs' continuum of design options places disciplined-based designs at one end of the

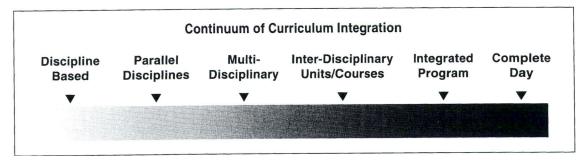

Continuum of Curriculum Integration

Discipline Based	Parallel Disciplines	Multi-Disciplinary	Inter-Disciplinary Units/Courses	Integrated Program	Complete Day
▼	▼	▼	▼	▼	▼

spectrum and the entirely integrated, complete program at the other end.

The *discipline based* option is the conventional approach of separate subjects, separate times. There is no attempt to link the various subjects. For example, students have a math lesson on multiplication tables, followed by a hands-on science unit about the life cycle of the monarch butterfly. Next comes recess, then reading. Lunch breaks the day, after which art, music or silent reading follows. The last activity of the day is a social studies lesson on the Pilgrims. Conventional junior and senior high schools have engineered discipline based curriculum to a science.

A *parallel disciplines* design orders subjects and topics, so that even though there is little additional attempt to coordinate or team teach units, at least there is some logical order and overlap among disciplines. The English class reads *To Kill a Mockingbird* at approximately the same time the history class focuses on the Depression Era. The math teacher introduces vectors, angles and use of protractor and compass while the earth science teacher begins a unit on topography and mapping.

The *multi-disciplinary* option purposefully combines two or three disciplines in a defined unit with a thematic focus. In preparation for annual Earth Day events, for example, science lessons address waste management, pollution and recycling. Skills-focused math lessons draw examples from those science activities. Students estimate the amount of trash produced by the school, by a neighborhood or household. They determine percentages of recyclable items in a conventional landfill and calculate how landfill capacity is affected by various recycling programs. In English class students read Rachel Carson and Edward Abbey and pursue library research regarding the local watershed and waste management systems.

Inter-disciplinary units take another step along the continuum and involve all the disciplines in curriculum design around an organized theme. Subject areas and classes are deliberately combined. The organizing question tends to be more global. The Earth Day unit is expanded and includes art, music, physical education, social studies and foreign language. The theme is reshaped and refined as "Caring: A skill for life."

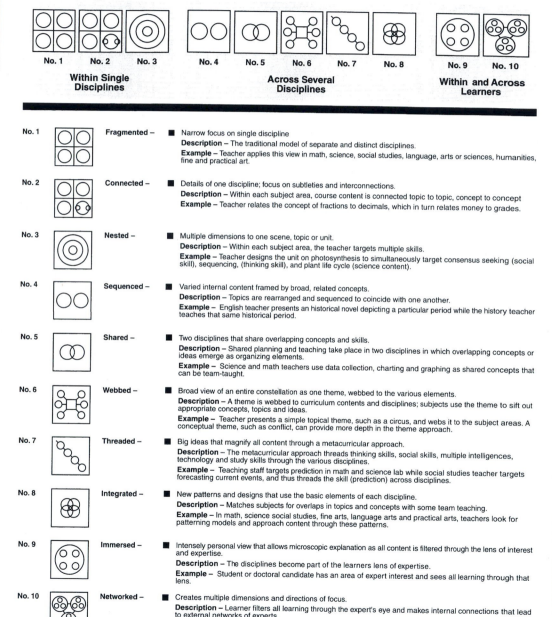

Toward an Integrated Curriculum*
Ten Views for Integrating the Curricula: How Do You See It?

| No. 1 | No. 2 | No. 3 | No. 4 | No. 5 | No. 6 | No. 7 | No. 8 | No. 9 | No. 10 |

Within Single Disciplines   **Across Several Disciplines**   **Within and Across Learners**

No. 1 — Fragmented —
- Narrow focus on single discipline
  Description – The traditional model of separate and distinct disciplines.
  Example – Teacher applies this view in math, science, social studies, language, arts or sciences, humanities, fine and practical art.

No. 2 — Connected —
- Details of one discipline; focus on subtleties and interconnections.
  Description – Within each subject area, course content is connected topic to topic, concept to concept
  Example – Teacher relates the concept of fractions to decimals, which in turn relates money to grades.

No. 3 — Nested —
- Multiple dimensions to one scene, topic or unit.
  Description – Within each subject area, the teacher targets multiple skills.
  Example – Teacher designs the unit on photosynthesis to simultaneously target consensus seeking (social skill), sequencing, (thinking skill), and plant life cycle (science content).

No. 4 — Sequenced —
- Varied internal content framed by broad, related concepts.
  Description – Topics are rearranged and sequenced to coincide with one another.
  Example – English teacher presents an historical novel depicting a particular period while the history teacher teaches that same historical period.

No. 5 — Shared —
- Two disciplines that share overlapping concepts and skills.
  Description – Shared planning and teaching take place in two disciplines in which overlapping concepts or ideas emerge as organizing elements.
  Example – Science and math teachers use data collection, charting and graphing as shared concepts that can be team-taught.

No. 6 — Webbed —
- Broad view of an entire constellation as one theme, webbed to the various elements.
  Description – A theme is webbed to curriculum contents and disciplines; subjects use the theme to sift out appropriate concepts, topics and ideas.
  Example – Teacher presents a simple topical theme, such as a circus, and webs it to the subject areas. A conceptual theme, such as conflict, can provide more depth in the theme approach.

No. 7 — Threaded —
- Big ideas that magnify all content through a metacurricular approach.
  Description – The metacurricular approach threads thinking skills, social skills, multiple intelligences, technology and study skills through the various disciplines.
  Example – Teaching staff targets prediction in math and science lab while social studies teacher targets forecasting current events, and thus threads the skill (prediction) across disciplines.

No. 8 — Integrated —
- New patterns and designs that use the basic elements of each discipline.
  Description – Matches subjects for overlaps in topics and concepts with some team teaching.
  Example – In math, science social studies, fine arts, language arts and practical arts, teachers look for patterning models and approach content through these patterns.

No. 9 — Immersed —
- Intensely personal view that allows microscopic explanation as all content is filtered through the lens of interest and expertise.
  Description – The disciplines become part of the learners lens of expertise.
  Example – Student or doctoral candidate has an area of expert interest and sees all learning through that lens.

No. 10 — Networked —
- Creates multiple dimensions and directions of focus.
  Description – Learner filters all learning through the expert's eye and makes internal connections that lead to external networks of experts.
  Example – Architect, while adapting the CAD/CAM technology for design, networks with technical programmers and expands her knowledge base, just as she had traditionally done with interior designers.

* From *The Mindful School: How to Integrate the Curricula* by Robin Fogarty. © 1991 by IRI/Skylight Training and Publishing, Inc., Arlington Heights, IL. Reprinted with permission.

The last two design options deliberately blur discipline boundaries, yet do not ignore particular skills or techniques best taught in small units that support the larger structure. For example, the *integrated day* concept builds on student-generated issues and then draws on subject-based skills to facilitate learning. In the Community Studies Project, developed by University Heights High School in New York City, students design research projects about their neighborhoods. One student centers his project around the question, "How does my neighborhood reflect the different immigrant groups that live here?" A classmate launches her inquiry with the question, "What do women in my neighborhood need to know and do to survive here?" Interview techniques, library research skills and mapping skills are taught as mini-units in what might have earlier been considered English or math classes. The difference is that the larger inquiry drives the particular lessons. The larger inquiry is both design element and architect of the curriculum.

Similarly, the *complete program* integrates the entire learning environment with the curriculum. Environmental education center programs like Nature's Classroom are complete program integrations. Not only do classes focus on environmental issues, but staff titles, after-dinner songs, management of mealtimes and rest times support the educational philosophy and goals of the curriculum. Students eat vegetarian meals and compete with themselves to reduce the amount of ort at the end of each meal. Games played after dinner reinforce the study of nocturnal mammals.

The Mindful School approach to integration

While Heidi Hayes Jacobs lays out design options to shape interdisciplinary curriculum, Robin Fogarty details ten distinct methods for operationalizing those designs. Fogarty's own graphic summary is the best way to scan her classification of approaches.

Two features of Robin Fogarty's paradigm merit a note here. First, Fogarty provides a substantial number of integration frameworks. While some people find this list daunting, others enjoy a delightful menu. A second interesting feature is the itemization of thinking, social and cognitive skills in two of the models as "metacurricula." In clearly distinguishing these areas from the academic curriculum of science, language arts, math and social studies, Fogarty opens the door to the larger meaning of curriculum integration and invites teachers to widen their horizons. Her work supports the kind of approach to curriculum integration characteristic of the AITC model.

Project-based curriculum

Finally, a word about an approach to curriculum integration that some consider the ideal of integration: this is project-based learning, where the curriculum is built around real-world challenges that students put their hands to solving. An entire curriculum focused on converting a vacant lot into usable recreation and leisure space, for example, becomes the purpose for studying literature, social studies, math, land management, biology, art and computer science. The MIT instructional model, where engineering students spend a semester designing a solar-powered automobile, is another example of project-based learning. Students deal with real-world issues at the same time that they learn content. They develop discipline-based skills along with team and social skills.

The Expeditionary Learning project, sponsored by the NASDC initiative, builds its curriculum around expeditions, or final projects where students go out into the community to present, explore and create. What has at other times been called the "peak experience" is legitimized as the rightful center of instruction. It is an opportunity for students to demonstrate understanding, mastery and application of their learning.

Options for Student Structures

Any design option for curriculum, however, still needs students! There are basically three structures used to organize students for curriculum integration:

1. Classroom or grade
2. Across grade or ability
3. School-wide

Classroom or grade

For many teachers, beginning the integration process at the classroom or grade level is the easiest to grasp. At the very least, there is no need to upset the existing school schedule. The classroom and grade level are the frameworks in which teacher education, schools and curriculum continue to function. Integration here is only one step. If we honestly commit to new visions of education, new ways of teaching and a wider understanding of learning, then we need to look beyond the conventions of grade levels.

Across grade or ability

Curriculum integration across grade levels and ability levels sometimes begins with "classroom buddies," a purposeful connection and commitment between two classrooms of different grades. Coordinating units of study between the two grades offers rich opportunities for learning. Specific content areas, activities or curriculum modules offer helpful first connections. Examples of successful ventures include hands-on science activities, art lessons, literature-based reading programs and journal writing.

Fifth graders at Winthrop Elementary School regularly meet with their kindergarten buddies during the school year to do hands-on, exploratory science lessons. The nature of the lessons intrigues both age groups. The presence of older students permits the inclusion of experiments that are interesting to the five- and six-year olds, but that require skills that five- and six-year olds are just developing—measuring, fine motor coordination and reading skills. Instead of one adult to twenty-six students, there is a 1:1 ratio. The older students often learn new material in preparation for teaching their buddies and gain deeper understanding of the content. Sometimes the tables turn, and the younger students teach their fifth-grade partners.

During the 1992–93 school year, second graders at Devonshire Elementary School shared with their fifth-grade buddies what they learned from their unit of the solar system. Each second-grade classroom became an "expert class" on a particular planet. When the fifth graders began their research projects on the planets, they tested out some of their initial questions with the second graders. Second graders were proud to teach fifth graders; and the older students began to see their younger schoolmates as knowledgeable partners.

A by-product of cross-grade buddying and curriculum integration efforts is the strengthening of the adventure learning community through healthy, mutual relationships among the children. One teacher explained, "My kids no longer see the first graders as 'babies.' For some of our students, the classroom buddies are the best part of their week. It's what they look forward to."

School-wide

If we can look at integrating curricular content across grade levels, then why not explore curriculum integration across the entire school? Full integration of all subject areas, social skills, thinking skills and well-defined sequencing of curriculum at every step may be an impossible task for some schools, but there are steps to initiate school-wide integration.

School-wide themes are an effective means to integrate curriculum throughout a school. The Cedarwood and Devonshire Schools have used both monthly and quarterly themes. With everyone in the school focused on a particular theme, resources are better utilized. School spirit improves. If everyone, from kindergarten through sixth grade, special needs and resource rooms, media and library operate inside the theme of "Diversity," for example, the shared

language strengthens everyone's sense of membership. A school-wide theme encourages more sharing among the school community members, including staff, parent volunteers, administration and faculty. For example, the door opens for the reading specialist to share with a group of third and fourth graders, students whom she might not otherwise teach, her experiences as a school teacher in Asia.

Common curriculum as center for school-wide integration. Another way to initiate school-wide focus on a theme is through an all-school curricular concentration. The Cambridge City Schools, Cambridge, MA, have developed district-wide health programs across the curriculum that have been the linchpin for staff development, integrated curriculum development, team building and restructuring efforts. Throughout the entire school system a range of efforts defines and integrates the notion of "health." Individual schools define what a healthy school looks like and identify necessary steps to nurture it. Teachers and staff reflect and redefine their classes with this shared lens. What does a "healthy class" look like? How do the members of a healthy class live and work together? How can we teach in ways that reflect our understanding and goals?

At the Cedarwood and Devonshire schools, classroom teachers go with their students to physical education class and assist the P.E. teacher. As they plan cooperatively within grade levels, the classroom teachers and P.E. teacher determine social skills that they all address simultaneously. Early in the year, for example, the focus throughout the school is on cooperation. Students play cooperative games in gym, talk about what makes a game cooperative, how to play cooperatively and identify skills necessary for cooperation. Cooperative learning skills are embedded in academic curriculum back in the classroom. In the gym and in math groups, the children pay attention to developing cooperative strategies.

Parallel or similar activities throughout school to implement theme. The common experiences of an annual field trip, local celebrations or experiences at a camp, environmental, historical or arts center foster school-wide curricular integration. Cedarwood and Devonshire schools use the facilities of a local camp, Camp Mary Orton. Each school has designed its particular sequence of camp experiences for its students. But in both cases, students from the entire school, over the course of the year, have anywhere from a one-day to a three-day challenge ropes course experience at the camp. This becomes a school-wide organizing center and opportunity for school-wide curricular integration. Teachers can better sequence the various environmental studies, science, math and writing projects. The entire camp experience becomes a way to shape the larger curriculum of subject matter along with the "metacurriculum" (Fogarty, 1991) of group social skills and thinking skills.

Another example of a school-wide activity is the all-school sleep-over that Devonshire and Cedarwood organize each year. Sleeping bags, pajamas, teddy bears, popcorn and snacks, movies and games are scattered throughout various rooms on the night of the sleep-over. Everyone, from kindergartner to custodian, secretary to student

teacher, proud fifth grader to principal, stays overnight at the school. Students participate in the planning process. They determine how much popcorn their grade will need, how many parent chaperones they will need, what movies should be on hand. Students manage permission slips, develop checklists for overnight gear, plan activities for each other and make arrangements for local businesses to donate beverages.

Beyond the various writing, language arts, math and group management skills, students practice in preparation for the event, the school community grows with the shared experience. Students see teachers as human beings, bundled in bathrobes and slippers, washing sleepy faces and brushing teeth. This experience goes a long way to strengthen commitment to school and to each other. The rough and tumble fourth grader is a little less likely to snatch a playground ball from a group of second graders who snuggled in sleeping bags next to her on the gym floor. A first grader, confused about where to go for indoor recess, is more likely to ask the third-grade teacher with whom he had shared popcorn during school sleep-over night.

While these various instructional designs enrich the repertoire of structures for integration, they remain incomplete. Curriculum integration within these models focuses on integration of academic subjects. While blurring the boundaries of disciplines is an important step in improving curriculum, the step is limited. The omission that shackles existing models of curriculum integration is the omission of the human experience of learning.

The power of the AITC model is its purposeful and consistent attention to personal and interpersonal growth and development, and the deliberate shaping of curriculum and instruction to facilitate that growth and development. The challenge, then, is to embrace something bigger and more significant: consistent instruction, facilitation, practice and processing of interpersonal skills and personal growth along with cognitive and metacognitive learning.

A Broader, Deeper Meaning of Curriculum Integration: Intentionality and Curriculum Integration

Though curriculum has been defined in many ways, I… use it… to mean all of the experiences of learners in the context of the school.

— *James Beane*

Regardless of the labels—*metacurriculum*, *critical and creative thinking skills* or *affective domains*—the processes of learning academic content and learning about self and each other must be incorporated into the school curriculum for truly effective, meaningful learning to occur. Integration must be an intentional integration of —

- The two curricula of school
- Content and processes of learning

- Individual, curricular and learning community needs

Integrating the Two Curricula of School: The Shape of the Matter

We need to acknowledge that two curricula operate in schools: 1) the obvious subject or discipline related curriculum; and 2) the curriculum of relationships. This second curriculum is the unwritten curriculum that is so intricately connected to how we go about our teaching and learning and that we are so often inarticulate and unintentional about it. This second curriculum may be more visible in classes with names like "Senior Decisions" or "Peer Mediation" or "Family and Society." But the fact of the matter is that interpersonal skills and self-management require attention in the science lab, the computer class, physical education and French.

In discussing content, then, we must include the content of interpersonal and intrapersonal learning along with academic learning. In other words, *content* includes the conventional subject areas as well as the content of interpersonal and intrapersonal knowledge and skills. In the high school classroom this means that students study the factors that led to the American Civil War and learn about effective decision making; and they learn about both experientially. Students read, explore, engage in the issues surrounding the Civil War just as they read, explore and engage in decision-making strategies. Fifth graders not only study the Pilgrims and learn to set STAR goals (see Chapter Six), but set goals around their study of Pilgrims as well as their problem-solving skills.

Intentionality is key. Teachers cannot wait and address interpersonal or intrapersonal growth when a crisis occurs. Teachers cannot wait until the day after a weekend riot to talk about managing conflicts. Managing conflicts is an intimate, intentional part of the visible curriculum of science, math, English and social studies.

I think back to my early days of teaching when I considered myself responsive to adolescent development and student needs. I was friendly with my students. I engaged in conversations about things that had personal interest for them. But those conversations were not connected to *Macbeth* or English poetry or the American short story. When interpersonal conflicts arose, I treated them as separate from the curriculum, something that had to be dealt with in order to go ahead with what we have to study. This compartmentalized approach to teaching isolated the "real" curriculum from the classroom, ignoring rich opportunities for learning that addressing interpersonal growth in the context of the classroom and in connection with the academic curriculum would have permitted.

Integrating Content and the Processes of Learning: The Mind of the Matter

Intentional integration of the two curricula of schools must also address the processes of learning and not just the content. A fully integrated curriculum incorporates metacognitive learning. A thematic unit of study that hinges on a school-wide theme and incorporates skill development of problem-solving strategies is incomplete if it does not include consistent reflection and learning about the processes of the learning. As the Experiential Learning Cycle reminds us (see Chapter Four), we must consciously attend to reflecting, generalizing and abstracting learning in order to transfer new knowledge and skills. Curriculum integration must unite metacognition with cognition in both the academic and behavioral or social skills subjects.

Educators and students today benefit from the research that demonstrates the role metacognition plays in the learning process. In addition, the various approaches to teaching critical thinking validate the significance of metacognitive instruction and increase the strategies from which teachers can draw.

Processing the content and learning of social skills

The term affective education suggests that somehow affect can be isolated from episodes in which its form will be educated...we should avoid use of the term affective education and instead speak of the place of affect in the curriculum.

— *James Beane*

There are two primary reasons for the deliberate focus on processing of behavior and social interactions in the AITC model. First, reflection and feedback are necessary for one to learn about the effects of one's behavior and the success of one's efforts to make behavioral changes. Second, the mere existence of community means people interact with each other, need effective skills to do so and have feelings about those interactions. To refuse to acknowledge feelings or address behaviors is like ignoring the "check oil" light on the car dashboard. Something is happening under the hood. The oil is low and the car is heating up, but the problem won't disappear because the driver doesn't check.

In the same way, students have feelings about what is going on in the classroom and need to process their attempts to develop social skills. Laura worries about finding her lunch money. Jermain is thrilled to be finishing his lab report. Tanya and Will can't agree on the right answer for the last question on the lab quiz. The adventure classroom must teach students the skills to identify, monitor and appropriately manage their behavior. Ordering behavior ("You need to control your temper!" or "Don't get so upset next time!") is not managing behavior. Ordering group norms ("You need to listen to each other.") is not developing group norms. Students must learn strategies and practice skills to be more effective members of their learning community.

Processing the process of learning content

Effective teaching and learning incorporates regular reflection and attention to the thinking and problem-solving skills related to the subject at hand as much as it involves rigorous academic content. Students need to learn how to approach content, not simply receive the lessons. Some folks identify this part of learning as the *critical thinking curriculum*. Skill building around how to grapple and work with content is as important as the material itself. Learning how to analyze the opening scene of Tennessee Williams' *The Glass Menagerie* is only important as having a reason to carry out that analysis and the ability to apply those analytic skills to other pieces of literature, art, music or social science. The ability to process how one learns lays the groundwork for life-long learning.

Integrating Goals: The Heart of the Matter

In mapping out this chapter, I colored and highlighted the various topics to indicate connections that were apparent to me. Next I drew circles and arrows to remind myself which diagrams illustrated which points. Interestingly, the circles that I drew around integrating individual, curriculum and learning community goals formed a heart shape. I saw this pattern of goals that address the various needs within the adventure classroom as the heart of integration.

The adventure classroom addresses three sets of goals throughout its time together:

1. Curriculum goals

2. Individual goals

3. Learning community goals

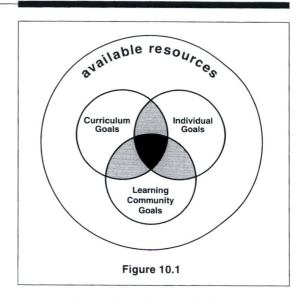

Figure 10.1

Curriculum goals include the content, skills, syllabus and the various learning goals for that class. These are the goals that we immediately think of when we make choices about what needs to happen in class.

Individual goals are the academic and behavior goals that each student has, the particular learning needs of each student, the various learning styles preferences alive in the class. These individual needs overlap with the curriculum goals. After all, the responsible teacher designs curriculum that responds to the various needs of his students. He designs lessons that connect to each of the learning preferences and incorporates opportunities for students to work towards their particular goals.

Learning community goals are the corporate, team goals. These are both academic and behavior goals. The entire group, for example, needs an operative understanding of the concepts of oxidation and reduction and needs to develop better listening skills. Again, there is some overlap. Four students in the class have chosen to work on their listening skills; and half of the class has made it clear that they are still confused about oxidation/reduction.

Optimal learning occurs where the three goal sets overlap. This is the place of in-depth, connected, meaningful learning (see Fig. 10.1). Because the individual goals are specific to each student, just what this place looks like and how it is experienced is slightly different for each student.

It would be nice if the overlaps were consistent and congruent, and each set of goals received an equitable portion of the available resources. However, the needs within each class are ever changing. Some days there is a remarkable balance. Other times one set of goals requires more of the available resources and overshadows the other two. For example, Chuck comes to class fuming about being pulled off the first string defensive line. For the next half hour, he cares more about football than English or the learning community (Fig. 10.2). If, on the other hand, the teacher is concerned that the class hasn't been making progress on their short stories, he is going to place more emphasis on the curricular needs, temporarily subordinating both the learning community and Chuck's individual needs. Choices also isolate learning community needs from individual needs (Fig. 10.3). The important question is, "Have I made careful and intentional choices? Are the choices the best ones with regards to the sets of goals?"

Unfortunately, the resource pool of time, materials, personnel, individual and collective energy and physical space is finite. Regardless of the waxing and waning of needs, the class period remains constant, the teaching staff fixed, the budget firm and the players set. The needs and their attending goals are complicated and many. The teacher's job

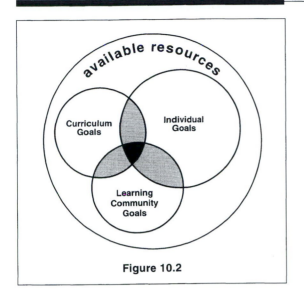

Figure 10.2

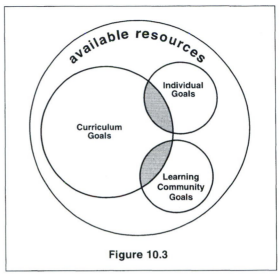

Figure 10.3

is to balance, integrate and make *intentional* choices. If Chuck chooses to spend half of class fuming about the football coach, he needs to be aware of what that means to his classmates. Any feedback from class members should address the issue. If the teacher decides to push the task of writing, he needs to acknowledge that some folks will not be able to work on behavior goals. The teacher must consider how those choices will affect the entire adventure learning community. Such dilemmas are not red flags. They are reminders of the need for intentionality and wise choices.

Getting Started

We have, to this point, looked at curriculum integration from the existing paradigms of curriculum integration and a new approach to integration that takes into consideration three levels:

1. Intentional integration of the two curricula of teaching

2. Intentional integration of content and the processes of learning

3. Intentional integration of three sets of goals in the classroom

The following are comments and practical suggestions gleaned from teachers in the field who integrate curriculum.

Learn From Others

There are many experts in the field of integrated curriculum. Among them are Robin Fogarty, Heidi Hayes Jacobs, David Perkins, James Bellanca and Robert Marzano. Some focus on the integration of subject areas. Others provide models that infuse teaching about the processes of learning into content. Read, hear, learn from those folks who address that area of integration you require. There is no need to re-invent the design process. In addition, there are classroom teachers who do excellent work integrating content and process, the two curricula of schools and subject areas. Learn from those who have done and are doing.

Keep Your Focus

Maintaining focus is just as important in the design process as it is in the actual teaching/learning and processing of the learning experience. A unit rich in both academic content and the processing of content learning, needs the infusion of social skills. Put new energy and focus there.

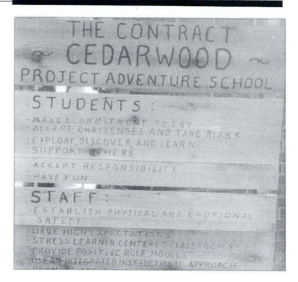

Before developing a newer version of the same content, complete the integration process.

Maintain focus during the processing of a lesson, too. If the initial reflection needs to be on the content, then use processing techniques that keep it there. If the class needs to process the interpersonal skill development or metacognitive activity, then maintain that focus. When it is time to shift gears, be conscious and transparent about it: "I can see that you have some other ideas about Hamlet's motivation to deceive his mother, but let's take the remaining time to discuss the strategies you used to analyze Acts III and IV," or "Let's reflect on your various behavior goals and what you did to reach them today."

Identify a Specific Time

Many teachers, anxious to intentionally integrate the interpersonal curriculum with the subject-related content, begin with a set time that is "interpersonal skills," or "communication skills," or even "Project Adventure time." When Beth Acinapura began incorporating adventure activities and integrating social skills, she began with Project Adventure time on Tuesday morning. She presented an activity to specifically address or introduce a new group skill, process a theme or behavior issue. This became a building block for the rest of the week. The *Two-Person Trust Fall*, for example, opened dialogue around the need for communication in order to build trust between team members. As the week progressed, and students worked in new cooperative groups, they related their experiences with the

Two-Person Trust Fall. They referred to the effectiveness of clear commands and learned to speak directly to each other about their needs in the group. The key was that students had processed their Project Adventure time and transferred those experiences and lessons to other classroom activities.

Kathy Moore and Michelle Harkins, at Cedarwood Elementary School, use the morning circle time to talk about behavior goals with kindergarten and first-grade students. Students set their goals for the day. Sometimes they do an activity that introduces or teaches a new interpersonal or group skill. This does not mean that interpersonal skills are left out of the conversations as the day progresses, but that circle time focuses the students on behavior goals, and brings those interpersonal skills to the front of the discussion. We set aside time to teach a particular writing or editing skill or introduce a new music concept. Why not do the same with the interpersonal and social skills curriculum?

Another way to foster integration of the two curricula of the classroom also comes from Kathy Moore. Right inside Kathy's classroom door is a large chart of twenty-four library tag board pockets that go in the back of library books to hold the checkout card. On each pocket is a face that indicates some feeling, such as *happy, tired, excited, mad, lonely, nervous* and *interested*. Each child's name is written on a wooden popsicle stick. As children come into class, they put their name sticks in pockets that identify their feelings at the time. Students are free to move their names to other pockets as the day progresses. The chart is a way for Kathy to get a general read on the collective state of her students. It also opens the door for communication about feelings and checking in with individuals. While this strategy is not directly tied to a particular academic curriculum, it raises the shade on the interpersonal curriculum.

Look for Connections

As you look at integrating social skills curriculum with academic curriculum, look for natural connections in the existing curriculum. For example, a three- week unit on *Charlotte's Web* lends itself to lessons about identifying feelings and using appropriate means to express feelings. Wilbur, early after his move to the Zukerman's farm, feels lonely. He struggles with his sadness. He tries to escape. He looks for his stomach to warm his heart. He asks other animals to play with him. He cries. How do *we* deal with loneliness? What are healthy ways? What are unhealthy ways? What makes us feel lonely at school? What do we do when we feel this way?

Four teachers from Torch Middle School in Los Angeles, CA, took advantage of the history and literature unit on the English Middle Ages to incorporate development of a Full Value Contract. They introduced the lesson with an adaptation of *Mine Field*, where objects (or mines) are strewn over a confined area and blindfolded participants traverse the area with the help of sighted partners. The students were Robin Hood's Merry Men attempting to return to the safety of Sherwood Forest with out being caught or wounded by the King's soldiers. The various objects strewn over the ground represented swamps, rivers, traps and weapons deployed by the King's men.

The teachers processed the activity in terms of obstacles preventing its completion and identifying skills necessary to avoid those obstacles. Students identified the need for "listening," "clear directions," "paying attention to my partner," "go slow," "praise" and "asking questions." The processing led the students to transfer those obstacles and skills to their academic work. The class then wrote the skills on a pair of oversized dice. The group rolled the dice three times. The six skills that came up were the processing and social skills for the class to focus on throughout the week.

These teachers extended the visual and kinesthetic learning for their students by taking the activity one more step. On a large archery target, they wrote the six skills according to where the students wanted to hit them by the end of the week. "Talking one at a time" was at the bull's eye, as was "praise." But the remaining four skills were targeted at other points based on an informal prioritizing of the skills. Through the week, as students demonstrated their work toward reaching the various goals, they wrote their names on paper arrows and placed them on the appropriate skill as a form of self-evaluation.

Identify Particular Skills

In a similar vein, explore one metacognitive or interpersonal skill to center curriculum over an extended period of time. The Devonshire Elementary School has identified four school-wide, quarterly themes that shape the interpersonal and metacognitive curricula and frame the academic topics. *Cooperation, problem solving, environmental awareness* and *community service/giving back* are the themes for each two-month cycle. As second graders study space and the planets of the solar system during December, they study it from the vantage point of problem solving. What are the challenges facing the exploration of Mars? When the second grade moves on to reading *Katie No-Pocket*, they look for the various problems that Katie faces and how she meets her challenges.

With the aid of the all-school, five-step problem-solving process, the children look at their own personal challenges in class, on the playground and in the lunchroom, as well as the challenges facing the historical or fictional characters they are studying. By the time the two-month theme is completed, the problem solving process is internalized by every student and at work in every corner of the school—from understanding Curious George and his problems to how to handle an argument in the classroom.

Plan with Intentionality

Whatever the beginning point, plan with intentionality. Be clear with yourself and your students about what metacognitive, cognitive or social skill is in focus. Know your goals. Know your choices. Know your reasons for making those choices.

There are a variety of ways to look at the intentional planning process. One tool, used by T. C. Motzkus, at Badger Middle School in West Bend, WI, focuses on the integration of social skills and clarifies each step to be considered—from team learning strategies to identifying the processing focus (Fig. 10.4).

The Experiential Learning Cycle (see Chapter Four) provides a structure for planning and facilitating the academic curriculum as well as the curriculum of group development, behavior change and social skills. These lessons can occur separate and distinct from each other, or integrated and facilitated as one lesson.

If a math lesson, for example, is presented apart from the proposed social skills lesson, it should, nevertheless, incorporate reflection upon interpersonal and/or personal learning, and tie into the various behavior or group process goals that the students have in place. This can happen in one of two ways. First, as the class moves through the Experiential Learning Cycle, and reflects, at step two, on the content and the processes of learning the content, they also take time to review and assess their group and/or individual process of the activity.

A second scenario is that the class moves through the four steps of the ELC with a distinct focus on the academic content—the math lesson, for example. The class then repeats the cycle with a focus on group process. In either case, be distinct and keep the target clear. "Right now we

Curriculum Adaptation to Include Social Skills to Promote "Eustress"*

1. WHAT IS THE TARGETED SOCIAL SKILL? _____

2. ACTIVITY CATEGORY TO ACHIEVE SOCIAL SKILL:
   _____ ICE BREAKER _____ TRUST _____ DECISION MAKING OR /PROBLEM SOLVING
   _____ DE-INHIBITIZER _____ COMMUNICATION _____ SOCIAL/PERSONAL RESPONSIBILITY

3. HOW WILL THE ACTIVITY BE BRIEFED
   _____

4. POSSIBLE ACADEMIC LESSON SOCIAL SKILL CAN BE INFUSED INTO:_____

5. GROUP SIZE _____

6. ASSIGNMENT TO GROUP: _____ PERSONAL GOAL _____ GROUP GOAL

7. TITLE OF ACTIVITY _____

8. MATERIALS NEEDED _____ _____
   _____ _____

9. PURPOSE/OBJECTIVE OF ACTIVITY _____
   _____

10. CRITERIA FOR SUCCESS/EXPECTED BEHAVIOR _____
    _____

11. METHOD USED TO PROMOTE POSITIVE INTERDEPENDENCE
    _____ TASK _____ FANTASY _____ IDENTITY _____ ROLE _____ RESOURCE
    _____ ENVIRONMENTAL _ _____ GOAL _____ REWARD _____ OUTSIDE ENEMY

12. TEAM ENCOURAGEMENT STRATEGIES LOOKS LIKE | SOUNDS LIKE

13. DEBRIEFING (PROCESSING) ACTIVITY WILL BE DONE BY:
    _____ TEAM (COUNSELING METHOD) _____ TEACHER (FEEDBACK)

14. OBSERVATION: _____ STUDENT (TEAM MEMBER) _____ TEACHER _____ BOTH

15. DEBRIEFING WILL FOCUS ON: _____ WHOLE TEAM _____ INDIVIDUALS

16. EVALUATION +1 -1 (CHANGES FOR NEXT TIME) _____
    _____

* Good Stress

Figure 10.4

are just going to look at this lab experiment and the mechanics, logistics and learning of the material. After we have done that, we will talk about how each of you worked in your small group." The important task of the teacher is to clarify the issue on the table and keep the reflection, generalizing and transfer of the experience focused on either the content or the processes of learning at any given time. There are times when you might have to say, "I know you want to argue the validity of this theory right now, and we are going to come back to that in about ten minutes; but at the moment we are looking at how you handled disagreements and misunderstandings in your group."

Start Somewhere

Whether you begin with curriculum mapping, weekly goal setting, daily reflection time or connecting literature and social studies curriculum, it's important to begin somewhere. Don't let the number of choices immobilize you. Gardening catalogs both excite and frighten me. The huge selection of plant varieties overwhelms me. At some point I have to make a decision and order some variety of blueberry bushes. If the new shrubs produce, that's information I have for next year.

Regardless of your satisfaction with the results of your first steps, consider the experience as information which informs your next choices. The revised "Heroes and Heroines" unit, which incorporates history, music and science, works well. The next time around you are ready to be more direct about teaching social skills along with it. If the originally planned implementation of individual journal time on a daily basis ends up to be too repetitive, then you know to look for one or two more methods of personal reflection to vary the processing.

Nike has good advice: "Just do it!"

"Yeah, but..." A few Words about Two Dilemmas

You may agree that learning is a function of perceiving information and processing the experience, but the voices of caution ring out, "Yeah, but..." There is, "Yeah, but I don't have time to talk about feelings," and "Yeah, but on Friday we do affective education." These are the two dilemmas facing attempts to integrate curriculum—the *dilemma of time* and the *dilemma of compartmentalization*

The *dilemma of time* is an incessant irritation. As one social studies teacher lamented, "My students have to be ready for state exams by the end of May. I'm supposed to cover all the pertinent material in this three-hundred page history book, teach in cooperative groups, require one piece of formal writing from the students every two weeks and include a unit on multi-culturalism. And you want me to spend time leading class discussions about interpersonal skills?" Making a choice to incorporate instruction, practice and feedback around social skills is making a choice to spend time. Initially it might feel like, and even look like, time spent here is time lost to World War II, calculus, French or reading. In fact, efforts to teach students specific skills for team learning and how to give effective feedback to each other are investments. They are investments in student involvement, classroom management, student achievement and academic excellence.

The *dilemma of compartmentalization* also challenges teachers. Uncomfortable and ill-prepared about how to "do it," curriculum coordinators, teachers, department chairpersons assign an isolated place in the week or in the curriculum where "affect can be taught," as if human beings only have an emotional life at prescribed moments of the day. This is similar to the conventional approach to teaching academic subject areas—"Math is what we do in the morning." While there is a need to identify particular behavior goals or social skills to emphasize at a particular time, we are short-sighted if we think the only time these skills are important is "on Friday." After all, "Affect is one dimension of humanness and functions simultaneously with other dimensions in learning experiences. Therefore, education *must* be affective and cannot be otherwise, just as it must be cognitive and cannot be non cognitive" (Beane, 1990).

Summary

Curriculum integration is messy business. But then an integrated curriculum mirrors life; and life is messy business, too. Curriculum integration cannot be ignored in school. Human beings have a basic need to integrate the many experiences of life. At the same time, otherwise esoteric or uninteresting material comes alive and elicits personal meaning for students through curriculum integration.

Curriculum integration typically focuses on various design options for integrating subject areas as well as strategies for grouping students. A broader, deeper look at curriculum integration highlights the need for intentionality in curriculum integration and attention to integrating—

- The two curricula of school
- Content and processes of learning
- Curricular, individual and learning community goals

For all its mess, however, curriculum integration is necessary for in-depth learning. Intentional, comprehensive curriculum integration is imperative if we expect students to meet their intellectual potential and emerge from our classrooms as competent, skillful, thinking, caring and creative human beings.

Adventure Activities

The adventure activities described in this appendix are activities mentioned in preceding chapters. There are hundreds of other activities appropriate for the range of classroom purposes suggested throughout the book. The following examples present only a sampling of that wealth. See page 233 to learn more about Project Adventure's activities books.

Toss-a-Name Game (Name Game/Memory Circle)

Object

To learn or review factual information. While this activity was originally intended as a way for students to learn each other's names, the game lends itself to content review and checking for understanding.

Props

Gentle throwable (GT) (fleece ball, softie, squishy or rubber animal)

How to Play (name game version)

The group of between eight and fifteen students stands in a circle, arm's distance apart. One at a time, going around the circle in sequence, each member calls out her or his name, passing the GT along the way. When the GT passes around the group and returns to the first person, that student calls out someone's name in the circle and lofts the GT to her. That person calls another individual's name and tosses the GT. Remind students that it's important to get eye contact before throwing the ball.

After a few rounds, add "thank you's." As students receive the GT, they thank the thrower *by name*, before calling on someone else to pass along the GT.

Variations

To learn or review factual information, students come into the circle prepared with two or three true/false or single answer questions appropriate to the topic being reviewed.

The key is that questions must be brief and answers unambiguous (yes/no; correct/incorrect). Someone begins the process by asking a question, then calling on someone in the group to answer. Toss a GT along with the question to remind folks to keep focused, be clear on who is asking the question and who is answering. But have fun, too.

After answering the question, that person asks a question, then calls on another student to answer.

Allow for passing and for collaborating as appropriate in the group. For example, if students have been working in cooperative teams, team members can assist each other in answering or forming questions. Also encourage building on questions. For example, if the question about Macbeth is "What is Macbeth's tragic flaw?" an extension question might be, "Where is the first evidence of this flaw?"

Other ways teachers have adapted this activity include:

- **Multiplication tables** — Each child needs to be ready to call out and/or answer multiplication problems ("Five times three" or "Seven times four").

- **Spelling or vocabulary** — Children call out spelling or vocabulary words for the "catcher" to spell or define or put into a sentence. This works with teaching both primary and secondary languages.

- **Reading comprehension** — Students come to the circle with short answer or true/false questions to ask of each other. The thrower asks the question, then tosses the GT to someone who answers the question.

Speed Rabbit

Object:

This activity elicits a good deal of laughter. While you can use *Speed Rabbit* as a tone-setter activity, it is also appropriate to use in introducing the concept of cooperation. It can also be used to introduce the class to characters, animals or concepts that can be pantomimed, or as a review of traits or characteristics.

Props

None

How to Play the Basic Game

A willing game initiator (the teacher?) stands in the center of the circle. His responsibility is to point to a person in the circle and name one of several animals: elephant, rabbit and cow are good starters. The signified individual, and the partners to her immediate right and left (this makes a three-person team) must make the pose of that animal before the center person can count to ten.

If the sequence is not done correctly or in time, then the offending person must take the place in the center. If the sequence is performed correctly, then the initiator points to another person, calls out one of the animals and counts to ten, hoping that someone will make a mistake. When someone eventually makes a mistake or doesn't complete the sequence within the allotted time, that individual changes places with the person in the center.

The animal sequences are as follows and, of course, can be (should be) amended or added to as play continues.

Elephant

The person pointed to:

1. Extends her right arm forward, palm down, hand lightly cupped.

2. Brings the left hand under the right arm and up to pinch the nose.

3. Flaps the right arm up and down, as if flapping a trunk. The two players to the right and left of the flapping trunk must flap their "ears" by waving their hands next to their ears.

All this happens simultaneously before 1, 2, 3,...10 is reached.

Rabbit

1. Center person hops up and down.

2. Person to the right stomps his right foot. Person to the left stomps her left foot.

Cow

1. Center person interlaces fingers of both hands and presses both palms out away from his body, resulting in both thumbs point to the ground.

2. Side people must grab a thumb and mime a milking motion.

Variations

This activity works well in units on rain forests, biomes or geographic regions. The animals the class uses are those critters indigenous to the region (this may be your only chance to get a half dozen marsupials in one room!).

A middle school team of teachers once used this activity with their mythology unit. The students picked out various characters from Greek and Roman mythology and figured out how to demonstrate them in *Speed Rabbit* fashion. This mythology version of *Speed Rabbit* ended up helping kids get a better handle on those characters they had trouble remembering. It also sparked discussion about the essential qualities of the various characters and helped students internalize material they had been reading.

Fire in the Hole

Object

This activity is basically a chance to laugh and make a lot of noise, so it's not a good choice when the class next door is taking an exam.

Props

- Balloons, inflated and many!

How to Play

Find out if anyone knows what the exclamation, "Fire in the hole!" means. This is one activity where the name really sets the tone.

With one or two partners, students place a balloon at about mid-torso level between them. The placement of balloons is just as important as the appropriate placement of dynamite. With arms around each other, partners shout, "Fire in the Hole!" and hug each other vigorously.

For a variation, five or more people form a circle, all facing in one direction (so that one person's chest is facing the next person's back) with a balloon between each player. Again, after the warning, "Fire in the Hole!" each person hugs the person in front. If all goes well, balloons will be popping in firecracker fashion amidst a bit of laughter.

Variation

This activity is a good way to culminate a series of balloon activities (*Boop, Balloon Frantic* , etc.).

Boop

Object

This cooperative activity requires non-threatening touching, a little ingenuity and some group flexibility and coordination. The group's goal is to keep a balloon off the ground while staying connected.

Props

- Inflated balloons

How to Play

Players, in small groups of three or four, join hands. The groups are spread out enough to allow for moving around. Each group has a balloon that it tries to keep aloft while holding hands. Any body part can be used to accomplish the task.

After a minute or two of "freestyle," the teacher can call out a particular method to use to keep balloon aloft; e.g., "Chins, only," or "Knees, only," or "Elbows, shoulders and pinkie fingers."

Variations

This game can be played while students are sitting on the floor. Rather than holding hands with each other, students must keep their bottoms on the ground.

Friendly competition can be introduced, so that groups compete for the best time without dropping the balloon or the fewest drops in a set length of time. The class as a whole can compete against itself, working to improve their overall time or reducing the number of drops within a two-minute period.

As a cooperative activity, *Boop* works well to introduce elements of cooperation — setting goals, working collectively toward the same goal, joining strengths, strategizing together, talking and listening to each other.

Traffic Jam

Object

Two teams work together to completely exchange places on a line of markers that has one more place than the number of people in both groups. The players need to be in the same order when they arrive on the other side. While this is a great problem-solving initiative, it also addresses the themes of communication and leadership. Questions to consider include, "How does one get to be a leader in this activity? How does one's place in the line affect participation? How does it feel to be in the back of the line, away from the action? How does the group address these issues?"

Props

Something to mark places—masking tape, paper plates, rug squares, rubber spot markers.

How to Play

One half of the group stands on places to the left of the middle, open spot; the other half of the group stands on places to the right of the middle, open spot. Relying on legal moves only, the students on the left side must end up in the places on the right side, and vice versa.

Legal Moves

- Students can only move in one direction. No backward moves permitted.

- Students can only pass someone facing the opposite direction. In other words, team members cannot pass one of their own group.

- Students may only jump or pass one person at a time.

- A student may only move into a spot that is already open.

- Only one person can move at a time.

Variations

This activity has been used successfully to illustrate algebraic equations. Students chart the number of steps necessary to complete the activity. They determine the number of steps necessary to complete the activity if the group size is 4, 6, 8 and 10. Patterns begin to emerge and it is possible, then, to predict the number of steps necessary for a group of 20 to complete the activity, a group of 50, even a group of 1,000,000. Students can write a mathematical formula that predicts the total number of steps required by a group of any size to complete the activity.

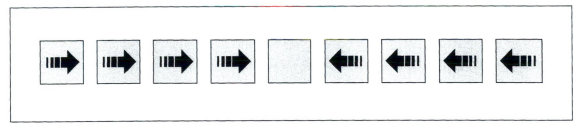

Impulse/Squeeze

Object

To pass a hand squeeze around the group. This activity works in several contexts and for several curricular goals.

How to Play

The class forms a circle with everyone holding hands. Someone starts the impulse by squeezing (gently) the hand of the person on either the right or left. The one who receives the squeeze squeezes the hand of the next person, and so on. This hand squeezing continues so that the impulse goes around the circle until it gets back to the person who started it.

Variations, Thoughts and Other Ideas

Impulse usually works best with groups of fewer than thirty players. If the group gets too large, action gets slow and people can get bored.

Among the various curricular goals this activity lends itself to are the following:

- *Stimulus /Response.* From either a science, health or social studies standpoint, this activity illustrates the concept of stimulus/response, both physiologically and metaphorically. Students experience the sensation of receiving and then sending a stimulus. They see that people have different reaction times. They can speculate on the shortest amount of time it takes for a reaction and consider the contributing factors. Challenges can be introduced, such as closing eyes, outside noises or distractions, crossing hands.

- *Goal setting and problem solving.* The group can challenge itself to break its own record and try to set a time for passing the impulse.

- *Rhythm and music.* Notice what happens when the group sends around a hand clap or other percussive sound. How does establishing a rhythm affect the maintenance of the *Impulse*? Why?

- *Opening or closing a class time.* The impulse can be introduced as a non-threatening hug or gentle welcome or good-bye. As people pass the hand squeeze, they may offer a thank you to the group, extend a wish for the group or for themselves, share a thought or hope for the day.

An impulse can be made more challenging by introducing one of several variations:

- Send the impulse in a different direction from the first time you went around.

- Send two impulses simultaneously but in opposite directions. The impulse will cross somewhere near the halfway point of the circle and both impulses should get back to the starter at about the same time.

- Pass around a word, silly sound, funny face, whistle or tune.

Monarch

Object

This is a tag game that begins with one It, or Monarch, who tries to turn all of the Anarchists into members of the Monarchy.

Boundaries vary according to the size of your group, but allow enough room to run around.

Props

Gentle throwable (GT) such as a Nerf ball, fleece ball or softie

How to Play

A volunteer begins as the first lonely Monarch. The Monarch has possession of the Nerf ball, fleece ball or other GT (symbol of the Monarchy) and tries to tag the Anarchists (other players) with the ball. When an Anarchist gets tagged, that student becomes a member of the Monarchy. The two Monarchs then work together to hit another Anarchist, etc., etc. Anarchists, of course, don't want to join the royal family, and try to avoid being caught. Once they are tagged, however, their allegiance quickly changes, and they become enthusiastic loyalists, eager to convert the insurgents.

Include two balls (two Monarchs) at the start of the game if the group numbers more than 20 players.

Rules

- If an Anarchist runs out of bounds, she or he automatically becomes a Monarch.
- Monarchs cannot run when they have the ball in their possession. The only Monarch who can run with the ball is the first one, when he or she is acting alone. Once someone else joins the Monarchy, there is no more running with the ball in hand. The ball can be passed to another Monarch.

Variations and Other Thoughts

This activity works well to address a number of group or membership issues, including the following:

- What does it feel like to be a member of the minority group? The majority group?

- How do allegiances change when membership changes?

- How do you maintain membership as an Anarchist? What strategies do people use to keep from being caught?

- How do members of either group assist each other?

- How is membership in the Anarchy different or similar to membership in the Monarchy? What differences, if any, did you experience as a member of one group in contrast to the other?

- How is this like what happens at school? In society?

In addition, the experiences and processing around this activity can provide an effective bridge to various social studies topics, including civil strife, changing citizenry, immigration and balance of power.

One elementary school teacher calls this game *Monarch Butterflies*, and the opposing factions are caterpillars and butterflies.

People to People

Object

Have some fun, a few laughs and play cooperatively. This is a good activity for dismantling anxieties about appropriate touching. If students are willing to tag and hold hands (occasionally, if it's not for long), *People to People* is a great game to extend that willingness in a non-threatening manner.

How to Play

Students stand in a circle with partners. A caller stands in the middle of the circle (it's a good idea for the teacher to be the first one in the middle).

Set an easy finger-snapping rhythm that everyone can join in on. A nice blues or rock beat works well. When the group gets warmed up, snapping together and bouncing to the beat, the caller begins calling out body parts, in beat. The partners join with each other using that body part. For example, if the caller announces, "Elbow to elbow," partners touch elbows to each other. If the caller calls, "Thumb to shoulder," partners join their thumbs to each other's shoulders. The caller gives a series of contact points, trying to keep the beat, and allowing a few beats for partners to figure out and remain joined together. Partners make the appropriate changes each time until the caller finally shouts, "People to People."

When the caller yells, "People to People," everyone changes partners while the caller tries to enter the circle and find a partner. This means that someone else becomes the caller.

Play continues until it appears that all reasonable combinations have been exhausted, everyone has had a chance to be in the middle, forty-five minutes have passed, or whichever comes first.

Variations

I've known some teachers who have used this to reinforce vocabulary of human skeletal system ("tibia to humerus" or "patella to femur") as well as second language vocabulary (can you do, "Ellbogen und Schulter?").

Quail Shooters

The object of *Quail Shooters* is to focus and catch as many objects thrown to you as possible. The problem is that are as many objects, or more, as there are people simultaneously lofting them into the air!

Props

Lots of gentle throwables like softies, rubber chickens, Nerf balls, fleece balls. There should be one or two objects per student.

How to Play

Students stand in a circle, about arms distance apart, each person holding one or two GT's. A volunteer stands in the middle of the circle. On a collective count of "Three," the players loft their GT's high into the air and toward the person in the middle, who tries to catch as many as possible.

Students should be allowed to volunteer to go into the middle. This is an activity that challenges the common notion of success, and the initial feeling of failure at being unable to catch very many objects can be intimidating. As the activity continues, though, and it becomes clear that "success" is measured in small amounts (one or two balls caught), the willingness to give it a try increases.

Variations, Thoughts and Considerations

This activity illustrates a number of group development and process topics, such as:

- *Community or team building* — How does the group work to both challenge and support the person in the middle? Where does the leadership need to be? How does the group respond to different leadership?

- *Success* — What is it? Who defines it? How do we measure it? What does it feel like when we don't achieve it?

- *Goal setting* — Who sets the goals? How are they determined? How does setting goals affect outcomes? What considerations must be part of goal setting?

- *Making choices and setting priorities* — How are priorities and choices made? What role does leadership have?

If you have a large group or want a different way of playing this, more than one person can go in the middle. The score is the total number of balls caught by the students in the middle.

The group can work as a whole to "break its record" with each new catcher or pair of catchers.

Establish restrictions for catching, for example, you can only use your hands and arms, or only use what you have on your person.

Assign values to the various objects and work towards a goal; e.g., fleece balls = 1 pt., rubber animals = 5 pts., softies = 10 pts.

Object Retrieval

This activity is a great problem-solving initiative that elicits numerous themes for processing or focusing on various community issues; e.g., leadership, communication, decision making, including all members, asking for clarification, allocating resources. The object is for a group to retrieve an object that is located near the center of a "danger zone," an outlined diameter of approximately 30', and to set it down in a safe area approximately 10'-12' away.

Props

- A length of rope that is longer than 60' to mark the perimeter of the circle
- Two lengths of rope or 1" webbing that measure 18'-26' long
- A bucket with a quart or two of water in it
- A bicycle tube cut in half or two, 2'-3' sections of bungee cord
- Hoola-hoop or 6' piece of rope to mark a safe area 10'-12' away from the danger zone.

Play

Set the bucket with water inside the circle, which has been marked off with the rope. Explain that the area inside the rope is a toxic waste area, lethal to all living organisms. The bucket, however, holds some vital material necessary to manufacture a new inorganic compound that can potentially neutralize toxic waste of all kinds. But if the material is lost or exposed to toxins before the manufacturing process is complete, it will be unusable in the process.

The group has a limited amount of time and resources with which to retrieve the material in the bucket and safely transport it to the manufacturing site (the safe area marked off by the hoola-hoop, and set several feet away).

Rules for Play

- Only the props listed can be used to retrieve the object.
- If *anyone* or *anything* touches the ground inside the circle, the retrieval efforts must start all over again.
- The bucket cannot be dragged over the ground, through the toxins.
- Human hands cannot touch the bucket (it is a sterile container).
- Set a time limit of somewhere between 20 and 30 minutes.

Variations, Considerations and Thoughts

This initiative can be adapted in numerous ways. For one thing, don't worry about having the exact equipment.

If you don't have a bicycle tube or bungee, add a couple of extra ropes or twine for props. Throw in a few balloons. A wastepaper basket or No. 10 tin can works if a bucket is unavailable. Pebbles, ping pong balls, tennis balls or sand can replace the water. Just be careful to choose something that makes carrying the bucket a challenge, but not so heavy, awkward or full that the task is impossible (just appears so!).

Add some items to the props that don't seem to be usable but might add some fun, inventiveness, as well as challenge the decision making ("Do we have to use all these things?")—kitchen utensils, sticks, noise-makers, for example.

The scenario can be adapted to meet your goals or themes. Have students label the balls or objects in the bucket: various strengths or skills of the students; the goals of the class or the individual students; resources; oxygen, carbon atoms; Congressional legislation or bills to be passed.

Spider's Web

This is one of the all-time classic Project Adventure problem-solving initiatives. The *Spider's Web* is a put-up/take-down, customized, fabricated "web," constructed of a frame, measuring approximately ten-feet wide and six-feet high and strung with bungee cord in such a fashion that no two openings are the same size or shape.

Object

The group must try to get through the web without touching any of the web material. After a web opening is used by someone, it is "closed" to further passage by anyone else until the entire class has passed through safely.

Rules

- If a student touches a section of web during passage, that person must return and start again.
- If a student who is helping another pass through the web touches the web for any reason, the helper also must return and start again.
- Once a web opening is used, it cannot be used again.

Some Considerations

The *Spider's Web* generates excitement and curiosity with its strong visual appeal. Most students see the *Web* as challenging but achievable, and they generally anticipate active roles in solving the initiative. The critical pieces for the teacher are: 1) framing the activity, and 2) observing and facilitating the processing of behaviors which this activity elicits.

The *Web* is either a simple exercise or an exasperating challenge, depending upon the consequences for touching. Touches can result in any of the following:

- Only the person touching returns
- All people in contact with the person touching return
- Any touch means all people return

Choices around consequences depend on the teacher's assessment of the group and the *Web*. No two *Webs* are identical in the number and size of holes, and no two groups are identical in the number and size of people. Likewise, the goals of your group, and its stage of developmental readiness, must enter into the decision making regarding consequences.

Once the consequences are clear, stick to them. The tendency to overlook a touch here, a brush there says, "Hey, consequences and rule breaking don't really matter," and students will soon take advantage of your leniency. As hard as it is to hold the class to consequences, the experience, behaviors and learnings from maintaining the integrity of the challenge generally prove to be worth the temporary discomfort.

This activity is effective in raising a number of themes:

- Organization and planning
- Group needs vs. individual needs
- Stereotyping according to physical strength and gender
- Honesty, truthfulness and integrity
- Facing obstacles, challenges and difficulties
- Lines of communication and changing leadership

5-5-5 Duo Stretching

Object

The body needs flexibility and movement during the day. Sitting at a desk for a four- or six-hour stretch in unhealthy. The brain also needs a change of pace, time to relax and change focus. Stretches can be part of any day's activity. In addition, partner stretches remind us to enjoy and learn more about each other.

Play

The following isometric partner stretches balance a menu of individual and group stretches.

- Facing one another with arms extended, students put both hands on each other's shoulders. (Try this exercise with a partner of near equal height.) Partners gradually begin trying to push each other into the ground. Increase pressure over a 5-second time span, maintain full pressure for about 5 seconds, and then gradually decrease pressure for about 5 seconds until back to normal. Ask one of the partners to count aloud in order to regulate and coordinate pressure applied. If this psyche contact is too "heavy," delete the audio ploy.

- Facing one another, have the students extend one hand forward as if they were going to shake their partner's hand. Keeping hands open and flat (not clasped) and with each arm fully extended, begin to exert lateral pressure on a partner's arm using the 5-5-5-second counting pattern as before. This is not a contest, so don't allow students to twist their bodies to gain a leverage advantage. Partners should remain laterally parallel to each other at all times. If done well, both students' hands should not move from side-to-side more than about an inch. The increased, maintained and decreasing pressure, with no movement, is a satisfying feeling of shared struggle.

There are numerous spatial variations to this cooperative exercise sequence. Ask the students to use their imaginations to come up with other 5-5-5 isometric exercise positions. Don't forget the use of legs.

Wall

The *Wall* is another classic low ropes course element. It presents a challenge that's both visually and physically imposing. Standing at the base of a twelve-foot, flat-fronted wooden wall, most students know that they cannot single-handedly scale this formidable obstacle. Fifteen minutes later, the group pats itself on the back for having achieved the impossible. On reflection, it becomes clear that the word "impossible" is too often and casually used. Even more important than that, the *Wall* reminds us that we are all capable of more than we imagine possible.

Objective

To physically, efficiently and safely move a group over an 8'-14' wall.

An 8' wall works well for students in grades four, five and six. A 10'-12' wall provides plenty of challenge for middle school and high school groups. Fourteen feet challenges older high school and adept college students.

Rules

- No more than four people are allowed on the wall at a time, including the person in transit.
- The sides of the wall may not be used in any way.
- The vertical support trees or poles cannot be touched.
- Cracks and knotholes cannot be utilized for hand-holds or climbing maneuvers.
- After someone ascends the front of the wall and climbs down the back, (there is usually a platform on the back side of the wall with a ladder or steps from there to the ground) that student cannot come back to the front of the wall and offer physical aid. They can and should assist in spotting.
- Anyone not physically involved in helping people over the wall should be in a spotting position, front or back.
- If a person leans over the wall in an attempt to get the last student over, that person must be supported by two other participants, both of whom have their feet on the standing platform.
- Articles of clothing cannot be used to aid a climber.

Safety Considerations

The most common fall experienced while ascending the wall happens in the initial attempts of the climber to get a hand hold, either with a helper on top of the wall, or on the top of the wall itself. Spotters must position themselves on either side of the climber, as well as underneath, and move with and in anticipation of the climber.

Anyone who is off the ground must have an active spotter.

The teacher needs to stay actively involved, because even students who work well together can lose focus or become overwhelmed with everything that is going on.

No two students climb the same way. Climbers sometimes need the teacher's intervention if they are unable to express themselves, or if the group isn't listening.

Clothing unintentionally torn off turns a wonderful group experience into hideous embarrassment for the student whose pants are accidentally pulled off or whose shirt ripped down the front. Talking about this in the beginning provides the group an opportunity to develop some strategies.

Adaptations and Other Thoughts

The *Wall*, as a metaphor, is that which separates the group from its goals—poor communication, lack of focus, unresolved conflict. The *Wall* is the challenge that we must meet in order to proceed or grow. The *Wall* is a group goal that cannot be accomplished without everyone's full effort.

Participation in this initiative is the opportunity to identify what the group can do to overcome the challenges. "Giving a hand" and "spotting" are really the concrete ways students help each other. "Listen to the person who is climbing" reminds the class to take an active role in helping each other academically and interpersonally.

Teachers have used the metaphor of the *Wall* to help students experience and understand the challenges others have faced in lessons on the civil rights movement, women's suffrage, immigration, diversity and cultural change. Students not only have a personal experience with overcoming the *Wall*, but transfer that to the experiences of others and more easily identify with the struggles of those who have overcome the walls of segregation, hatred and misunderstanding.

Another way to frame the *Wall* is in terms of personal walls. Students can look at the *Wall* as signifying those things that stand in the way of their personal, academic or behavioral goals. From here they identify what they need and how others can assist them in reaching those goals.

NOTE: For further guidelines about spotting and preparation for falling activities, refer to *Cowstails and Cobras II* (1989).

Two-Person Trust Fall

This activity, often referred to as a "trust activity" is, in my thinking, a communication activity. After all, honest, clear communication is a building block of trust; and trust grows as the communication and the experience of trusting increase.

Object

Student partners take turns spotting and falling, maintaining safety and good communication.

Play

The activity begins by having the faller stand in front of the spotter. The faller should cross her arms against her chest and stand straight, with knees locked.

The spotter faces the faller's back, standing with one foot slightly in front of the other and knees slightly bent to maintain balance. The spotter's hands are raised to match shoulder height with the faller.

The faller and spotter set up a communication sequence, which they commit to always using. A typical sequence might sound like—

> ***Faller:*** "Are you ready to catch?"
>
> ***Spotter:*** "Ready to catch."
>
> ***Faller:*** "I'm ready to fall."
>
> ***Spotter:*** "Fall away."

The communication always ends with the spotter—the person who has ultimate responsibility and the final word on safety. The faller should be reminded to secure her arms across her chest to ensure not throwing out arms and elbows.

After the spotter announces, "Fall away," the faller leans back to fall directly into the hands of the spotter.

The faller must remember to fall backwards, as tightly and as straight as possible. The faller must keep knees and body straight and fall directly backwards.

Willow in the Wind

This communication exercise brings the entire group into the circle of communication and support.

Object

For the group to support a person standing in the middle as he leans into the group and is then gently passed around and across the circle.

Play

Ten to fifteen students stand shoulder-to-shoulder in a circle with one person (the faller) standing in the center, rigid, with arms folded across his chest. The spotters hold the spotting position as above (one foot slightly in front of the other, hands raised to shoulder height).

The group establishes a communication sequence similar to that of the *Two-Person Fall:*

Faller:	"Are you ready to catch?"
Spotters:	"Ready."
Faller:	"I'm ready to fall."
Spotters:	"Fall away."

Remaining rigid, the faller leans slowly in any direction, maintaining a straight, stiff body and locked knees. Before he moves very far off plumb, the circle people redirect the faller's impetus and begin to move him around the circle, passing the faller from spotter to spotter in a very gentle fashion.

After one or two rotations, the spotters can gently nudge the faller to different places in the circle, if the faller will want this less predictable motion.

This fall-catch-nudge sequence continues in a gentle fashion until it becomes obvious that the center person is relaxing (but remaining rigid) and that the spotters have gained confidence in their ability to work together toward handling the occasional weight shift of the faller.

The group needs to stay focused with the faller until he is guided to stand up in the center of the circle and has regained his balance.

Change people in the center until everyone who wants to has an opportunity to be a *Willow in the Wind*.

Adaptations and Considerations

This activity lends itself to numerous metaphors for classroom and group development application. Some of the themes that emerge from it include—

- Physical, intellectual and emotional safety
- Building trust
- Reliability
- Lines of communications
- Individual and shared responsibility

Curriculum

Curriculum development is a complex and dynamic process that challenges the various methods teachers use to document it. The outlines and brief descriptions in this appendix are only snapshots from a sampling of curriculum that teachers have developed within the framework of the AITC model. While these few pages do not do justice to the work and creativity of the many teachers who have developed adventure curriculum, I hope these snapshots provide a glimpse of the possibilities.

Space Travels

First-grade unit developed at Cedarwood Elementary School, Columbus, OH

It's grey and cold with winter dampness outside, but inside first-grade classrooms the mood dances with anticipation. Today is "Astronaut Training Day," the culminating activity of the month-long unit entitled "Space Travels." This grade-wide thematic unit has introduced students to the solar system, the study of gravity, the phenomenon of orbits and methods of space study.

Children wear "space suits"—jogging suits, wind suits and sweat pants and sweat shirts—and "moon shoes," also called sneakers! The excitement pulses, as today's activities are part celebration, part evaluation of the unit. The children make badges and review the role and preparation of an astronaut. "They have to be in good shape," announces Brian. "They're squeezed into a rocket together, so they really have to know how to work together," explains Talisha. "And they have to be good with computers," offers Sandy.

Today's activities tend toward more physical challenges, with an emphasis on the importance of fitness, good health and habits for astronauts. Each child carries a training card for the day which lists the various activities:

- Exercises — These warm-ups and stretches set the tone for the day and help to direct early morning energy.

- Space information test or "space challenge" — Here the children respond to questions from the unit which test both factual and analytical understanding of the material from the unit.

- Nurses station — Children have their height and weight measured and recorded.

- Zero Gravity Climb — This is the indoors ropes course challenge typically named the *Zip Line.*

- Moon Walk — This is another renamed initiative, the *Trolleys.*

- Cooperative Moonrover — The children will maneuver with partners through this cooperative obstacle course.

- Illustrations — As the soundtrack from *2001: A Space Odyssey* plays, the children illustrate their ideal space journey.

The day ends with awards presented to each child, an exchange of appreciations or thank-you's and a processing activity of writing postcards to family "back home."

Unit Design

In deciding upon and developing this unit on "Space Travels," the teachers began with what interested their students. Space had been a high-interest topic and provided a wealth of opportunities to address the academic and social skills mandated by the Ohio State Course of Studies for first graders and identified by the school. The teachers brainstormed activities, paying close attention to both the school's commitments to Project Adventure skills (problem solving, trust, cooperation, risk and challenge) and to the subjects stipulated by the state (language arts, science, health, social studies, math, reading, art, music, physical education). They chose activities from their brainstorming which provided a balance of subject areas and skills, and refined lessons to ensure as comprehensive a curriculum as possible.

Astronaut _____		
Height	**Weight**	**Cal**

Moonwalk	Zero Gravity Climb	Cooperative Moonrover	Space Challenge

Training Card

All activities integrated skills or concepts that are traditionally isolated to separate subject areas. For instance, students wrote books about their imaginary trips to the moon. Study about the moon's surface and atmosphere led to a problem-solving activity identifying survival needs for human beings on the moon. Students worked collaboratively on their books, relying on collaborative skills as they developed language and writing skills. Illustrations for the books were "art" projects, but also demanded that the children think about how pictures could elaborate on words and blend fact with fiction. Similarly, a lesson about stars and constellations incorporated art with reading, language arts and science.

A lesson built around Byron Barton's *I Want to be an Astronaut* began with the reading of the book. The children then chose partners in order to trace each other onto kid-size pieces of paper. The children then had to imagine how the outlines would look different for an astronaut who is suited up, ready to head off on a mission. The children altered the outlines accordingly. Later in the day, as the discussion turned to the planets, each student chose a favorite planet. The class graphed the choices to see the spread of answers and then shared reasons for their respective choices. Comparisons between different pairs of planets reviewed the students' skills in identifying "more than/less than" and articulating relationships as number facts. The day concluded with a cooperative initiative where students worked in groups of four to design a space craft. They built the craft with a variety of household materials—cans, construction

Space Travels

Project Adventure Planning Tool

Grade Level: 1st   Unit: Space

Activity	Problem Solving	Trust	Cooperation	Risk	Challenge	Language Arts	Science	Health	Social Studies	Math	Reading	Art	Music	Physical Education
① Paper Mache Earth with Key	✓		✓	✓			2.01		1.01 1.02 1.04 1.05 1.06 5.01		1.28	1.05 3.04 3.08 3.12 3.13		
② Astronaut Training Camp	✓	✓	✓	✓	✓	2.01 2.13 2.15	2.04 2.05	5.05 8.01	2.08 3.01 3.02 3.03 5.01					2.01 2.02 2.03 2.04
③ General Discussion on Solar System	✓	✓	✓	✓	✓	3.02	2.01 2.02 2.04		5.01	8.01 8.03 9.10	1.05 1.06 1.28			
④ Planet mobile with information	✓	✓	✓	✓	✓	2.01	2.01 2.02		5.01		1.28	1.05 1.06 3.04 3.12 3.13		
⑤ Role play orbits science book	✓	✓	✓	✓	✓	2.01 2.07	2.01 2.02		5.01	2.01	1.05 1.06 1.28			
⑥ Problem solve- needs a moon-book 4 Trip to the Moon	✓			✓	✓	2.01 2.07 2.13	2.01 2.03		5.01		1.05 1.06 1.28			
⑦ graph- sim. and diff. between sun-moon-earth	✓	✓	✓	✓	✓	3.02	2.01 2.02		5.01	8.01 8.03 9.10				
⑧ Flashlight experiments	✓		✓		✓		1.02 2.02 2.03 7.07		5.01					

Project Adventure Planning Tool for *Space Travel*

paper, cotton, rubberbands, paper rolls, toothpicks, yarn, egg cartons, etc.). As each group shared its creation, it also had to explain the reasons behind the choices of building materials.

Evaluation and Extension

While student and unit assessment were ongoing, the culminating day, "Astronaut Training Day," focused teachers and students for a final evaluation.

This unit was a favorite of students and teachers, as it grew from an area of interest to the children and tapped into their curiosity about space and space travel. It is a unit that can fit into other larger thematic contexts. A study of the solar system fits easily into themes such as systems, community, risk taking or cooperation.

Over the Rainbow

Third-grade unit developed at Devonshire Elementary School, Columbus, OH

Sheets of newsprint checkerboard the floor of Room 23. Third graders huddle over papers labeled "Problem Solving—Wizard of Oz actors." In small groups, the children tackle the problem of researching biographical information on Judy Garland, Ray Bolger, Margaret Hamilton, Bert Lahr and the cast of the well-loved movie, *The Wizard of Oz*. Having recently watched the movie, the class prepares to embark on its own journey entitled, "Over the Rainbow." Before the six weeks are over, these children will have read, written and studied about rainbows, tornadoes and other weather phenomenon. They will have presented oral reports about the actors from *The Wizard of Oz* and written comparison and contrast studies of the other titles in Frank Baum's Oz series. For now, though, they prepare to do some library research and begin to establish classroom norms around team learning.

The teacher calls the class back together from their small groups and asks, "What problems did you have when you were working on your charts?"

"It was hard to hear!" exclaims Beth. "The group next to us was too loud, and they kept asking us what we were doing."

For the next few minutes, the class looks at the problem, "Noise in the classroom," and comes up with shared solutions to dealing with this very real challenge. Since the school-wide theme for these first two months of the school year is "Adventures in Cooperation," the

social skills woven into the Over the Rainbow unit will focus on such behaviors as "six-inch voices," "sharing materials," "asking for ideas," and "attentive listening"—all skills necessary for a cooperative learning environment.

As lunch rolls around, the teacher asks, "How is our classroom like a rainbow?"

"Different colors come together to make a rainbow," offers one boy. "I guess in our class different people have to learn how to work together."

Beginning with the familiar: *The Wizard of Oz*

In developing this curriculum, the teacher saw the familiar story of *The Wizard of Oz* as a "hook" for the children. It was something familiar, but the same time it opened the door to the new and unfamiliar. In addition, the theme provided numerous connections and textures, full of possibilities for exploration and learning. As they researched information about the actors, for example, the students learned about the making of the movie, and began to look at the familiar with new lenses. None of the students had read the novel which inspired the movie, nor were they aware that Frank Baum had written an entire series. The story about Dorothy, Toto and her traveling companions opened a door to a host of language arts activities and skills. Students interviewed family members on the topic, "There's no place like home." They published a newspaper from Munchkinland and

> **"Problem Solving -
> Dorothy wants to get home"**
>
> **1. Fact-Finding**
> >   Gather information
> > >   Dorothy wants to go home
>
> **2. Problem-Finding**
> >   Finding THE problem
> > >   Dorothy doesn't know how
> > >   to get home
>
> **3. Idea-Finding**
> >   Brainstorm solutions
> > >   see the wizard
> > >   ask Glinda
> > >   click her heels
> > >   wish real hard
> > >   pray
> > >   just stay with her friends
> > >   don't fall asleep in the
> > >   poppies
>
> **4. Solution-Finding**
> >   Select best solution
> > >   see the wizard
>
> **5. Acceptance-Finding**
> >   Make a plan of action
> > >   the friends stick together
> > >   to help each other get to
> > >   the wizard
> > >   don't give up

printed the front pages of Dorothy's hometown newspaper and *The Oz Gazette*. As they read *The Road to Oz*, *The Marvelous Land of Oz* and other titles in the collection and wrote journal entries of various characters.

Unit Design

On a practical level, the Over the Rainbow unit blurred traditional subject area boundaries. Students conducted and wrote about experiments with prisms and bubbles. The children learned about the color wheel, played with primary, secondary and complementary colors, and made their own rainbows using only the primary colors of red, yellow and blue paint. They learned about tornadoes, studied weather cycles and wind currents, created a "tornado in a jar." Hot air balloons captured the interest of some children who built their own hot air balloon models, relying on research, math, art and science skills. Writing and reading were integral to each of these projects, and lessons on punctuation and writing paragraphs addressed specific skills. But rather than relying on a sheet of drills to teach or review the various math or writing skills needing attention, the teacher used the work at hand as a context and a reason for learning.

The social skills aspect of this unit focused on skills necessary for effective cooperation and the sharing of tasks and responsibilities. The students determined their own goals. They identified appropriate group and individual rewards, and explored the nature of shared responsibility in a cooperative group. They developed their personal definition of cooperation, then came to a consensus as to the working definition they would use in their classroom. Their common vocabulary helped build the foundation of cooperative operating norms at work not only for this unit, but for the entire school year.

To initiate discussion around the topic of goals and rewards and shared responsibility, the students compared and contrasted the various jobs of the characters in the story—Glinda, Dorothy, Tinman, Lion, etc. They compared and contrasted these characters with people in the school and in the classroom. Who are the organizers? The encouragers? Who is a good listener? They made charts of the long-term and short-term goals that the various characters had, and then made charts of their own goals for the unit. Using the five-step problem-solving tool that is part of Devonshire life (see Chapter One), the students identified problems that the characters faced along their journey and outlined the steps that either the individual or the group took to meet the challenge. From here the children assessed and evaluated the different approaches then defended their decisions by making speeches. With this process, the students learned skills necessary to analyze choices, motivate others, make decisions and apply reason —skills necessary for their own development in problem solving.

Evaluation and Assessment

As the Over the Rainbow unit progressed, the room was transformed into a museum of rainbows and Oz. Student-made rainbows, newspapers, goal sheets, cooperation charts and Oz characters adorned the room. Large problem-solving posters outlined the challenges faced by Dorothy and her companions. Story maps summarized the various titles in the *Oz* series that students read. Displays about atmospheric changes, weather patterns and different types of storms demonstrated the students' understanding of meteorology.

There was evidence of learning and internalizing of the skills of cooperation and problem solving. Students worked in groups, took on the responsibilities of various tasks, checked up with each other on their work, asked each other for help. They gave each other "appreciations" at the end of the day and reminded each other to use "six-inch voices." They shared resources of time, material and ideas. As they lived the challenges and advantages of cooperation in their classroom, and saw from their own experiences the benefits of teamwork, these students laid the foundation for an operating norm that guided them throughout the year. "Cooperation" was more than just an easy answer to the question, "So what helped you?" or "What's important about working together?" Cooperation had real-life meaning.

Student Experts

Each student has become an expert on a particular animal and has researched, read, written about, mapped the habitats, graphed the reductions in that species' environments, measured the dimensions of the animal ("Hey! the blue whale is as long as the hallway from the boys' bathroom to our classroom!" "My tree frog is only as long as this eraser!"). They have probed such questions as, "Why is this species endangered?" "Why do people 'use' this animal? Is there something else they could use?" "What happens if this animal disappears from the earth?" and "What can I do to help?"

Even though the "Expert" status is individual, the skills, resources and learning outcomes have been shared. This means that students have approached each other for help and information. They have collaborated on aspects of their projects. They have also been responsible for teaching each other about the individual species under study and have been accountable to learn information about each other's animals at the same time they develop various reading, math, inquiry and team skills.

In addition, the fourth graders have written ABC books about endangered animals with their first-grade buddies. They put into practice their learning about self, each other and the content. The opportunity to explain information to others helped reinforce and refine their understanding. After all, leave it to a first grader to ask the hard questions: "Do panda bears ever lose their teeth?" and, "Where do the frogs lay their eggs?"

Endangered Species

Fourth-grade unit developed at Cedarwood Elementary School, Columbus, OH

It's Thursday, and fourth graders at Cedarwood Elementary School talk excitedly as they prepare for the "Zoo Architectural Convention." For the past several days, each cooperative student group has focused on the needs of a particular animal in captivity. Students have brainstormed and drawn up plans to best meet those needs. They have built models and prepared presentations. Today is the day that they unveil their plans and give oral presentations at their mock convention.

The children put the finishing touches on posters and models of various structures to house animals. They shuffle note cards, rearrange desks, set out paper mâché sculptures of blue whales, harbor seals, tigers and tree frogs. At the front of the room, two children arrange four chairs for the invited guests, parents and community people who have agreed to judge the designs based on thoroughness of research, detailed planning, practicality and cost effectiveness.

The zoo facility project pushed students to hone their research skills. It required students to calculate, measure and draw to scale. They had to be accurate with their information and accurate in their scale model. This project taught students about the procedures necessary to carry out a building project and helped students to transfer this learning to other complex problem-solving needs. Students strengthened their problem-solving and communication skills. They applied team skills, established and monitored group goals. In many ways, this project pulled together various skills and subjects integral to the entire unit.

Unit Design

Early in the unit the classes went to the Columbus Zoo to see loggerhead turtles that had been hatched in captivity and were in preparation for transport to the Virginia shoreline for release. This visit introduced the topic of protection of animals and the involvement of zoos in carrying out that work. The students grappled with such questions as, "Why should we care about loggerhead turtles and the seacoast?" and "What makes an animal endangered, anyway?" The visit to the zoo also initiated a research project on the housing of endangered species. This included mapping zoos who care for these animals as well as the locations from which threatened animals come and where they are released. Students quickly recognized that people all over the United States and beyond care about endangered animals. The children also learned that there are many creatures in the world that are in peril, and that many strategies and programs exist to protect them.

These first activities provided an overview of endangered species, so that by the time students needed to choose an animal for their own study, they were familiar with a wide range of possibilities. In other words the opening activities broadened the students' horizons so that the children were better able to make educated choices. These

youngsters knew that there were more creatures in jeopardy than just whales and panda bears!

As the students researched various organizations involved in the protection of animals, they wrote letters of inquiry regarding the institutions' operations. Charting of organizations, the species with which they work and the types of action they take (studying, protecting habitats, raising young, creating legislation, providing veterinary/medical treatment) became material for various math lessons. These included different graphing techniques and the use of ratios and percentages. All of the unit's activities were language rich with reading, writing, editing, proofreading and speaking. Students researched with the aid of books, tapes, zoo keepers and computers and learned about their particular animals. Learning about a rhinoceros, for example, meant finding out what it eats, where it lives, what it needs to survive and thrive, what its "family life" is about, what its play is like. After all, we can best take care of a rhinoceros in its natural habitat or in captivity only if we know what it needs.

The literature used in the unit, *Charlotte's Web,* by E. B. White; *Old Yeller,* by Fred Gibson; *Cricket in Times Square*, by George Seldon; and *Help! I'm a Prisoner in the Library*, by Eth Clifford, opened the discussion around the social skills central to the unit ("How did Charlotte show her concern for Wilbur?" "Why was it important for the farm animals to cooperate?" "How did the settlers care for each other?" "How do you let someone know when you are disappointed or hurt?"). Similarly, lessons

Zoo
Designer's
Checklist

Checklist -How well will your zoo take care of animals?

To the Designer: Don't forget these items as you design your zoo.

- Do the animals have privacy? Can they get away from visitors?
- Is it convenient for the animal to get food and water?
- Are all enclosures adequate in size and space? Can the animal walk at least four times its own length?
- Is there adequate sun or light for diurnal animals?
- Are nocturnal animals safe from direct or bright light?
- Is there good ventilation and air circulation in the enclosures?
- Do animals have easy access to heat and shade?
- Can the temperature be kept at an appropriate temperature for the animal?
- Are animals safe from harm from their cage? Are bars, doors, walls secure? Is the floor safe and appropriate for the animal?
- Is it easy to keep the area clean?
- Do animals have appropriate and safe stimulation? Are there toys, trees, things to rub against or dig in or climb, as appropriate to the animal?
- Are the sound conditions appropriate for the animal?
- Do birds have at least two separate perches or roosts?
- Do birds have ample space for flight?

— adapted from Living Trophies by Peter Batten

regarding animal communication presented opportunities for the students to compare animals' needs of communication for survival with human beings' needs to communicate for survival in life, in school, on the playground. The class examined the qualities of "good" or effective communication as communication that is appropriate to a situation and to other beings.

Evaluation and Assessment

As the three teachers of this fourth-grade team developed their unit, they knew that the students would recognize connections between their lives, their actions and the needs of other human and non-human living beings. They planned for the transfer of learning to other subject areas and to behavior in and around school. What they hadn't anticipated was that the students would recognize a responsibility they had right in their own school to the creatures in the school *Cocoon*, a room-sized zoo of birds, small mammals, amphibians and reptiles.

Having studied about the survival needs of blue whales, Amazon sloths and Bengal tigers, the

Schedule

While the unit was initially designed to be the emphasis of the afternoon for the opening six weeks of school, various topics ran throughout the entire day or were picked up at other places in the school schedule. For example, physical education class focused on the roles of nutrition and physical exercise as keys to good health. Another feature of the units' structure was the dedication of morning class time to particular skills necessary for the thematic unit. The morning was time for review, remediation or learning new skills. For example, reading groups met for specific instruction during the morning. Students who needed additional help in calculating percentages or ratios had lessons focused on those during the morning.

students asked, "But what about our hamster?" Very quickly these young zoologists made changes to better the conditions of their Cocoon charges. They purchased and sought donations of larger cages. They acquired additional shavings for bedding. They upgraded the food for the hamster and took it out of the cage daily so it could exercise. In true experiential learning fashion, the students acted on their new knowledge and applied it not only to their class work on endangered species, but to the very real, very alive charges right in their own community.

Biomes

Fourth-grade unit developed at Devonshire Elementary School, Columbus, OH

A five-foot paper maché cactus, tubs of sand, murals of desert scenery and rolls of fabric draped for shade from the burning sun greet the visitor to Room 24. At another part of the school, in Room 11, a Baobab tree bulletin board and a cardboard giraffe stand guard. These, too, are student made. Charts with riddles about the savannah are posted along with stories about life on the savannah. Around the corner and down another hall, monkeys, tree frogs, sloths and gorillas (all kindly made and stuffed by Dakin, of course!) inhabit Room 6. Vines drape from the classroom ceiling, richly hung with flowers, leaves, insects and animals who make the rainforest their home. And at another end of the school one enters the world of the seashore where a saltwater aquarium, collections of shells, sea stars and horseshoe crabs create places to explore. Students sit under a large beach umbrella or on beach towels to read.

No, the fourth grade is not "out to sea," or "lost in the woods." The fourth graders have become experts on four biomes of the Earth. The students in each classroom have researched and learned about one of the four biomes by immersing themselves in the environment. They have also learned about themselves and each other.

District curriculum requirements stipulate that fourth graders learn basic information about biomes and their ecology. Rich extensions and overlays of perspectives, subject areas and skills weave into a study of biomes and easily match the school theme of *environmental awareness.*

Expert Class Model

As is often the case in curriculum/unit development at Devonshire, the teachers decided to use an "expert class" model, whereby each class becomes experts about one phase of the topic, then teaches its material to the other students. Second graders participated in this model during their study of the solar system, where each class became experts in one or two planets. The basic inquiry questions for each expert group are the same as for the teaching strategies.

When it came time to teach each other about their biomes, students in each class had to come to consensus about what was important for the others to learn and how they were going to teach the material. They had to determine and delegate tasks. Did they need guides? What teaching materials did they need, and who was going to put them together? What questions were they going to ask of their students? What kind of experience did they want their students to have? Riddles, measurement activities ("Measure the height of the cacti."), estimation ("Estimate the number of prickles on each cactus."), spelling, calculation activities ("A mountain gorilla eats forty pounds of food a day. How many pounds of food would she eat in five days?") were among the activities students developed for their peers.

The Desert

_____ Rm. _____
name
and room #

A Desert is a place that is _____, _____ and _____, Very little rain falls here.

There are many deserts around the world. Some of them are in _____ and _____.

The animals of the desert sleep during the _____ because _____.

The people of the desert are called _____.

This means that they _____.

They live in _____ and _____.

Draw a picture of each [ ] and [ ]

group activity

With your class list how a cactus is different from a plant in the classroom.

Have your teacher write on your Room number's large paper

Exploring
Native American Cultures

Middle School Curriculum—Solomon-Lewenberg Middle School, Boston, MA

By focusing on a holistic approach to a study of Native American cultures, the eighth-grade teaching team of an urban middle school met the daily challenges of teaching in a school where more than half the children speak English as a second or third language and where urban violence batters these young students. Disciplinary boundaries were less important than meaningful connections between the history of others and the students' personal experiences. Disciplines became unique lenses from which to learn content and skills as students conducted original research and demonstrated the relevance of Native American cultures to their own lives. At the end of the unit, students praised the success of the study on the front page of the January, 1995 issue of the *Lewenberg News*, the monthly student newspaper:

The Solomon Lewenberg 8th-grade students studied Indians and their cultures for eight weeks. During the last two weeks we split up into eight groups by activities. Each teacher picked an activity and we signed up for which one we wanted.

The activities included beading, blanket weaving, building houses like teepees, long houses, and Pueblo Indian houses, and making things like dream catchers, corn husk dolls and totem poles.

We actually built a real life teepee and Pueblo Indian house. The teepee was about nine feet tall, and the Pueblo Indian house was big enough to fit three people.

At the end of eight weeks all of the different groups met together for a whole day to talk about their tribes.

It was a great experience and all the students enjoyed it. But it was more than that. You could see that the teachers also enjoyed it. They were very proud and happy that they could have helped us learn about different tribes.

On behalf of all the students, we would like to thank them!

During a final pow wow, the culminating activity for the unit, the students shared stories, gave performances, displayed artwork and celebrated their accomplishments. Visitors to the school were greeted by banners depicting various Native American tribes. Classrooms had been transformed into museums of Native American history and culture, complete with dioramas of dwellings, charts depicting accomplishments of numerous Native Americans, student published books of mythology and maps of various tribal boundaries. The students' pride in their achievements, skills and knowledge rivaled the excitement of connected learning and deep experience.

Interdisciplinary Approach and the School Schedule

The teaching team took advantage of the school day structure, where students moved between subject-related classes by turning subject areas into lenses with which to study various aspects of the larger unit. The social studies class provided a framework for looking at various cultural themes on a weekly basis, for example. Students explored the themes of displacement, communication, protest and images of Native Americans in our society. They read biographies and recognized that Native Americans are not just anonymous "cultures" but real people with real life stories. English, reading and bilingual education classes used the lenses of literature, especially mythology, to explore similarities and differences between not only different Native American groups, but also between the students' own understandings of such themes as love and friendship, world creation, heroes, war and fighting. In math, students developed computation skills necessary for working to scale; and in science, they focused on the relationship between humans and their physical environment.

A unique feature of the unit was that students worked in cooperative groups of four or five to conduct research on selected Native American tribes. As each group researched and studied cultural aspects of their tribe, they divided responsibilities and became experts on particular topics that enhanced the entire team's study. One group, for example, structured their research so that one member focused on family structures and tribal organization, while another became the group's expert on food and dress. Another team member researched customs regarding marriage, burial and rites of passage, while someone else learned about games, sports and art of the tribe. At the same time, the entire group was responsible to learn from each other and integrate the various topics as they wrote reports, gave oral presentations and constructed dioramas and scale models of dwellings.

Students remained in their cooperative groups throughout the day as they moved from class to class, refining their knowledge about their tribe and learning skills and concepts to further that study. For example, a student whose group focused on the Kwakiutl tribe and who took responsibility for learning about methods of transportation, learned research methods in social studies and gathered information about canoes. She relied on computation and conversion skills learned in math to construct a scale model of a canoe.

Personal Connections

In addition to focused, in-depth work, students continuously made personal connections throughout the unit. In English, for example, students read and wrote about Native American mythology. They studied literary devices such as irony, personification and symbol. They compared, contrasted and categorized stories, as the folklorist does, to identify common narrative conventions, plot structures and myth morals, along with the variants within each type of story. They made Venn diagrams to

Teachers learn through adventure: Excerpts from an interview with Larry Donnelly, social studies teacher, conducted by Gail Matthews-DeNatale, 1/5/95

LD: I had gone to an expedition down in North Carolina…When I came back, I was full of ideas and especially when I was doing this, I was getting influenced, because I was all full of the Cherokee. We looked over the treaty of Lachota. We were given names to pick and choose to role play…the various Native Americans, John Ross, Andrew Jackson, and all of the rest of the people. But we also tried to renegotiate it, where we got the people back together and the ones who didn't want to sign it the first time around, you know. We did every type of thing that you would do in a regular type of expedition in the school. Where usually I get hung up with the book and the fact and the book and the fact and question and answer. I went down there not knowing anything about the Cherokee…. And it was wonderful. We learned something….So coming back to teach the kids about things, I had pictures. I had slides. I had things to show the kids. And I was just talking about the Cherokee. It's instilled in me that I didn't realize the way they made a living and how they adapted and how they intermarried and how they had Scottish blood in them. I knew nothing about that.

…When I came back I really had a lot of stuff to give to the kids.

The point is that I got excited about the whole thing. And the more things become aware to you when you're…finding things in the paper…"Wait a minute—this is on Native Americans."

compare and contrast the versions, and saw that this method of graphic illustration is not limited to math class. As a culminating project, students created personal mythology books in which they compiled personal mythologies which they had written, edited and illustrated. Selected pieces from these books were later compiled into a school-wide literary magazine, thereby further extending the audience for these compositions.

The importance of making personal connections and constructing meaning and knowledge influenced the structure of the various learning activities as well as the processing methods woven into the unit. Students kept journals, for example, and in some cases, responded to writing prompts, questions or selected topics. In other situations, journals offered a place for free writing. Journals were used not only to address specific content learning or reflection on the literature or history under investigation, but also to assist students as they reflected on their own participation, strengths and growth areas.

Two early math and science activities which demonstrated the relationships between personal experience and new knowledge involved mapping and descriptive writing. In their cooperative groups students drew detailed maps of the school-yard flora and fauna, determining the number and exact location of trees and bushes, and noting inanimate objects. They measured, identified and labeled trees and assessed the rate of growth of saplings in the school yard. They recorded information in field notebooks, then used that information to

---

**The Full Value Contract
as written by students at
Solomon-Lewenberg School**

We Agree:

1. To work together and participate as a group so we can be successful at what we are doing. To help each other feel safe and not scared by saying good things and not de-value each other.

2. To understand each other so that we can work more and give more cooperation to get what we want in class, school, and life.

3. To receive and give meanings. To listen to what your teammates are saying. After that, you have to give your ideas to them in return.

4. To not call anyone names. Respect each other and help others. Try to cooperate with your team members. Do not put anyone down so their feelings won't get hurt. Be nice to each other. Do not leave out anyone or your-self when doing group activities.

5. To not hide our negative feelings about something that you are not comfortable with; get the situation settled and resolved.

---

determine how, as a tribe, they could best use those resources to survive in that limited territory.

The second assignment required students to write a detailed description of their bedrooms. When the students returned to class, they shared these with their group. After comparing backyard maps and bedroom descriptions, they developed charts about their yard inventories and the contents of an average student bedroom. However, they were not allowed to add information to either the map or description once they were back in the classroom. While students recognized from this first hand experience the need for detailed field documentation and gained practice in translating qualitative and quantitative data into charts, this also opened discussion regarding the interrelationship between natural environment, human-made living space and daily culture.

Because students worked in cooperative groups for most of the unit, addressing group needs, individual responsibilities within the group and interpersonal skills for effective collaboration were essential focus areas. Early activities, such as the school-yard research, provided initial practice in group collaboration and the opportunity to identify the needs and challenges for each group. Processing this activity focused on the content and related skills; e.g., looking at both the techniques for information gathering and recording of data, prediction of how a tribe would adapt to live in a territory circumscribed by the school's boundaries, description of culture based on this limited territory as well as interpersonal skills; e.g., assessment of the group's ability to work together, communication needs within the group, rights and responsibilities of group members.

A mask-making activity set the stage for a study on the role of masks in Native American culture, the creation of personal masks based on that study and also an opportunity for team building. Working in pairs, students molded plaster masks on each other. While the subject had to cover her face with Vaseline, the partner dipped plaster-coated gauze in water and placed it on the subject's face. The model had to wait ten to twenty minutes before removing the mask so the plaster could dry. The students then reversed roles. As students processed

---

Sample Math Self-Assessment Guide

Use this guide each day to monitor your progress and the quality of your work
(Not-So-Hot, Good, Very Good, Excellent!)

	NSH	G	VG	E!

1. Written Report:

Predictions........................... >_____

Information Gathered................ >_____

Ecological Description.............. >_____

Variables............................ >_____

Menu (3 meals)..................... >_____

Paragraph 1........................ >_____

Paragraph 2........................ >_____

Paragraph 3........................ >_____

Paragraph 4........................ >_____

Graph 1............................. >_____

---

this activity, they answered such questions as, "What did you learn about yourself while doing this activity? What did you learn about your partner? What was the most difficult part of this exercise? How did you get through these difficult spots?" They continued reflecting on the activity and identified specific ways that they could assist each other on their academic projects that would make their work more rewarding and more enjoyable.

The Role of the Full Value Contract

According to the teachers, the unit owed much of its success to the structure for processing student experience, reflective communication and awareness of behavioral norms which had been established before the unit actually began. The students had been operating with a Full Value Contract and continued to process much of their work during the unit in terms of the contract. In addition, extensive problem-solving responsibility rested in the hands of students who repeatedly challenged the Full Value Contract. Students had the power to voice their opinions and contribute to the success of the school, and those students who actively engaged in speaking up and making a difference modeled positive behavior for others who found it difficult to work toward a common good.

The Full Value Contract also maintained a context for self-assessment throughout the entire unit. On a daily basis students filled out self-assessment guides for math and science. Students also did self-assessments for their individual and group presentations and their final projects.

Teachers spent time with students to establish evaluation criteria as well as expectations. They discussed criteria for each letter grade and how the group would determine whether work was *A* quality or *B* quality. As the weeks progressed, students learned how to evaluate and assess their work. One teacher explained, "They were able to look at what was expected of them because there were some standards that we set at the beginning of the year regarding how we were going to do things and how we were going to assess what got done." Students were able to match their behavior and their work against those standards.

Another teacher made a point of listing for students the specific criteria for reports that would be critiqued. Before handing in their reports, students checked off the list and identified immediately what grade range their work fit. In addition, the students wrote a statement at the bottom of their reports about what grade they thought they deserved, along with a rationale for that grade. They then exchanged their reports and statements with a partner and gave each other feedback before finally handing in the work to the teacher.

As one teacher commented, "With self-evaluation, students get better at judging their work. They are willing to be constructively critical and not just say after the first draft, 'That's it.' Students know that what they are doing may be published, so they try to create works that are publishable. The students take ownership for producing high-quality work, rather than waiting for it to be edited by an adult."

Exploring Motion

High School, semester-long curriculum developed at Middle College High School and International High School, New York City, NY

The Motion Program is a twelve-week set of connected courses for students in grades nine through twelve which explores the concept of motion from the points of view of physics, math, English, physical education and health. Students see, predict and effect motion from the vantage of physics, describe and calculate it with the language of mathematics and play with it in writing. They physically participate in swinging, lifting and carrying in physical education where they also address the social skills and group norms necessary to carry the forward movement of the class.

Motion in Physics, Math, English, Physical Education and Health

During the physics concentration one day, students cluster in groups of three or four, talking, arguing, writing, explaining. With meter sticks, stopwatches, dollar bills and dominoes, they measure speed and reaction time, calculate velocity and plot graphs. No two groups are "on the same page." No one sits complacently. One group appears to have completed their activity while another group appears to be in the early stages of their's.

Four students at one table take turns timing how far a meter stick falls between a poised thumb and forefinger before the catcher stops the fall. Diligently recording the data, they note the differences in each other's reaction times, and discuss why this is so. At another table three girls line up a set of dominoes on their ends, careful not to knock one over into the mad tumble of a chain reaction.

Later in the day, these students look at speed, reaction time, measurement and calculation with the lens of mathematics. They drop weights so they hit the ground at equal and successive intervals and take measurements. Students with lower abilities in math look for patterns in the number sequences of drops. Those with stronger math abilities explore the contrast between differential calculus and integral calculus. In an activity using colored wooden sticks, another group predicts and calculates patterns of probability.

In English class literature and fictional writing further the exploration of the theme of motion. With Jack London, May Swenson and Carson McCullers as their guides, the students consider the relationship between motion and emotion and examine the ways authors "move" their characters and their readers. The students experiment with writing from different points of view to effect the motion of a story. When the curriculum turns to graphing, English class looks at the ways people's lives can be "graphed," at the effects certain events have on the course of one's life, at the ways one can learn from the shape of one's own life as well as another's.

In physical education, the students toss rubber chickens, fleece balls and deck rings as they call out each other's names and play tag games that help them to get to know each other better. Physical education is the world of motion, certainly; but in this program, it is the place where students develop the operating norms, goals and Full Value Contract which will frame their twelve weeks together.

Staffing and Structure

Originally, the motion curriculum supported twenty-five students and eight teachers—an expensive program. Team participation in developing the program and development of the teaching staff as a team were seen as essential to the program's success. Eventually, the team decreased to four teachers, so that one teacher is present at all times and the other three rotate. Each teacher is generally with the class for a seventy-minute period, during which time students work on interdisciplinary activities in self-selected cooperative groups of two to four members.

While each teacher has a primary subject focus, each activity has applications to all the subjects and blurs the boundaries. The teachers are intentional in their efforts to show students the interconnectedness of everything they study. This occurs both in the curriculum and design of the activities and in the relationships teachers have with each other and the subjects. Students see the physics teacher as a history teacher and an English teacher also. This happens because teachers move in and out of each others' classes and co-lead lessons and activities. In addition, classroom conversations include the various perspectives of the program. For

---

The Domino Effect   Name: _____

Partners: _____

_____

Date Completed: _____

Consider the Following situation:

Dominoes are placed in a line equally spaced from each other. See diagram below.

d = Spacing between dominoes

When the domino is toppled, describe what will happen?

Explain how your group would determine the average speed at which the dominoes are toppled over after the chain reaction is started.

---

example, students compare their reading of a Jack London story with their experience with predictions in a math activity.

In all classes students work in cooperative learning groups. The operating norms of the Full Value Contract and Challenge by Choice are consistent throughout the program and mean that students take responsibility for supporting and challenging each other. A student who is consistently late to class, for example, and complains that she can never get to the activity she wants, is confronted by the class who points out the effects of her lateness on her choices in class. When another student sug-

Sample Motion Worksheet

By varying the spacing between the dominoes and determining the toppling speed, your group can investigate how the spacing affects the speed. Vary the spacing of the dominoes and determine the toppling speed of the dominoes for each spacing. Complete the following table and graph your results.

Spacing,d (cm)	Time, t (sec)	Distance,D (cm)	Speed (cm/sec)

Consider the data you have just obtained. How can you find the spacing for the fastest toppling speed?

gests that his best friend get an *A*- on the unit, without considering that his buddy only completed half of the activities he committed to, it is other members of the class, not the teacher, who confront the incongruity.

Activities — The Starting Point

The experiential activities, the foundation of the program, are designed to work with multi-level abilities. For example, *The Domino Effect*, which asks the group to determine the average speed at which dominoes are toppled after a chain reaction is started, includes averaging, prediction, maximum and minimum curves, interpolation and extrapolation. *Traffic Jam*, where two teams exchange places in a restricted sequence, prompts algebraic expressions, explores pattern recognition and introduces calculus-based sequencing.

When students go to class, they sign in to do any one of two to four activities that are set up for the particular unit of study. This procedure serves to establish the working groups for the day as well as take care of attendance. Students gather with the other two to four classmates who have chosen that activity for the period. All activities take from two to three periods to complete, but none of them is precisely timed. The open-ended nature of the activities, along with the heterogeneity of the group, requires this flexibility. Students set goals in each class as to the number of activities they will complete, so that each student is cognizant of the work she or he needs to do in order to satisfactorily participate in the program.

Excel Program

High School English and Social Studies Curriculum developed at Groves High School, Birmingham, MI

Groves High School, in Birmingham, MI, enjoys the unique opportunity of having its own Experiential Learning Center right on campus. The Center provides a range of integrated course offerings, various service learning and wilderness courses and support for other departments interested in integrating adventure learning in their classrooms.

The EXCEL Program is an elective course that grants credit in English and social studies and is taught concurrently with existing English and social studies curriculum. A team of teachers representing both departments instructs in this course, which typically has an enrollment of about sixty students.

The students who take EXCEL tend to be highly motivated young people. The students must meet high expectations in the course, primarily in the form of individual and group responsibility for work and learning, group process and evaluation. Discussion of the topics and exploration of the EXCEL curriculum are the responsibilities of the students. The staff works hard to let the students know that they expect much, but are willing to be involved in the students' academic lives to ensure success. Both staff and students, therefore, are invested in the process of learning, and the students rise to the level of these expectations.

Urban Issues Project

An on-going theme of the EXCEL program is the exploration of social issues. Students look at these issues in their historical context through literature and writing. In small teams students choose and research outside of class those social issues that they study in the classroom setting. Among the issues addressed are—

- Public Transportation—What is the current state of public transportation in Detroit? What role does the size and demographic layout of Detroit play in this? What was the purpose of the People Mover? What is its function? What role does the expansion of air services play in the development of metropolitan Detroit?

- The Elderly—How do service providers define the elderly? What is the status of the quality of service for the elderly? What determines the quality of health care for elderly citizens? What should/could be done to improve services for this population?

- Ethnic Cultures of Detroit—What are the major ethnic groups that comprise the population of greater Detroit? Which ethnic groups were prominent in the past? How have demographic shifts affected the development of Detroit? What have been the patterns of urban migration in the last half century?

- The Legal System—How does the criminal justice system work in the city of Detroit?

How has the legal system met the needs of low income citizens? How are juvenile offenders handled? What are the challenges for the future?

- Cultural Detroit—Explore art in public places. What is the state of public support for the arts? What is the status of professional music organizations in Detroit? What is available in the area of theater?

- Environmental Issues—What environmental concerns face the city? What is being done about noise abatement? What are the citizens' groups actively involved with environmental issues?

- Gentrification—Define this issue. What effect has it had on the quality of life in Detroit?

- Physically Challenged—Gain an appreciation of issues facing those with physical challenges. What barriers face citizens with physical challenges? What improvements can be enacted to facilitate change?

- The Homeless—Why are individuals homeless? What services are available to this population? What can be done to better meet the needs of homeless people?

The students use a variety of formats to both direct and present their research: oral histories, news articles, legislation, court briefs, photo-journalism essays, docu-dramas and position papers. While the group must come to consensus about their topic and their format, they also must appoint a group editor who coordinates the research findings and presentations with the other research groups. The working teams, then, are responsible for both a topic and a product that must be presented to the rest of the teams and to their parents.

The Scheduling Challenge

In order to allow all sixty students to be actively involved in the urban issues project, yet maintain protected time for other English and social studies curriculum, teachers have staggered the schedule and each group's involvement. Each team has one class period to plan, two class periods to go off campus to conduct research, and one class period to coordinate their findings. Since this is a cooperative program between the English and social science departments, each class "period" lasts two periods, and students are scheduled into a study hall that backs up to this block, thereby allowing Experiential Learning Center staff to work with them for a half day each time (see Urban Excel diagram).

Real Life, Real Needs

Students are excited about the opportunity to work together and to be in charge of their curriculum. The issues they pursue have faces, real stories and real needs. The students learn social studies and English as they immerse themselves in real social issues. For example, a group studying issues relating to people with physical disabilities linked up

ADVENTURE ACTIVITIES

- Team-building initiatives
- Excursions into the city— Urban Exploration!

PROCESSING

- Done in small groups & whole class
- Students maintain individual journals

TEAM LEARNING & TEACHING

- Cooperative games & Initiatives at beginning of semester to develop teams
- All research must be coordinated within and between teams
- All projects are collaborative. Students must jointly do tasks, assign roles, facilitate small group processing.

INTEGRATED CURRICULUM

Social Studies

- Meeting individual needs within the community
- Historical background to the issue
- Evaluate issues that feed the issue
- Balance of Power

English

- Speeches before city council
- Presentation of findings to class & parents
- Letters to the Editor
- Writing letters to agencies
- Writing articles

Urban EXCEL
Social Studies & English

EXPERIENTIAL LEARNING CYCLE

FULL VALUE CONTRACT

CHALLENGE BY CHOICE

- Activities follow ELC, including, reflection, generalizing & transfering

- Established at begining of semester
- Processing of teamwork always addresses FVC

- Students choose topic
- Students choose group editor

with a blind rehabilitation group. The students visited the clients in their agency and brought them back to the high school. To better understand the challenges facing people with physical disabilities, the class went to downtown Detroit, with half of the group in wheelchairs and half in blindfolds. The students traveled the city as if they lived and worked there. They chronicled their experiences with pictures and wrote a paper describing what they felt were the pertinent issues facing physically disabled people. From this experience, the group wrote to the Chamber of Commerce and pointed out the lack of accessibility in the downtown area.

Another group pursued the issue of inequality in the court system. The students interviewed a public defender, an assistant district attorney and an attorney in a large law firm. They tracked the cases of two clients—one represented by the public defender and one represented by a private attorney. The students attended court sessions of both clients. Their conclusions supported their assumption that the legal system favors individuals on the basis of class. The team wrote up its findings in the form of a position paper to the Bar Association and the district court.

Bringing It Back Together

Through this unit, students additionally study the ethnic neighborhoods of Detroit as they look at the city as a resource. Together they study such topics as the impact of an incinerator on the ecology of the city and the resurgence of specific neighborhoods in the city. The various team projects are bound together into a book that is shared with the parents and the rest of the class. Staff and students alike emerge with a better understanding of the units of study, an appreciation of the diversity of the city and its environs, a more comprehensive knowledge of their group and themselves, and a sense that they are able to take on a large piece of their own learning. In addition, many of the students who become involved in service projects continue their involvement after the course is completed, testimony to the fact that learning is significant to the extent that it has personal meaning.

Bibliography

Ackerman, David and Perkins, David N. 1989. Integrating Thinking and Learning Skills Across the Curriculum. In Heidi Hayes Jacobs (ed.), *Interdisciplinary Curriculum: Design and Implementation.* Alexandria, VA: Association for Supervision and Curriculum Development.

Aronson, E. 1978. *The Jigsaw Classroom.* Beverly Hills, CA: Sage.

Bandura, A. 1986. *Social Foundation of Thought and Action: A Social Cognitive Theory.* Englewood Cliffs, NJ: Prentice-Hall.

Bandura, A. 1977. *Social Learning Theory.* Englewood Cliffs, NJ: Prentice-Hall.

Barth, Roland. 1991. *Improving Schools from Within: Teachers, Parents, and Principals Can Make the Difference.* San Fransisco: Jossey-Bass.

Beane, James A. 1990. *Affect in the Curriculum: Toward Democracy, Dignity, and Diversity.* New York: Teachers College Press.

Belenky, Mary Field; Clinchy, Blythe McVicker; Goldberger, Nancy Rule; Tarule, Jill Mattuck. 1986. *Women's Ways of Knowing: The Development of Self, Voice, and Mind.* New York: Basic Books.

Bellanca, James and Fogarty, Robin. 1991. *Blueprints for Thinking in the Cooperative Classroom.* 2nd ed. Palatine, IL: Skylight Publishing.

Bennett, Barrie; Rolheiser-Bennett, Carol; Stevahn, Laurie. 1991. *Cooperative Learning: Where Heart Meets Mind.* Toronto: Educational Connections.

Blanchard, Kenneth and Johnson, Spencer. 1982. *The One Minute Manager.* New York: William Morrow and Company.

Blanchard, Kenneth; Zigarmi, Patricia; Zigarmi, Drea. 1985. *Leadership and the One Minute Manager.* New York: William Morrow and Company.

Brandt, Ron. 1994. *On Making Sense:* A Conversation with Magdalene Lampert. *Educational Leadership* 51.5, pp. 26-30.

Brooks, Jacqueline Grennon and Brooks, Martin G. 1993. *In Search of Understanding: The Case for Constructivist Classrooms.* Alexandria, VA: Association for Supervision and Curriculum Development.

Caine, Renate Nummela and Caine, Geoffrey. 1991. *Making Connections: Teaching and the Human Brain.* Alexandria, VA: Association for Supervision and Curriculum Development.

Carnegie Council on Adolescent Development. 1989. *Turning Points: Preparing American Youth for the 21st Century: The Report of the Task Force on Education of Young Adolescents.* New York: Carnegie Corp.

Clifford, Margaret M. 1990. Students Need Challenge, Not Easy Success. *Educational Leadership* 48.1, pp. 22-26.

Cohen, Elizabeth G. 1986. *Designing Groupwork: Strategies for the Heterogeneous Classroom.* New York: Teachers College Press.

Costa, Arthur L. 1992. The Learning Community. In Arthur Costa, James Bellanca, Robin Fogarty (eds.), *If Minds Matter, Vols. I and II.* Palatine, IL: Skylight Publishing.

Csikszentmihalyi, Mihaly. 1991. *Flow: The Psychology of Optimal Experience.* New York: Harper & Row.

DeVries, D. L. & Slavin, R. E. 1978. Teams-Games-Tournament (TGT): Review of Ten Classroom Experiments. *Journal of Research and Development in Education* 12, pp. 28-38.

Dewey, John. 1938. *Experience and Education.* New York: Macmillan.

Duckworth, Eleanor. 1987. *The Having of Wonderful Ideas and Other Essays on Teaching and Learning.* New York: Teachers College Press.

Duckworth, Eleanor. 1991. Twenty-four, Forty-two, and I Love You: Keeping it Complex. *Harvard Educational Review* 61.1, pp. 1-26.

Dunn, Rita. 1990. Rita Dunn Answers Questions on Learning Styles. *Educational Leadership* 48.2, pp. 15-19.

Ewert, Alan W. 1989. *Outdoor Adventure Pursuits: Foundations, Models, and Thories.* Columbus, OH: Publishing Horizons.

Fogarty, Robin. 1991. *The Mindful School: How to Integrate the Curricula.* Palatine, IL: Skylight Publishing.

Fogarty, Robin and Bellanca, James. 1992. Capture the Vision: Future World, Future School. In Arthur Costa, James Bellanca, Robin Fogarty (eds.), *If Minds Matter, Vol. I.* Palatine, IL: Skylight Publishing.

Fullan, Michael. 1982. *The Meaning of Educational Change.* New York: Teachers College Press.

Garger, Stephen. 1990. Is There a Link Between Learning Style and Neurophysiology? *Educational Leadership* 48.2, pp. 63-65.

Gardner, Howard. Multiple Intelligences: Implications for Art and Creativity. 1990. In William J. Moody (ed.), *Artistic Intelligences: Implications for Education.* New York: Teachers College Press.

Gould, Stephen J. 1993. *The Mismeasure of Man.* New York: Norton.

Gibbs, Jeanne. 1987. *Tribes.* Santa Rosa, CA: Center Source Publications.

Gilligan, Carol. 1982. *In a Different Voice: Psychological Theory and Women's Development.* Cambridge, MA: Harvard University Press.

Gilligan, Carol; Ward, Janie Victoria; Taylor, Jill McLean (eds.). 1988. *Mapping the Moral Domain.* Cambridge, MA: Harvard University Press.

Glasser, William. 1993. *The Quality School Teacher.* New York: Harper Pernennial.

Hand, Kathi L. 1990. Style is a Tool for Students, Too! *Educational Leadership* 48. 2, pp. 13–14.

Heath, Douglas H. 1991. *Fulfilling Lives: Paths to Maturity and Success.* San Francisco: Jossey-Bass.

Heath, Shirley Brice. 1983. *Ways with Words: Language, Life, and Work in Communities and Classrooms.* Cambridge: Cambridge University Press.

Jacobs, Heidi Hayes. 1991. The Integrated Curriculum. *Instructor* 101.2, pp. 22–23.

Jacobs, Heidi Hayes (ed.). 1989. *Interdisciplinary Curriculum: Design and Implementation.* Alexandria, VA: Association for Supervision and Curriculum Development.

Johnson, David W. and Johnson, Frank P. 1991. *Joining Together: Group Theory and Group Skills,* 4th ed. Englewood Cliffs, NJ: Prentice Hall.

Johnson, David W. and Johnson, Roger T. 1992. Cooperative Learning: A Theory Base. In Arthur Costa, James Bellanca and Robin Fogarty (eds.), *If Minds Matter, Vol. II.* Palatine, IL: Skylight Publishing.

Johnson, David W.; Johnson, Roger T.; Holubec, Edythe Johnson; Roy, Patricia. 1984. *Circles of Learning: Cooperation in the Classroom.* Alexandria, VA: Association for Supervision and Curriculum Development.

Johnson, David W.; Johnson, Roger T. and Holubec, Edythe Johnson. 1988. *Cooperation in the Classroom,* rev. ed. Edina, MN: Interaction Book Company.

Kagan, Spencer. 1992. *Cooperative Learning.* San Juan Capistrano, CA: Resources for Teachers.

Kamii, Mieko. 1993. Having Wonderful Ideas: An Interview with Eleanor Duckworth. *The Web* 1.9, pp. 2–3.

Kamiya, Art. 1985. *Elementary Teacher's Handbook of Indoor and Outdoor Games.* West Nyack, NY: Parker Publishing.

Kelley, Earl. 1947. *Education for What is Real.* New York: Harper & Row.

Kolb, David. 1985. *Learning-Style Inventory,* rev. ed. Boston: McBer & Company.

Lewin, Kurt. 1944. The Dynamics of Group Action. *Educational Leadership* 1.4, pp. 195-200.

Lewin, Roger. 1992. *Complexity: Life on the Edge of Chaos.* New York: Macmillan.

Lightfoot, Sara Lawrence. 1983. *The Good High School: Portraits of Character and Culture.* New York: Basic Books.

Lofquist, William. 1989. The Spectrum of Attitudes in *The Technology of Prevention Workbook.* Phoenix, AZ: Association for Youth Development.

Lopez, Hector; Hirschy, David; Rugger, Kathleen; Krull, Alan. 1991. *The Motion Program.* New York: The International High School and Middle College.

Marshall, Carol. 1990. The Power of the Learning Styles Philosophy. *Educational Leadership* 48.2, p. 62.

Maslow, Abraham. 1962. *Toward a Psychology of Being.* Princeton, NJ: C. Van Nostrand.

McCarthy, Bernice. 1996. *About Learning.* Barrington, IL: Excel, Inc.

McCarthy, Bernice. 1981,87. *The 4MAT System: Teaching to Learning Styles with Right/Left Mode Techniques.* Barrington, IL: Excel, Inc.

McCarthy, Bernice. 1990. Using the 4MAT System to Bring Learning Styles to Schools. *Educational Leadership* 48.2, pp. 31-36.

McCarthy, Bernice and Susan Morris. 1995. *4MAT in Action: Sample Units K-6.* Barrington, IL: Excel Publishing, Inc.

McCarthy, Bernice and Susan Morris. 1995. *4MAT in Action: Sample Units 7-12.* Barrington, IL: Excel Publishing, Inc.

McKeachie, W.; Pintrich, P.; Lin, Y.; & Smith, D. 1986. *Teaching and Learning in the College Classroom.* Ann Arbor, MI: University of Michigan.

Meek, Anne. 1991. On Thinking About Teaching: A Conversation with Eleanor Duckworth. *Educational Leadership* 48.6, pp. 30-34.

Noddings, Nel. 1984. *Caring: A Feminist Approach to Ethics and Moral Education.* Berkeley, CA: University of California Press.

Noddings, Nel. 1992. *The Challenge to Care in Schools: An Alternative Approach to Education.* New York: Teachers College Press.

Oakes, Jeannie. 1985. *Keeping Track: How Schools Structure Inequality.* New Haven, CT: Yale University Press.

Paley, Vivian Gussin. 1986. *Mollie is Three.* Chicago: The University of Chicago Press.

Perkins, David. 1993. Thinking-Centered Learning. *Educational Leadership* 51.4, pp. 84-86.

Perkins, David and Salomon, Gavriel. 1992. The Science and Art of Transfer. In Arthur Costa, James Bellanca and Robin Rogarty (eds.), *If Minds Matter: A Forward to the Future. Vol. I.* Palatine, IL: Skylight Publishing.

Perkins, David and Blythe, Tina. 1994. Putting Understanding Up Front. *Educational Leadership* 51.5 pp. 4-8.

Perrone, Vito (ed.). 1991. *Expanding Student Assessment.* Alexandria, VA: Association for Supervision and Curriculum Development.

Piaget, Jean. 1968. *Six Psychological Studies.* New York: Vintage Books.

Pribram, Karl. 1987. A Systematic Analysis of Brain Function, Learning and Remembering. Paper presented at *Educating Tomorrow's Children.* Neuropsychology Services. San Fransisco.

Rico, Gabriele Lusser. 1983. *Writing the Natural Way: Using Right-Brain Techniques to Release Your Expressive Powers.* New York: Jeremy P. Tarcher/Perigee Books.

Rogers, Carl. 1951. *Client-Centered Therapy.* Boston: Houghton Mifflin.

Rohnke, Karl E. 1989. *Cowstails and Cobras II.* Dubuque, IA: Kendall/Hunt.

Rohnke, Karl E. 1984. *Silver Bullets.* Dubuque, IA: Kendall/Hunt.

Rohnke, Karl and Butler, Steve. 1995. *QuickSilver: Adventure Games, Initiative Problems, Trust Activities and a Guide to Effective Leadership.* Dubuque, IA: Kendall/Hunt.

Schoel, Jim; Prouty, Dick; Radcliffe, Paul. 1988. *Islands of Healing: A Guide to Adventure Based Counseling.* Hamilton, MA: Project Adventure.

Senge, Peter. 1990. *Fifth Discipline: Mastering the Five Practices of the Learning Organization.* New York: Doubleday.

Sharan, S. and Sharan, Y. 1976. *Small-group Teaching.* Englewood Cliffs, NJ: Educational Technology Publications.

Slavin, Robert E. 1970. *Cooperative Learning: Theory, Research, and Practice.* Englewood Cliffs, NJ: Prentice-Hall.

Slavin, Robert E. 1983. When Does Cooperative Learning Increase Student Achievement? *Psychological Bulletin* 94.3, pp. 429–445.

Slavin, Robert E. 1978. Student Teams and Achievement Divisions. *Journal of Educational Psychology* 12, pp. 39–49.

Slavin, Robert E. 1980. *Using Student Team Learning,* rev. ed. Baltimore, Md: Center for Social Organization of Schools.

True Colors. 1989. Corona, CA: Communication Companies International.

Tyack, David B. 1974. *The One Best System: A History of American Urban Education.* Cambridge, MA: Harvard University Press.

Vygotsky, Lev S. 1978. *Mind in Society: The Development of Higher Psychological Processes.* Michale Cole, Vera John-Steiner, Sylvia Scribner and Ellen Souberman (eds.). Cambridge, MA: Harvard University Press.

Waldrop, M. Mitchell. 1992. *Complexity: The Emerging Science at the Edge of Order and Chaos.* New York: Simon & Schuster.

Wheatley, Margaret. 1993. *Leadership and the New Science: Learning About Organization from an Orderly Universe.* San Fransisco: Berrett-Koehler.

Project Adventure Services and Publications

Services

Project Adventure, Inc. is a national, non-profit corporation dedicated to helping schools, agencies, and others implement Project Adventure programs. Toward that end, the following services are available:

Project Adventure Workshops. Through a network of national certified trainers, Project Adventure conducts workshops for teachers, counselors, youth workers and other professionals who work with people. These workshops are given in various sections of the country. Separate workshops are given in Challenge Ropes Course Skills, Counseling Skills for Adventure Based Programs, Project Adventure Games and Initiatives, and Interdisciplinary Academic Curriculum.

Challenge Course Design and Installation. Project Adventure has been designing and installing ropes courses (a series of individual and group challenge elements situated indoors in a gymnasium or outdoors in a grove of trees) for over 15 years. PA Staff can travel to your site and design/install a course appropriate for your needs and budget.

Challenge Ropes Course Source Book. A catalog service of hard-to-find materials and tools used in the installation of Challenge Ropes Courses. This catalog also contains climbing rope and a variety of items useful to adventure programs.

Executive Reach. Management workshops for business and professional persons. These workshops are designed for increasing efficiency of team members in the workplace. The trust, communication, and risk taking ability learned in the executive programs translate into a more cohesive and productive team at work.

Program Accreditation. The Accreditation process is an outside review of a program by PA staff. Programs that undertake the accreditation process are seeking outside evaluation with regard to quality and safety. The term accreditation means "formal written confirmation." Programs seeking confirmation are looking to ensure that they are within the current standards of safety and risk management. This assurance may be useful for making changes in program equipment and/or design, and in providing information on program quality to third parties such as administrators, insurance companies and the public.

Publications

If you would like to obtain additional copies of this book, an order form is provided on the next page. Project Adventure also publishes many books and pamphlets in related areas. Described below are some of our best sellers, which can be ordered on the same form. Call or write to Project Adventure for a complete publications list.

Cowstails and Cobras II — Karl Rohnke's classic guide to games, Initiative problems and Adventure activities. Offering a thorough treatment of Project Adventure's philosophy and approach to group activities, *Cowstails II* provides both the experienced practitioner and the novice with a unique and valuable resource.

Silver Bullets — More Initiative problems, Adventure games and trust activities from Karl Rohnke: 165 great games and activities that require few, if any, props. Use this as a companion to *Cowstails and Cobras II* or a stand alone guide to invigorate your program.

Youth Leadership In Action — All too often young people have little access to the resources necessary to improve their skills and develop their leadership potential. *Youth Leadership In Action* addresses this need by providing a guide for youth leaders to implement experiential, cooperative activities and techniques into their programs.

But the most striking and unique feature of this book is that it was written by a group of youth leaders. This group of eight leaders have taken 54 of Project Adventure's most popular Adventure games and activities and rewritten the instructions and rules in the way *they* present and play them. They also give a brief history of Project Adventure,

present their own definition of Adventure, and explain some of PA's basic concepts and techniques — Full Value Contract, Challenge By Choice, debriefing, sequencing, etc. They also provide a section on effective leadership and how to start several types of programs.

By combining the magic of Project Adventure activities with the power of young people leading them, *Youth Leadership In Action* provides youth leaders with a valuable tool to help their programs get even better and to Bring the Adventure Home!

Islands Of Healing: A Guide to Adventure Based Counseling — Long a standard in the field, *Islands* presents a comprehensive discussion of this rapidly growing counseling approach. Started in 1974, ABC is an innovative, community-based, group counseling model that uses cooperative games, Initiative problem solving, low and high Challenge Ropes Course elements, and other Adventure activities. The book contains extensive "how-to" information on group selection, training, goal setting, sequencing, and leading and debriefing activities. Also included are explorations of model ABC programs at several representative sites— junior and senior high schools, a psychiatric hospital, and court referred programs.

To get further information about Project Adventure services and programs, contact one of the following offices:

Project Adventure, Inc.

P.O. Box 100
Hamilton, MA 01936
978/468-7981
FAX 978/468-7605

P.O. Box 2447
Covington, GA 30015
770/784/9310
FAX 770/787-7764

P.O. Box 14171
Portland, OR 97293
503/239-0169
FAX 503/236-6765

In New Zealand:
Project Adventure New Zealand
P.O. Box 5303
Welington, New Zealand
04/384-8096
FAX 04/384-8146

In Australia:
Project Adventure Australia
332 Banyule Road
View Bank, Australia
03/457-6494
FAX 03/457-5438

Request Form

Please send information on the following programs:

O *Project Adventure Training Workshops*

O *Challenge Course Design and Installations*

O *Ropes Course Equipment Catalog*

O *Executive Reach Programs*

O *Publications List*

O *Program Accreditation*

O *Project Adventure Membership*

O *Project Adventure's new headquarters —Moraine Farm*

O *Please add my name to your mailing list.*

Ship to:

Name _____

Address _____

City _____ State _____ Zip _____

Phone (___) _____

Copy or detach this form and return to:

Project Adventure, Inc.
P.O. Box 100
Hamilton, MA 01936
978/468-7981
FAX 508/468-7605
or
P.O. Box 2447
Covington, GA 30015
770/784-9310
FAX 770/787-7764